LIVING A JEWISH LIFE

Updated and Revised Edition

Also by Anita Diamant

NONFICTION

The New Jewish Wedding

The New Jewish Baby Book

Choosing a Jewish Life: A Handbook for People Converting to Judaism

Saying Kaddish

How to be a Jewish Parent

Bible Baby Names

FICTION

The Red Tent

Good Harbor

The Last Days of Dogtown

ESSAYS

Pitching My Tent: On Marriage, Motherhood, Friendship and Other Leaps of Faith

LIVING A
JEWISH
LIFE

Updated and Revised Edition

Jewish Traditions, Customs,
and Values for Today's Families

ANITA DIAMANT

with Howard Cooper

<u>HARPER</u>

NEW YORK . LONDON . TORONTO . SYDNEY

HarperCollins books may be purchased for educational, business, or sales promotional use. For information, please e-mail the Special Markets Department at SPsales@harper-collins.com.

First edition was published in 1991

Designed by Joy O'Meara

Library of Congress Cataloging-in-Publication Data has been applied for.

ISBN: 978-0-06-117364-6
ISBN-10: 0-06-117364-9

19 WBC/LSC 20 19 18

PERMISSIONS:
Blessing the Children © Danny Siegel. Reprinted with permission of the author.

Copyright © 1996 by Marcia Lee Falk. Excerpted from *The Book of Blessings: New Jewish Prayers for Daily Life, The Sabbath,* and *the New Moon Festival* by Marcia Falk (Beacon, 1999). Used by permission. For more information: www.marciafalk.com.

For my daughter, Emilia Diamant
"She is a gift and a wonder."

A. D.

For my mother, Annette S. Cooper
"My mother was a perfect tzadik."

H. C.

CONTENTS

Contents

PREFACE

Dear Reader:

While I was writing this book, I thought a lot about who you might be, why you might pick up this title, and what you needed from an introduction to Judaism. I did this because I wanted to write a book that you would be comfortable with, a book that you could really use.

Since my image of you guided the contents, the organization, and the tone of *Living a Jewish Life,* I think it's only fair to tell you who I think you are.

I think you are a graduate student, and that you are an empty-nester. I think you have two children under the age of five, that you hope to become a grandparent soon, and that children are not part of your life-plan at all. I think you went to Hebrew school as a kid, and that you grew up only vaguely aware that you were Jewish but never belonged to a synagogue or any other Jewish organization. I think that you cherish memories of your mother lighting candles every Friday night, and that you've never seen anyone do that in your whole life. I think you are interested in Judaism because the person you are in love with is a Jew, and that you have been a Jew-by-choice for many years. I think you are not Jewish at all but are raising a Jewish child with a Jewish spouse. I think you are the Christian grandparent of Jewish grandchildren.

I think you know not a single word of Hebrew and that you can still read a little Hebrew from when you prepared for your *bar* or *bat mitzvah*. I think you believe deeply in the existence of a Holy One, and that the question of religious faith is meaningless to you.

I think you are married, divorced, single; straight and gay; active in the Jewish community and alienated from it.

In other words, I think you are a very diverse bunch. What you have in common is a genuine interest in Judaism as a way of life. I think you are curious about how to make Jewish choices in ways that do not deny the importance of all the other parts of yourself and your world. I think you are eager to learn from tradition and confident of your own ability to interpret ancient sources and ways.

I think we have a lot in common.

I was born to Jewish parents, both Holocaust survivors, who gave me an undiluted and positive Jewish identity. Yet, I consider myself a "Jew-by-choice" and I only started studying my heritage and making Jewish choices in my late 20s. That was when I fell in love with a non-Jew and realized how little I knew. So my then-boyfriend and I joined a Jewish reading group and discovered the vastness of the Jewish library. I wrote newspaper articles about the Jewish community and learned how varied and vital it is. I started to light candles on Friday night and made a place for meaningful ritual in my life.

When my fiancé decided to convert to Judaism, we found wonderful teachers and studied together. And together we started making Jewish choices, a process we continue day by day, year by year.

The Jews have often been called the Chosen People. They have also been called the Choosing People. *Living a Jewish Life* is intended as a guide to help you make meaningful choices in this ancient, life-affirming tradition. Remember that every Jew, regardless of training or accomplishments, is a student. Judaism is as wide and as deep as the ocean itself, which means that we are all, even the most learned among us, beginners.

I hope you find this book a welcoming and intriguing place to begin your exploration of Jewish life. May your journey be pleasant, your paths peaceful, and your discoveries fulfilling.

Anita Diamant
January 5, 2007
15 Tevet 5767

For the modern Jew, observance is no longer a matter of "the all or the nothing." One only has to start. Nobody can tell where this beginning will lead.

—FRANZ ROSZENWEIG (1886–1929)

INTRODUCTIONS
and DEFINITIONS

Opening this book and reading these words might constitute one of your first Jewish choices as an adult. Your reasons for wanting to explore Judaism are uniquely your own. Perhaps they have something to do with the desire for a more examined life, or a need to acknowledge spiritual or religious feelings. Maybe you are looking for an honest way to provide your children with a sense of their place in a great religious, ethical, cultural, and ethnic tradition.

Whatever your motivation or background, the first goal of *Living a Jewish Life* is to open the door to that tradition; the second is to help you make your own Jewish choices, at home, in the community, for years to come. The first section, "Home," describes the core elements that define a self-consciously Jewish home, which is the heart of Jewish life. These chapters cover everything from the contents of the kitchen cabinets, to the books on the shelves, to the observance of *Shabbat*—the Sabbath—the most important and sweetest of all Jewish holidays.

The section titled "Community" introduces the larger context for Jewish choosing, with information about how to find your niche through synagogues, educational institutions, and other kinds of organizations. This section also contains a discussion of Jewish learning, from preschool through adult education, and a chapter about Israel and traveling the world.

"Observance" provides an overview of the Jewish calendar, the annual holiday cycle, and the events that celebrate the human life cycle.

In order to make *Living a Jewish Life* as accessible as possible, Hebrew and Yiddish words and references have been kept to a minimum. Every non-English term used in this book is defined at least once in the text, and there is both a glossary and index for easy reference. A listing of recommended readings and resources is included, as is a timeline for historical reference.

While it is not a book of "do's and don'ts," *Living a Jewish Life* does have a point of view, and even an agenda—which is to encourage readers to make Jewish choices, to try on some of the rituals, observances, and customs described in the following chapters—to see how they feel and to explore what they can mean. Although there is a great deal of practical information in these pages—suggestions, instructions, and menus for everything from prayers to arts-and-crafts projects—the "how-to" materials are not presented as ends in themselves, because one of the hallmarks of liberal Judaism is its insistence on finding and creating meaning, on considering the "why" of everything: Why light candles on Friday night? Why forgo shrimp? Why get married under a canopy? Why join a synagogue?

For liberal Jews, the answers to these questions are not fixed, but open, dynamic, and personal. The answers come from many sources: through the process of studying traditional Jewish texts, such as the Torah, the literature of Jewish law (*halachah*) and imagination (*Midrash*); through the sweep of Jewish history; through discussion with teachers and peers; through a sense of God's presence; and through personal reflection and experimentation.

Living a Jewish Life takes a descriptive rather than a prescriptive approach to Judaism. The word "should" does not appear in these pages. Since Jews do things—well, actually nearly everything—in many different ways, this book contains "menus" of choices about the hows, whens, and whys of modern Jewish life. This embrace of Jewish pluralism is an expression of "liberal Judaism," which requires an introduction of its own.

Liberal Judaism

Liberal Judaism is a category that embraces the broad range of religious practices, beliefs, and institutions of Jews who identify themselves as Conservative, Reform, Reconstructionist, post- or transdenominational, egalitarian, humanist, New Age, or "just Jewish." Although there are substantial differences among these groups, what they share is an acknowledgment of their Jewishness as a choice. In other words, they practice Judaism not necessarily on God's authority, or because their parents would be horrified if they didn't, but because they find meaning, joy, and strength in Jewish practice and community. *Living a Jewish Life* is an expression and a celebration of the diversity that comes of this choosing.

Liberal Judaism is just over 200 years old, which in the context of Jewish time is relatively young. However, since the destruction of the Temple in Jerusalem in 70 C.E.,* Jewish life has been pluralistic, contentious, and constantly changing, and in that sense, this current incarnation of Judaism is heir to that long tradition of diversity and choice.

Nonetheless, Judaism certainly appeared more uniform in the past. Before the late 18th century, virtually all Jews experienced birth, education, marriage, family, work, recreation, worship, and death as mediated by Jewish law and custom. The non-Jewish world perceived and treated Jews not as individuals, but in accordance with prevailing attitudes, laws, and prejudices about them as a group.

The philosophical revolution of the Enlightenment and subsequent political changes transformed that reality. The ghettos were unlocked, as were the doors to the great universities of Europe. Jewish men shaved their beards; Jewish women removed their traditional head coverings. More Jews worked and even socialized with Christians. Alternatives to an all-encompassing Jewish lifestyle began to emerge, but they were limited: Jews could either remain as separate as possible from the larger secular world, or they could abandon their traditions altogether and convert to Christianity, or they could try to live a kind of double life, an existence that Jewish reformers of the time described as "Jews at home, but men (like all others) on the street."[1]

Within a few generations, the American experience and the drive to assimilate pushed this paradigm much further; one was a Jew precisely the way the neighbors were Presbyterian. What had once been

---

* Jews use C.E. (Common Era) and B.C.E. (Before the Common Era) rather than the designations A.D. and B.C., which refer to the divinity of Jesus (*Anno Domini* means "in the year of our Lord").

an all-embracing view of life shrank to nominal affiliation with once-in-a-while or even once-a-year observance. In other words, one was identified as a Jew on the street but was a secular person at home. For a time, liberal Judaism seemed to mean doing less and less in the way of ritual, study, or commitment.

In the 1960s, the Six Day War in Israel forged a renewed sense of urgency and pride among Jews around the world. That change coincided with a broader cultural shift away from the notion of a "melting pot," a society in which ethnic, national, and religious differences disappear, in favor of the ideal of a "mosaic," in which individual differences add to the richness of the whole. Within this context, liberal Judaism has thrived.

Today, Jews who are fully at home in the secular world, participating in every aspect of public life and culture as equals and as leaders, also light candles on Friday nights, study Jewish books, and are active members of synagogues and other Jewish institutions. From this integrated perspective, there are Jewish dimensions to many seemingly value-neutral choices of daily life: everything from donating blood to planning vacations, from deciding how much to give the United Way campaign to ordering lunch becomes a Jewish decision.

Less is no longer more. Liberal Jews now embrace once-rejected traditional customs and rituals at home, in synagogues, and in other settings. Traditions such as wearing *tallit* and *kippah,* signing a *ketubah,* immersing in a *mikveh,* and keeping kosher are choices on the menu of liberal Judaism. These and other *mitzvot* and customs are reimagined, reinterpreted, and reclaimed not only because they belong to the Jewish canon, but because they make living a Jewish life more beautiful and meaningful. And the choices made by liberal Jews are informed by contemporary wisdom; the insights of psychology and feminism, for example, are also part of the equation.

However, it is not easy to fix the boundary between liberal Judaism and the rest of Jewish practice. And as with liberal Jews, those who claim to be "traditional" or even "Orthodox" run a wide gamut, ranging from "traditional/egalitarian" groups, in which women lead part of the prayer service, to mainstream Orthodox Union congregations, to an array of Hasidic sects living in the United States and Israel. What such groups share, in the most general terms, is adherence to *halachah* (Jewish law), as set forth in rabbinic literature and as interpreted by their own rabbinic authorities; in practice this is expressed, most obviously, in more differentiated roles for the sexes, and stricter observance of Sabbath, holiday, and dietary laws.

Historically, there have always been deep divisions among Jewish factions, sects, and denominations, and our time is no different. Despite all the loud and even bitter disagreements that divide one Jew from another, the ethic of unity, *klal Yisrael*, transcends everything. We are all, ultimately, related to one another. We are all, ultimately, one people, responsible for one another.

Liberal Jews have long been challenged by charges of and troubled by feelings of inauthenticity. But the suspicion that only the Orthodox can lay claim to being "real" Jews is starting to fade. With the revival of study, commitment, and self-conscious Jewish decision-making in the liberal community, there is a growing sense of ownership, comfort, and legitimacy. Liberal Judaism offers a rich and engrossing way of life. Fed and fueled by the dialectic—the tension and resolution—of making Jewish choices, it is truly, "a tree of life."

Mitzvah

Making Jewish choices is traditionally expressed in the concept and execution of *mitzvot,* the plural of *mitzvah.* The word *mitzvah* does not translate well. It derives from a military term for "command," and it is often translated as "good deed." But Jews don't perform *mitzvot* like so many good Scouts. A *mitzvah* is a commandment from God, but a command that exists only when put in action by people. A *mitzvah* is an idea-given-form. It is value-action—praxis.

Obviously, the word "commandment" immediately raises the essential theological question. Since a commandment implies a Commander, the whole notion of *mitzvah* seems to rest on the existence of God—on a God who gives orders. For Jews who believe the Bible was divinely revealed, the authority of *mitzvot* is unassailable; God commands so people must obey each and every one.[2]

Liberal Jews, for whom the authority of the Bible does not necessarily reside in the idea of divine authorship, tend to emphasize the
fact that *mitzvot* are subject to human response—to a sense of being
commanded or directed, and thus to human interpretation.

Moses asks God to explain the laws for keeping kosher:

"Thou Shalt Not Seethe a Kid in Its Mother's Milk."
"Does that mean we should have two sets of dishes?"
"Thou Shalt Not Seethe a Kid in Its Mother's Milk."
"Does that mean that we should wait six hours between eating
milk and meat?"
"Thou Shalt Not Seethe a Kid in Its Mother's Milk."
"Does that mean we should check the label of everything we
buy and use only those items made with pure vegetable short-
ening?"
"Thou Shalt Not Seethe a Kid in Its Mother's Milk."
"Does that mean . . ."
"OKAY, HAVE IT YOUR WAY!"[3]

The Torah is said to contain 613 *mitzvot*. These include celebrating
Shabbat, giving money to the poor, refraining from eating pork and
shellfish, entering sons into Jewish life through the covenant of circumcision, teaching children the story of Passover. For liberal Jews,
not all *mitzvot* have the same weight because not all *mitzvot* provoke
the sense of feeling commanded. As one rabbi has written, "There will
be *mitzvot* through which my forebears found themselves capable of
responding to the commanding God which are no longer adequate or
possible for me, just as there will be new *mitzvot* through which I or
my generation will be able to respond which my ancestors never
thought of."[4] Indeed, for liberal Jews, the increasingly complex modern
world may suggest new and binding *mitzvot* regarding everything from
the proper application of medical technology for the terminally ill to
the ecological imperative to recycle.

Since each *mitzvah* is the occasion for reflection and for a choice,
liberal Jews take on *mitzvot* for many reasons. For some, there is a

compelling argument in following a particular discipline or practice simply because it has been and remains a part of Jewish identity. Many commit themselves to fulfilling those *mitzvot* that are consistent with a personal sense of right and wrong, such as giving to the poor and working to fulfill the prophetic call for justice. Some find *mitzvot* a way of maintaining a relationship with what is holy in life: "While I have and retain the freedom of choosing my specific means of response at a given moment, the essential fact of my life will be my intention to respond [to God through *mitzvot*]."[5]

The Hasidic masters discerned a relationship between the Hebrew *mitzvah* and a similar Aramaic word that meant "together."[6] Thus a *mitzvah* can be thought of as an act that unites people, and that unites people with God. Doing *mitzvot* can knit together the holy and the profane. Doing *mitzvot* can be a way to discover the sacred in the mundane.

However the idea of *mitzvah* is understood and for whatever reason a *mitzvah* is undertaken, the concept defies the rationalist, Western approach to the world, which posits that understanding should always precede action. (In other words, we tend not to open doors until we know what is behind them.) Doing *mitzvot* requires consciously setting aside that worldview. In the Bible, when the Israelites were given the Torah, their response was "We shall do and we shall hear."[7] In other words, they promised to act first, and hear (or understand) second; to leap before looking.

The logic to, benefits from, and understanding of *mitzvot* may be compared to human experiences that are endlessly described but ultimately available only through living. Such as making love. Such as becoming a parent. Or burying your own parents. The *mitzvot* are the methodology of Jewish choosing.

Jewish Parenting

Many people do not begin to make serious Jewish choices until they become parents. Then the question "What are we handing on to our children?" becomes a primary motivation in exploring Jewish questions: from selecting a religious education to figuring out how to impart a sense of Jewish identity.

The essential goal for Jewish parents through the ages has always been to raise a child to be a *mensch*—literally, "a person"; figuratively, a person who cares and shares, loves and studies, and acts righteously in the world. Just as it is difficult for a child to grow up to be a *mensch* without *mensch*-like parents, children rarely learn to cherish their Jewishness without witnessing their parents' commitment to Judaism.

Thus, if Judaism has nothing to do with family life, children cannot learn how to live a Jewish life. After-school programs or even a full-time Jewish day school is not sufficient because Jewish identity cannot be learned in a classroom. Jewishness is not simply a function of the intellect, but an expression of heart and soul, of psyche and senses.

To raise children who will care about Judaism, parents need to demonstrate their own Jewish commitment in ways that stimulate and satisfy them as adults. And this holds true for families where both parents are Jews, and for intermarried families where the non-Jewish parent is committed to raising Jewish children. Parents often begin making Jewish choices—lighting candles on Friday night, joining a synagogue, celebrating holidays—"for the children." If those practices remain essentially meaningless to the adults, children will see that Judaism is merely a matter of going through motions. If, however, those rituals and commitments—even if originally undertaken "for the children"—become important and fulfilling for parents as well, children will learn their Judaism as naturally as they learn their native language.

One of the great discoveries of parenthood is how much children teach us about life and time, joy and tenderness. Kids can help parents learn how to make Jewish choices, too, especially regarding ritual. American Jews are often unfamiliar and uncomfortable with ritual gestures, such as lighting candles and singing in public. Kids, however, are experts at learning through pretending and can enable adults to suspend their disbelief and make the leap to nonutilitarian language and actions. "Playing *Shabbat*" may be the best way to approach experimenting with Sabbath customs and rituals.

Raising Jewish children also means adding a whole new set of goals to the list shared with all parents (good grades, good manners, etc.). In two-parent families, Jewish parenting requires agreement on a long list of choices that may include the selection of a Jewish name for a new baby, or looking for a house in a neighborhood that is reasonably close to a synagogue and where there will be other Jewish children for yours to play with. Jewish parenting also means making decisions that may not be entirely popular with kids—like no television on Friday night, or the decision that religious school takes precedence over soccer practice. And that means tolerating some measure of Jewish conflict.

Ultimately, since children grow up to make their own decisions, perhaps the most important task for parents is to give children practice at making Jewish choices—appropriate to their age, of course. Youngsters can be asked how they would like to participate in Friday night rituals: by setting the table, by singing, by saying a blessing, by drawing a picture. Older children can be included in family decisions about where to send charitable contributions. A kid who announces he does not want to attend services with the rest of the family might be offered alternatives for those hours, such as reading a Jewish book, babysitting for preschoolers whose parents are attending services, or even doing volunteer work. In other words, the options presented require decision-making based on Jewish values and options.

Learning the Language

You don't have to speak Hebrew or know a lot of Yiddish to make meaningful Jewish choices. That said, it helps to know some of the vocabulary, which is not so much a matter of memorizing a list of words as it is mastering a few core concepts contained in words that do not translate very well. For example, *mitzvah,* which is not well served by a definition like "good deed" or "commandment." Or *tzedakah,* which means "righteous giving" not "charity." *Shabbat,* Torah, kosher, Reconstructionist, *shtetl, schlemiel:* these words are the Jewish cultural markers that will help you find your footing within the Jewish world.

Hebrew—the language of the Torah, the prayer book, the Passover *haggadah,* and the land of Israel—is the universal and sacred language of Judaism. And yet Hebrew, with its unfamiliar alphabet and right-to-left writing, can seem like a major stumbling block to feeling comfortable and authentic. This is a common problem, as the majority of American Jews cannot read or speak Hebrew.

Of course, almost all commonly used Hebrew texts and prayers are available in good English translations, and any home ceremony can be performed entirely in English. (It goes without saying that God understands no matter what language you're using.) If you do not know any Hebrew but want to incorporate its sound and flavor into home observances, many prayers are transliterated—the Hebrew sounds spelled out in the Latin alphabet—and can be learned phonetically thanks to recordings.

That said, basic Hebrew is not difficult to learn, and introductory courses are offered at all synagogues and in other settings, including online. Adults can learn Hebrew as an access language—for reading purposes—with a modest commitment of time in weekly or biweekly classes. Many people learn the basics by following along with their children's Hebrew lessons. Learning the aleph-bet along with some vocabulary and grammar provides unique insights into the tradition, because as every bilingual person can testify, something always gets lost in translation.

The best way to learn modern Hebrew is by spending time in Israel and/or attending an *ulpan,* an intensive Hebrew-language instruction course developed for immigrants to Israel.

Of course, Hebrew isn't the only Jewish language. There are three other languages written with the Hebrew alphabet that are part of Jewish history and culture: Aramaic, an ancient Semitic language, the language of the Talmud, was also Jesus' spoken tongue; Yiddish, a combination of Hebrew, German, and words borrowed from other languages, is spoken by Jews of Eastern European descent (Ashkenazi) and has infiltrated American popular culture; and Ladino, a combination of Hebrew and Spanish, is spoken among Jews of Mediterranean (Sephardic) background. Both Yiddish and Ladino have a rich literature that includes poetry, lyrics, prayers, jokes, and fiction. Yiddish language classes are taught in community and academic settings.

Getting Started

It is helpful to think about starting to make Jewish choices the way you would approach any life-enhancing discipline, such as taking up a new sport, changing your eating habits, learning to play a musical instrument, or studying a new language. In other words, this is going to take time, practice, and patience.

Especially patience. Without patience for the beginner's inevitable awkwardness and mistakes—at the piano, on the tennis court, in the synagogue—there can be no mastery of any new skill. Making new Jewish choices requires a suspension of the kind of standards (for competence if not excellence) to which adults tend to hold themselves. In other words, you have to allow yourself to learn as a very small child learns—without grades or deadlines, without too many expectations, and without fear of failure or embarrassment.

Of course, for adults and children alike, impatience is inevitable, and as with any discipline, there are times when the rewards just do not seem worth the effort. Sometimes you just don't feel like jogging. Sometimes you really want sour cream and butter on your baked potato. Sometimes, the last thing in the world you want to do is get out of bed on Saturday morning and go to services.

The rewards of making Jewish choices may be more difficult to measure or explain than dieting or jogging. For one thing, there is little support for liberal religious practice in American culture. Even with an idea as familiar and appealing as a real day of Sabbath, trying to explain that *Shabbat* is sacrosanct to you—no exceptions for basketball games or theater tickets—can mean that even supportive friends and family members may become suspicious or defensive: What are you, some kind of fundamentalist kook? Besides, if you're too Jewish to go out with me on Friday night, why are you eating that cheeseburger? Do you think you're better than me because I don't light candles on Friday night? Because I don't belong to a church?

Because liberal Jews tend to undertake *mitzvot* on a case-by-case basis, as they feel "commanded" or moved, there may be apparent inconsistencies in practice: not everyone who lights candles on Friday night maintains a kosher home; not everyone who keeps kosher goes to synagogue services, etc. Configurations of *mitzvot* vary enormously, and may change over time. Over the course of a lifetime, practices that once seemed alien can become deeply meaningful, while others that were once very important are abandoned.

Liberal Judaism's response to *mitzvot* is neither automatic nor defensive, but personal and open-ended: "This is how I do Judaism. It's not that my way is the only way or the 'right' way. But it is my Jewish way—for now."

Starting to make Jewish choices as an adult can feel very awkward, even for people who were born Jewish. There is a sense that you ought to know Hebrew, and when Passover begins, and what the Talmud is. Being uncomfortable in a synagogue or at the prospect of lighting Hannukah candles might seem to confirm the suspicion that you will never "get it," that you never will fit in.

Starting to make Jewish choices as an adult can feel even more awkward for people who were not born Jewish. Jews-by-choice and non-Jews living in Jewish-identified families may not carry the same emotional baggage as born Jews; however, there is a greater danger of feeling overwhelmed by the sheer amount of stuff—history, customs, traditions, languages—to be learned. And there is the fear that no matter how much you learn, you never will be comfortable or accepted.

However you begin this Jewish journey, remember that you are not alone. There are many other beginners just like you, and there are countless teachers and guides eager to help you find your way.

HOME

The Jewish home has been called a *mikdash ma'at,* a little sanctuary. It is an evocative image. From the moment you walk through the doorway of a sanctuary, you know you are entering a unique kind of space.

A sanctuary does not look like other places. It is defined and ornamented by ritual objects, books, and art. A sanctuary feels different from the workplace and the marketplace. In a sanctuary, the mundane criteria for success and failure fall away. What matters is not what you do but who you are.

A sanctuary is a place of safety and asylum. It is where the dispossessed go for shelter, where the hungry go for food, where the weary find rest. Sanctuaries are filled with voices, sometimes singing in unison, sometimes raised in disagreement. And sometimes, a sanctuary is as still as a garden.

Today, when so many families face the pressures of multiple roles, needs, and schedules, making a home into a sanctuary seems more difficult than ever—and thus more important than ever. The tools for making a home into a *mikdash ma'at* are the *mitzvot* described in the following pages.

"Your Own Sanctuary" elaborates the Jewish vision of the peaceful home as a place of hospitality and beauty. "The Sabbath" is an introduction both to Judaism's core insight and to creating a personal and family day of rest. "Good Deeds" explains the Jewish view of charity and social justice, and how they can be incorporated into daily life. "The People of the Library" defines some of the major Jewish texts and suggests books for the home library. "What Jews Eat" explains the Jewish dietary laws, their contemporary relevance and practice.

No sanctuary is perpetually filled with all the beauty or meaning it might contain. No home is ever fully or finally a sanctuary. But the ongoing process of making Jewish choices can help turn a home into a *mikdash ma'at,* a little sanctuary, an island of peace, a safe harbor, a beautiful Jewish place.

YOUR OWN SANCTUARY

With the destruction of the Second Temple in Jerusalem in 70 C.E, the focus of Jewish religious and ritual life had to change. The Jewish home became the new center of Judaism. However, this little sanctuary has never been a museum for vestigial rituals and ceremonies; it is home, the place where basic human needs are expressed and met. Home is the primary source of identity and education, as well as of affection, recognition, and sexual fulfillment. For Jews, making home into a little sanctuary means incorporating a range of beautiful and meaning *mitzvot* that make residents and visitors mindful of the blessings of peace, hospitality, and beauty.

Peace at Home

One of the primary reasons for adding a consistent Jewish dimension to family life is to create opportunities for sharing moments of peace. The Hebrew name for the goal of a "peaceful home" is *shalom bayit*.

Today, family peace and harmony are the province of psychologists and counselors, who often urge couples and families to set aside time to relax together, to talk, and to have fun. Experts have written about the positive impact of rituals on children's resiliency. Morning routines, family dinners, bedtime rituals, and annual holiday celebrations are powerful and positive ways of grounding and reassuring kids about the predictability of the world and their place in it. At its best, sharing Jewish rituals and practices can help to shape a healthy, happy, home.

Jewish tradition has always been quite explicit about the duties and obligations of family life, which are not meant to impose an external order on individuals and families, but to foster *shalom bayit.* The Jewish laws concerning family matters go into great detail and extend into the most intimate aspects of life. In matters of sexuality, for example, the rabbis codified the rights of women, making it clear that wives could expect their sexual needs to be met, and that husbands could not force physical attentions upon unwilling wives. Family violence of any kind is condemned in the traditional sources. Indeed, many of the rabbis even frowned upon disciplinary spanking.

The biblical call to honor parents, *kibbud av v'em,* was elaborated into a web of intergenerational obligations. While it is a child's duty to behave respectfully to elders, parents are responsible for educating their children, and not only in religious matters. For example, the Talmud tells parents that they should teach their children how to swim as well as how to read.

The Sabbath has always been the basic building block of family peace. Creating a restful island of time—turning off the television and turning to one another—is not just a nice family custom. It can actually help repair the wear and tear of the week. It can heal wounds that are not even apparent.

I am a father. I have a daughter and I love her dearly. I would like my daughter to obey the commandments of the Torah; I would like her to revere me as her father. And so I ask myself the question over and over again: What is there about me that deserves the reverence of my daughter?

You see, unless I live a life that is worthy of her reverence, I make it almost impossible for her to live a Jewish life. So many young people abandon Judaism because the Jewish models that they see in their parents are not worthy of reverence.

My message to parents is: Every day ask yourselves the question: "What is there about me that deserves the reverence of my child?"

Rabbi Abraham Joshua Heschel, 1907–1972

The peace of the house is really the health of the house. Traditionally, on Yom Kippur, the Day of Atonement, family members turn to one another and apologize for the hurtful words and thoughtless actions of the previous year. Today, the concept of *shalom bayit* can be extended to include support for family therapy and other forms of counseling when it is needed.

However, the concept of family peace is not a call for solemnity. The idea expressed in the Hebrew word *shalom* is not the same as that of the Latin *pax,* from which the English *peace* derives. *Pax* means "quiet." *Shalom* comes from the root *shalem,* which means "complete" or "whole." *Shalom bayit* does not refer to a quiet home, but a whole one. Quiet, somber observances miss the point. Laughter and foolishness are pretty good indicators of family harmony. With very few exceptions, the goal of Jewish observance is to open people up to the experience of joy—in Hebrew, *simcha*. In one family, *Shabbat* is greeted with a top-of-the lungs cheer: "Gimme an S. Gimme an H. Gimme an A. Gimme a B. . . ."

Hospitality

In every neighborhood, there is one house where children know they are always welcome to play. These are households in which, it seems, the couch is forever being made up for an out-of-town visitor. There are Jewish homes where it just isn't Friday night without guests at the table. Children who grow up under such welcoming roofs learn the pleasures of serving and sharing through the *mitzvah* of hospitality.

For Jews, hospitality is not simply a matter of good manners; it is a moral imperative, a sacred obligation called *hachnasat orchim,* literally, "the bringing in of guests." The biblical patriarch Abraham is the exemplar of hospitality; it was said that he kept his tent open on all four sides so that strangers would always know they were welcome. In the desert, of course, the offer of water, food, and a place to sleep could be a lifesaving act.

In the Middle Ages, Jewish communities ran charitable associations that provided meals and shelter for Jewish travelers, who were unwelcome, if not in danger, in the non-Jewish world. Likewise, it was considered a special honor to provide a bed and meal for scholars studying at a *yeshiva*, an academy of Jewish learning.

In the small communities and tight-knit ghettos of the past, everyone knew which families could be counted upon to make room for one more guest, and such people were considered praiseworthy and holy. There is a rich folk literature about poor people who, because they provided shelter and a crust of bread to a stranger, were rewarded with great wealth. The prophet Elijah, the legendary harbinger of the Messiah, is often portrayed as appearing in the guise of a beggar in search of a meal and a place to sleep, testing the practical morality of the Jews he encounters.

Today, hospitality tends to be the work of institutions. Jewish organizations provide help to newcomers to town, to immigrants, and to college students. However, there are still many opportunities for individuals to perform the *mitzvah* of hospitality for strangers: volunteering at a shelter for the homeless can be seen as an extension of *hachnasat orchim*—as can inviting students from a local college or university for a Friday night meal or a Passover *seder,* or contacting the Jewish chaplain at the local military base and inviting servicemen/servicewomen.

Hospitality is more important even than encountering God's Intimate Presence.

TALMUD: SHABBAT 127A

Beauty and Holiness

Home decoration is part of all known human cultures. But Judaism's tendency to blur the distinctions between sacred and secular, and its definition of the home as a holy place, suggests a special set of aesthetic considerations. Displaying Jewish art in a home or office is an act of identification and connection. Shopping for ritual objects and artwork can be a way of exploring Jewish identity and a way of deciding how to express Jewishness in concrete terms.

There is a long tradition of Jewish art, based both in custom and religious ritual. According to the rabbinic principle of *hiddur mitzvah,* when a physical object is needed to fulfill a commandment, the object should be made as beautiful as possible. While it is perfectly all right to make a blessing over wine in a paper cup, it is far better to use a beautiful goblet especially created for that purpose. Over the centuries, Jewish artists and artisans have fashioned ritual objects not only for large synagogues, but also for the homes of ordinary Jews. Embroidery and brocade have covered loaves of *challah* used in weekly Sabbath home rituals as well as synagogue Torah scrolls.

There are two kinds of Jewish decoration for the home: ritual objects and works of art. Ritual objects have a religious as well as a purely decorative function. They include: the *mezuzah* (a small container affixed to the doorposts of a home containing a piece of parchment inscribed with a biblical text; the *hannukiah* (the candelabra or *menorah* used at Hannukah); Passover *seder* plates; candlesticks used for *Shabbat* and holidays; and special goblets for blessing wine *(kiddush).*

Some families use ritual objects as decorative elements, displaying the family *hannukiah* year-round, or framing the *challah* cover Grandma embroidered in the old country. Others collect and display spice boxes, used in the ceremony that ends the Sabbath, or *draydls,* the spinning tops used during Hannukah.

The presence of ritual objects in a home, while not necessarily a sign of observance, acknowledges the religious and ritual aspects of Judaism. A *mezuzah* on the door, no matter how beautiful in its own right, says more than "this family enjoys lovely things." It is a sign and a symbol of identification.

Jewish works of art are more difficult to categorize and far more varied than ritual objects, comprising everything from fine-art photographs of Israel to framed examples of Hebrew and English calligraphy, from coffee-table art books and illustrated calendars to fine oils, lithographs, and sculpture. While the works of Marc Chagall, Ben Shahn, Chaim Gross, and others have been identified as "Jewish art," many other Jewish artists produce work that would never be labeled "Jewish." On the other hand, works on a biblical theme might be considered Jewish art, regardless of the artist's religion.

And of course, all art exists in the eye of the beholder. Some pieces might be immediately identified as Jewish—a painting of Moses, for example. But an abstract rendering of the Creation story may appear to a guest like nothing but a pleasing collection of shapes and colors—unless you choose to explain your understanding of it. One definition of Jewish art is that it is art that engages the viewer not only on an aesthetic level, but also in particularly Jewish emotional, intellectual, or spiritual ways.

There is a large selection of Jewish art especially for children's rooms, including mobiles that feature Jewish symbols, and posters of the Hebrew alphabet illustrated with bright, funny pictures. Of course, there's nothing like original art, even more meaningful when it's a Purim drawing or Passover painting created by your own budding Chagall.

The *Mezuzah*

The little box or cylinder affixed to the doorways of Jewish homes is a clue, a reminder, a sign of welcome, a decoration, an amulet, and a sentry box. The practice of hanging *mezuzot* on the doorposts of Jewish homes dates back to biblical times and they have been used, virtually everywhere Jews have lived, ever since. These ubiquitous objects have been assigned many meanings: they are reminders of God's presence, physical prayers for peace, a way of marking the difference between Jewish and non-Jewish space, a sign of Jewish pride, an opportunity for *hiddur mitzvah*, a good-luck charm.

Inside the container is a piece of parchment, called a *klaf,* containing the biblical reference to *mezuzah,* which means "doorpost." The words come from the book of Deuteronomy: "Write these words upon the doorposts of your house and on your gates." Also written on the parchment is the *Shema*, the proclamation of God's oneness, and biblical verses that follow it in the prayer book:

Listen, Israel, Adonai the Eternal, Adonai is One

You shall love your God with all your heart, with all your soul, and with all your might. And these words, which I command you this day, shall be upon your heart. You shall teach them diligently to your children, and shall speak of them when you sit in your home, when you walk by the way, when you lie down, and when you rise up. You shall bind them for a sign upon your hand, and they shall be for frontlets between your eyes. You shall write them upon the doorposts of your home and upon your gates.

And it will come to pass, if you will listen diligently to My commandments which I command you this day, to love your God and to serve Me with all your heart and with all your soul, that I will bring rain to the land in its season, rain in autumn and rain in spring and harvest rich in grain and wine and oil. And there will be grass in the fields for the cattle and abundant food to eat. But you must take care not to be lured away to serve gods of luxury and fashion, turning away from Me. For I will turn My face from you, and I will close the heavens and hold back the rain and the earth will bear no fruit and you will soon perish from the good land that I am giving you. Therefore impress My words upon your heart and upon your soul; bind them as a sign upon your hand and let them serve as frontlets between your eyes. Teach them to your children and talk about them when you are at home and when you are away, in the evening and the morning. Write them on the doorposts of your home and upon your gates. Then will your days be multiplied, and the days of your children, upon the land which I promised to give to your ancestors, as the days of the heavens above the earth.[1]

Mezuzot and scrolls are sold, usually separately, by Judaica shops and Jewish bookstores, and on the Internet. According to tradition, the scrolls are written by a *sofer*, a trained scribe. Thus, the parchment may cost as much as the *mezuzah* case.

Cases can be made of any material, adorned with all sorts of decorations, and are available in wondrous variety, including brightly colored *mezuzot* decorated with kites and teddy bears.

According to tradition, *mezuzot* are placed not only on the front door of a home, but on every doorpost inside, except for doors to closets and bathrooms. They are affixed on the right-hand side of a door (as you enter), at eye level, on the upper third of the doorway. The *mezuzah* is hung at an angle, with the top facing in toward the house or room. Two simple blessings are said before hammering the nails.

בָּרוּךְ אַתָּה יְיָ, אֱלֹהֵינוּ מֶלֶךְ הָעוֹלָם, אֲשֶׁר קִדְּשָׁנוּ
בְּמִצְוֹתָיו וְצִוָּנוּ לִקְבֹּעַ מְזוּזָה.

Baruch ata Adonai Eloheynu Melech Ha-olam asher kid'shanu b'mitzvotav vitzivanu likboa mezuzah.

Blessed be the Eternal One, Source of Life, by Whose power we sanctify life with the *mitzvah* of affixing this *mezuzah*.

בָּרוּךְ אַתָּה יְיָ, אֱלֹהֵינוּ מֶלֶךְ הָעוֹלָם, שֶׁהֶחֱיָנוּ וְקִיְּמָנוּ
וְהִגִּיעָנוּ לַזְּמַן הַזֶּה.

Baruch ata Adonai Eloheynu Melech Ha-olam shehecheyanu v'key'manu v'higianu lazman hazeh.

Blessed be the Eternal One, Source of Life, Who has given us life, helped us to grow, and enabled us to reach this moment.

Why do we affix the mezuzah *to the doorposts of rooms within rooms? This is necessary so that no one should think that only in public must one avoid doing wrong.*

ALSHEKH, 16TH CENTURY SAFED

Mezuzot are usually placed within 30 days of moving into a new house with a little ceremony called *Hanukat Habayit*, "dedication of the home." The blessing itself is the ceremony; however, you can add readings, songs, and prayers. One simple way to involve all your guests is to ask them to stand outside the door while you hang the *mezuzah*; then as each person enters, he or she gives a blessing for the new home.

Hanukat Habayit—Dedication of a Home
ADAPTED BY RABBI BARBARA R. PENZNER

We face the Eternal every moment we live.
We stand before God in every action we take.

The presence of the Holy One fills the whole world.
There is no place in the heavens or the earth that is
not touched by holiness.

If we but open our eyes we would recognize that the gateway to fulfillment is wherever we stand. It is to open our eyes to the holiness everywhere about us and within us that we perform the *mitzvah* of *mezuzah*.

We place the *mezuzah* on the gateway to our home, to remind us of the Holy when we enter and when we leave.

"Blessed shall you be in your comings and blessed shall you be in your goings."

Love Adonai with all your heart, with all your soul, with all your might. Take this teaching to heart. Transmit it to your children. Recite it at home and away, morning and night. Bind it upon your hands that your deeds be just. Keep it ever before your eyes that your vision be daring and true. Inscribe it upon the doorposts of your homes and upon your gates, that your going out and your coming in be for peace.[2]

(*Challah* is passed around.)

When the Temple in Jerusalem was destroyed twenty-five hundred years ago, the rabbis ordained that the Jewish home would replace the Temple. It would become a *mikdash ma'at,* a little sanctuary, and our table would be the altar, our bread and salt the sacrifice, and every meal a holy occasion.

בָּרוּךְ אַתָּה יְיָ. אֱלֹהֵינוּ מֶלֶךְ הָעוֹלָם. הַמּוֹצִיא לֶחֶם מִרְהָאָרֶץ:

Baruch ata Adonai Eloheynu Melech Ha-olam hamotzi lechem min ha'aretz.

Blessed be the Eternal One, Source of life, Who brings forth bread from the earth.[3]

(Holding the *mezuzah,* members of the household say:)

May our house be a place of holiness, by welcoming guests, *hachnasat orchim,* in the bonds of family, with deeds of loving-kindness, gifts of *tzedakah,* and words of Torah.

בָּרוּךְ אַתָּה יְיָ, אֱלֹהֵינוּ מֶלֶךְ הָעוֹלָם, אֲשֶׁר קִדְּשָׁנוּ בְּמִצְוֹתָיו וְצִוָּנוּ לִקְבֹּעַ מְזוּזָה.

Baruch ata Adonai Eloheynu Melech Ha-olam asher kid'shanu b'mitzvotav vitzivanu likboa mezuzah.

Blessed be the Eternal One, Source of Life, by Whose power we sanctify life with the *mitzvah* of affixing this *mezuzah.*

בָּרוּךְ אַתָּה יְיָ, אֱלֹהֵינוּ מֶלֶךְ הָעוֹלָם, שֶׁהֶחֱיָנוּ וְקִיְּמָנוּ וְהִגִּיעָנוּ לַזְּמָן הַזֶּה.

Baruch ata Adonai Eloheynu Melech Ha-olam, sheheche-yanu v'key'manu v'higianu lazman hazeh.

Blessed be the Eternal One, Source of Life, Who has given us life, helped us to grow, and enabled us to reach this moment.

(Affix *mezuzah*)

בְּרוּכִים הַבָּאִים

Bruchim Ha'baim

May all who enter be blessed.

THE SABBATH

We all have moments when the perfection of the world is revealed to us. A walk on the beach. A spectacular sunset. Our lover's eyes. A sleeping child. Sometimes, these moments take us by surprise, like rainbows. Sometimes, we engineer them: we plan vacations in the mountains, or tiptoe into the baby's room.

Shabbat is the way Jews arrange their lives to stay in touch with what is perfect in the world on a regular basis. It is Judaism's essential insight, its backbone, its methodology.

Shabbat, the Hebrew word for Sabbath, has been described a thousand ways. It has been called shelter, palace, fortress, bride, and queen. *Shabbat* is the only day of the week with a Hebrew name at all; the others are merely numbered in relation to *Shabbat*: the first day, the second day, the third day. In Yiddish, it is pronounced *Shabbes*.

The apparently simple idea that one day out of seven should be devoted to rest and reflection has always been a radical concept. Its earliest practice challenged the ancient world, which despised labor as the lot of beasts and slaves, and reserved leisure as the privilege of the rich and powerful. Today, when the hum of the machine never stops, when everyone has too much to do and not enough time in which to finish, *Shabbat* continues to pose fundamental questions about values and the value of life. For 21st century Jews, the challenge of *Shabbat* is literally radical, taking us back to our roots, recalling the biblical story of creation:

> *The heaven and the earth were finished, and all their array. On the seventh day God finished the work and stopped. And God blessed the seventh day and made it holy, because on it God rested from all the work of creation.*[4]

To the Talmudic rabbis who interpreted these words, the story does not mean that on the seventh day God rolled over, pulled up the covers and went back to sleep. On the seventh day, *Shabbat* came into being—and only then was the world completed, and perfect.

The Meaning of *Shabbat*

"The meaning of the Sabbath," wrote Rabbi Abraham Joshua Heschel, "is to celebrate time rather than space. Six days a week we live under the tyranny of things of space; on the Sabbath we try to become attuned to holiness in time. It is a day on which we are called upon to share in what is eternal in time, to turn from the results of creation to the mystery of creation; from the world of creation to the creation of the world."[5]

Millions of words have been written about the meaning of *Shabbat* in language ranging from legal to ecstatic. It has been associated with the great themes of Judaism: freedom, covenant, peace, and redemption. Sections of the *Shabbat* liturgy recall the time when the Jews were slaves in Egypt.[6] And although *Shabbat* celebrates freedom, it is also a reminder of the contrast between slavery and freedom. The Jewish notion of freedom entails both political and personal responsibilities; the mandate to work for the liberation of all oppressed people and the task of remaining free from enslavement to false idols, such as wealth, power, and fame.

Shabbat is called a covenant between God and the Jews. Just as the relationship between a loving couple is represented by a token, such as a wedding ring, *Shabbat* is the token between God and the people of Israel. "I have given them my Sabbath to be a sign between Me and them, so they will know that I am the One that sanctifies them."[7]

The charge of this covenant is to create wholeness, in Hebrew, *shalom*. *Shabbat* is about making peace with everyone: business associates, strangers, and especially within families. The highest priority is given to reconciliation and loving-kindness. Intimacy and sex are among the blessings of *Shabbat*.

Finally, *Shabbat* embodies the Jewish vision of redemption. Observing *Shabbat* fully means behaving as if the world were redeemed—complete, safe, perfect—right now. *Shabbat* is the opportunity to focus on what is right with the world, and thus to be refreshed to do the work of redemption: of repairing the world *(tikkun olam)*. Indeed, the Talmud says that if everyone on earth were to observe two consecutive Sabbaths, the world would be redeemed.[8]

History

The word *Shabbat* appears almost two hundred times in the Bible. ("Bible" refers to the Hebrew Bible, which consists of the Torah, or Pentateuch, the Writings, and Prophets. See "People of the Library" for a discussion of these terms.) The earliest mention of Sabbath rest is found in Exodus, when the Israelites who escaped from Egyptian slavery are told to gather a double portion of manna on the sixth day so they do not have to work on the seventh.[9] By the time of the First Temple (the 10th century B.C.E.), *Shabbat* was associated with joy as well as rest. The prophet Isaiah said, "And you should call the Sabbath a delight."[10]

During the Second Temple period (the first century C.E.), the nature of *Shabbat* was the subject of an intense and passionate debate whose outcome has shaped Jewish practice ever since. Among the sect known as the Sadducees, *Shabbat* was given an extremely ascetic interpretation: virtually all movement and all indoor illumination were forbidden. However, the Pharisees (forerunners of the rabbis) permitted far more latitude, declaring *Shabbat* laws moot in cases of helping the sick or saving a life. The Pharisees also made the lighting of candles on Friday night a precept that developed into the most evocative of all Jewish rituals.[11] After the destruction of the Second Temple by the Romans in 70 C.E., *Shabbat* observance came under the purview of rabbis, who have been interpreting and debating its meaning and practice ever since.

Although *Shabbat* has been a constant feature of Jewish life throughout history, its observance changed over time and varies among Jews living in different lands. For American Jews, most of whom have Eastern European roots, *Shabbat* associations—smells, tastes, sounds, and images—tend to have a Yiddish flavor mediated through American popular culture. Thus, *Shabbat* conjures up not only memories of chicken soup and braided *challah,* but also scenes from the musical comedy *Fiddler on the Roof.* Less familiar to most Americans are the customs of Mediterranean and Middle Eastern Jews, whose *Shabbat* was permeated by the aroma of lemons, food seasoned with fresh mint and garlic, and syncopated melodies.

Regardless of the particulars, however, *Shabbat* has always been experienced as different from the other days: it is the day for wearing new clothes, for inviting guests to share the best meal of the week, for singing at the table, for giving and receiving blessings. Jewish life and Jewish time are oriented around *Shabbat,* which takes precedence over almost everything else. Jewish weddings are not permitted on the Sabbath and neither are funerals because *Shabbat* is meant to be savored on its own, undiluted by other celebrations and unclouded, as much as possible, even by death.

Jews have often suffered for their loyalty to *Shabbat.* Antiochus Epiphanes, the villain of the Hannukah story, outlawed it and many Jews died defying his order. Marranos, Jews who publicly converted to Christianity during the Spanish Inquisition but practiced Judaism in secret, lit *Shabbat* candles in their cellars.[12] And there are heart-wrenching stories of Sabbath observances in the darkness of Hitler's death camps.[13]

More than Israel has kept the Sabbath, the Sabbath has kept Israel.

AHAD HA-AM, MODERN HEBREW ESSAYIST

Choosing *Shabbat*

The first appearance of *Shabbat* in the Torah is as a verb, *shavat.* "And God ceased/rested/stopped."

Shabbat is re-created weekly as Jews make *Shabbat.* The first verb for most Jews today, however, is not "make" but "choose." And *choosing Shabbat* is not one decision, but many. Choosing *Shabbat* means making a commitment to a weekly period of rest and peace. It means making distinctions between activities that are *Shabbat*-like from those that are workweeklike. It means avoiding things that might violate a sense of peace and planning ways to enhance that feeling.

These choices vary from one household to the next. Many Jews let voice mail pick up all their calls during *Shabbat,* but some find telephone conversations with family members and friends are relaxing and appropriate. Though traditionally, money is not handled on *Shabbat,* some people make a distinction between a day at the mall and taking the kids out for ice cream.*

Because *Shabbat* is often defined in terms of prohibitions against certain kinds of activities, Sabbath observance has been seen as a series of restrictions, a weekly sentence of self-denial.[14] But *Shabbat* is not an exercise in asceticism, and "making *Shabbat*" is not only a matter of refraining, but also of doing. The Talmud says "the affairs of heaven" are permitted on the Sabbath, which was specifically meant to include teaching children and arranging weddings.

Resting, eating, and praying are not only permitted, but mandated. There are other verbs appropriate to *Shabbat,* too; sleeping, reading, thinking, studying, talking, listening, meditating, visiting the sick, laughing, singing, welcoming guests, making love.

The real and the spiritual are one, like body and soul in a living man. It is for the law to clear the path; it is for the soul to sense the spirit.

RABBI ABRAHAM JOSHUA HESCHEL

Oddly, it turns out to be difficult, this choice to focus on peace and rest. All choices have consequences. If Friday night is going to be time at home, that means turning down invitations for dinner and a

---

* This kind of decision-making is a prime example of liberal Jewish practice, which focuses as much upon the spirit of the law, or *halachah,* as on the letter of the law.

movie with friends or family. And for chronically overscheduled people, sitting still for an hour, much less an afternoon, can be a real challenge. However, these are precisely the reasons that many people view
Shabbat as an opportunity to reorient a too-hectic life around the need
for relaxation and time with family and friends.

This is not always an easy change. The decision to start making
Shabbat requires planning and discussion, which may lead to some
discomfort and disagreement. Although it is common for one member
of a family to be the instigator and guiding force behind a commitment
to making *Shabbat*, it is important to include as many family members
as possible in the idea. This is rarely a problem with young children,
who tend to enjoy the specialness of *Shabbat* for its own sake, and
quickly come to look forward to the magic of Friday night. For older
kids, however, beginning *Shabbat* observance may seem restrictive or
just plain weird. Parents need to be secure in their own desire and
enthusiasm for *Shabbat*, and ease the transition by emphasizing the
playful and joyful aspects of the day, encouraging children's input as
well as their participation.

It is essential for family members to talk not only about how to make
Shabbat, but also why. Reasons can range from the practical to the mystical: *Shabbat* is something constructive and pleasant the family can do
together; it is an opportunity to learn; it is something Jews have done for
thousands of years and it can connect us to our heritage; it creates an
opportunity to visit with friends and family we otherwise don't see; it is
something beautiful and positive we want our family to share and remember; it is a way of finding and building community with other Jews.

Regardless of the whys or the ways, however, a commitment to
consistency and regularity is important. Most important, always remember that *Shabbat* is not something you do for or to your family; it
is something you make together.

Making *Shabbat*

While it would be difficult to overemphasize *Shabbat*'s intellectual and
theological significance, the Jewish Sabbath is not an abstraction or

disembodied idea that can be attained through revelation or prayer. *Shabbat* must be understood in its uniquely Jewish form—as a *mitzvah.*

A *mitzvah* is a command from God, chosen and enacted by people. The *mitzvah* of *Shabbat* asks us to be human in the most humane context that we can imagine and create.

The rest of this chapter is a kind of cookbook for making *Shabbat.* Just as it would be self-defeating for a novice in the kitchen to attempt an elaborate, multicourse dinner, it is not a good idea to take on every aspect of *Shabbat* observance all at once. Most people begin with Friday night table rituals: lighting candles, eating *challah,* singing songs. It may take weeks before even simple acts feel natural, but after a few months of repetition, comfort and a sense of expertise will come.

And just as cooks learn through apprenticeship, the best way to learn how to make *Shabbat* is with and from others. Sharing Friday night meals, attending services at different synagogues, getting together with friends on Saturday afternoon, can provide you with ideas, models, and support for developing personal *Shabbat* observance. Some synagogues run *Shabbat* retreats, a weekend at a camp, inn, or estate, where people study, pray, relax, and practice the fine art of Sabbath rest and joy.

On the following pages, *Shabbat* observances are divided into four sections: The first is devoted to preparing for the seventh day. The second part describes Friday night, the eve of the Sabbath, *(erev Shabbat),* where the focus is around the dinner table. The next section describes Saturday morning, and the synagogue service and Torah reading. And the last section is about *Shabbat* afternoon, which begins with a special lunch and ends with *havdalah,* the ritual that separates *Shabbat* from the new week.

Preparation

Shabbat is a vacation from the demands of the week, an invitation to shift gears, to slow down. For some, preparing for *Shabbat* starts with avoiding late-afternoon appointments on Friday and trying to be home at a specified time.

Shabbat also creates a deadline for finishing up things like getting the house clean, making sure that essential errands have been run, and that *challah,* wine, and flowers have been purchased. A traditional analogy compares making *Shabbat* to inviting a queen to your home. If you knew that royalty would be having dinner at your house, you would surely run the vacuum, take out the good china, think about the menu, and familiarize yourself with the special protocols and conventions of the event.

Food. Although Jewish law calls for three "feasts" on *Shabbat* to ensure a sense of celebration, it also forbids the lighting of fires, which traditionally means "no cooking." Thus, the biggest job of preparing for *Shabbat* tends to be food preparation. But even if you do cook on Saturday, preparing some food in advance can create more time for rest, relaxation, and fun.

Historically, Friday night dinner has always been the gustatory highlight of the week for Jews, no matter what their financial circumstances. Making it special does not necessarily mean making it elaborate, nor does it mean conforming to the chicken-soup-and-brisket menus of Eastern Europe. Some people find that making the same special meal every Friday night has its advantages: not only is it easier for the cook, it also reinforces the soothing, repetitive ritual nature of the meal and establishes a family tradition.

Any menu can be made special with a tablecloth and flowers on the dining room table. Ritual objects such as an embroidered cloth for the *challah,* candlesticks, and special wine goblets will immediately identify this meal as an *event.* And remember, anything you reserve for *Shabbat* use only, can become an heirloom. An inexpensive bread knife that never cuts anything but challah on the Sabbath may someday be a priceless family treasure.

Slowing down. *Shabbat* brings a release from the usual patterns of doing and being and celebrates some of the sensual, creative aspects of ourselves that may be sacrificed during the workweek. Celebrating the sensual can mean lowering the lights, taking time to smell as well as taste food, making sure to hug and kiss the people you love. And for those who cannot be with you, a few phone calls to say *"Shabbat Shalom"* is a two-way blessing.

In the rush to prepare home and table for *Shabbat,* it is easy to forget the importance of readying yourself. Nothing accomplishes the major shifting of gears from work to rest better than a hot shower or a bath. If you can find the time, meditate, listen to music, or read something to help you "get in the mood." But even taking a few minutes to wash hands and face, shave, comb or brush hair, put on perfume or cologne, or change clothes can help. Some people get into the spirit of *Shabbat* by listening to Jewish music as they set the table.

Traditionally, best clothes and new clothes are worn on *Shabbat*. However, if dressing up feels too much like work, a change into casual clothes might better facilitate your shift into *Shabbat* mode. Some people put on a skullcap (*kippah* in Hebrew, *yarmulke* in Yiddish), before beginning Friday night rituals.

Children. *Shabbat* easily becomes a focal point of anticipation and fun for children. The celebration can begin with a baking session or trip to the bakery for *challah* and other goodies. Setting the *Shabbat* table with children can be both a game and a reward, with special jobs assigned to each child: candlesticks and candles for you, the *kiddush* cups for you because you're so grown up and responsible. Kids can also create *Shabbat* place cards for guests, and centerpieces of LEGOs, or paper flowers, or dandelions from the yard.

Shabbat can inspire all sorts of arts-and-crafts projects. Since most small children love wearing hats—*kippot* (the plural of *kippah*) can be part of the fun. Some kids collect them, and a "custom-made" *kippah* can be created with some felt, a little glue, and a plain satin *yarmulke*. To make a Sabbath plate or set of dishes, apply Jewish symbols and lots of imagination to a melamine kit available in many toy stores. (Special pens are provided, and the dishes are then sent to a factory where the child's design is permanently baked on.)

Finally, when everything and everyone is ready, remove your watches. Empty your pockets. Ignore the phone. You are going to a party. *Shabbat* is not a solemn occasion. Along with the candles, the wine, and the *challah,* smiles and laughter belong at the table.

Friday Night

The four core ritual elements of a home *Shabbat* evening (*erev Shabbat*) celebration are: (1) blessings over candles, (2) wine, (3) bread, and (4) the eating of the meal. Friday night rituals vary from one Jewish household to the next. In some, there are many songs; in others, there is no singing. Some families recite all the blessings in Hebrew only; in others, there are English translations. Some discuss the weekly Torah portion at dinner; others use the time to reflect upon the week past. Some eat earlier than usual in order to attend services; others eat after services, lingering at the table as the candles burn down.

The various elements of Friday night observance are a menu from which a personal *Shabbat* home ritual can be created. As with any menu, all sorts of combinations are possible. Once you find a comfortable way to proceed, it can be helpful to make a one-page guide to the rituals and blessings in English, transliterated, and/or in Hebrew. This summary of your *"Shabbat seder"* can be decorated, laminated, and given to guests.

Despite the fairly detailed explanations below, *Shabbat* cannot be understood by reading a book. The best way to learn it is to live it—by watching and participating with others.

Friday night rituals:
Giving *tzedakah*
Singing
Lighting candles
Blessing for spouses
Blessing for children
Blessing for wine (*kiddush*)
Blessing for hand washing
Blessing for *challah*
The meal
Blessings after the meal
More singing
Synagogue
Making love

Giving tzedakah. Giving money to the poor is associated with nearly all Jewish celebrations and festive occasions. In moments of great joy, *tzedakah* is a way both of sharing happiness and of recalling that the world requires our attention.

It is traditional to put aside money for *tzedakah* before candles are lit. Many people cherish childhood associations of *Shabbat* with little tin cans called *pushkes,* which represented different Jewish charitable organizations. Making a collection box by decorating a can or jar, or making a container out of clay or paper, is a great project and a wonderful way of introducing children to the concept of *tzedakah.* (See "Good Deeds.")

"We will sing," said Rabbi Nachman of Bratslav, "and God on high will understand us."

Singing. Beginning a meal with a song breaks the week's routine and inaugurates *Shabbat.* While almost any song will accomplish this, many Hebrew songs *(z'mirot)* are associated with the *Shabbat* table. One of the simplest and best known is *"Shabbat Shalom,"* whose lyrics consist of those two words. *Shabbat* is a wonderful time for children to show off new songs they have learned.

But words are not really necessary. According to one tradition, a wordless melody, or *niggun,* is itself a prayer, and one of the purest forms of prayer at that. *Niggunim* (the plural) are usually fairly simple, repetitive, and easily taught.

One song most closely associated with Friday night is *"Shalom Aleichem,"* which is an invocation of angels who are thought to hover close on *Shabbat.*

שָׁלוֹם עֲלֵיכֶם. מַלְאֲכֵי הַשָּׁרֵת. מַלְאֲכֵי עֶלְיוֹן.
מִמֶּלֶךְ מַלְכֵי הַמְּלָכִים. הַקָּדוֹשׁ בָּרוּךְ הוּא:

Shalom aleichem.
malachei hasharet
malachei elyon.
Mi melech malchei hamlachim
Hakadosh Baruch Hu.

Peace be yours, angels of peace
Angels of the most high

Angel of the King who is King of kings
The holy blessed One.

Candlelighting. In cultures throughout the world, fire is considered one of the basic elements, a universal symbol of power, mastery, and divinity. Friday night candle lighting dates back to the first century C.E., and the blessing is as old as the eighth or ninth century.[15] For Jews, the lighting of candles is the act that formally ends the week and begins *Shabbat.*

Candlelighting is the most evocative of all Jewish rituals. Children who watched mothers and grandmothers *bench licht* (Yiddish for "blessing the light"), carry the image with them for the rest of their lives. Remembering her mother's *Shabbat* ritual at the turn of the 20th century, Bella Chagall wrote:

> *With a match in her hand she lights one candle after another. All the seven candles begin to quiver. The flames blaze into Mother's face. As though an enchantment were falling upon her, she lowers her eyes. Slowly, three times in succession, she encircles the candles with both her arms; she seems to be taking them into her heart. And with the candles her weekday worries seem to melt away.*
>
> *She blesses the candles. She whispers quiet benedictions through her fingers and they add heat to the flames. Mother's hands over the candles shine like the tablets of the Decalogue over the holy ark.*
>
> *I push closer to her. I want to get behind her blessing hands myself. I seek her face. I want to look into her eyes. They are concealed behind her spread-out fingers.[16]*

According to Jewish law, candles are lit not at dark but at sunset—technically, no later than 18 minutes before sunset. Candlelighting times are listed on Jewish calendars and in Jewish newspapers. Among liberal Jews, the common practice is to light candles when the whole household is gathered at the table for dinner.

The candles are lit before the blessing is recited or sung. There is a custom of circling the candles with hands and arms after lighting them, and then covering the eyes during the blessing. This practice can feel awkward or artificial to people who have never tried or even seen it done. If these gestures make you too self-conscious to get into a *Shabbat*-like mood, they defeat the purpose. Some people simply take a moment to inhale and release a very deep breath before lighting candles and reciting the blessing.

בָּרוּךְ אַתָּה יְיָ. אֱלֹהֵינוּ מֶלֶךְ הָעוֹלָם. אֲשֶׁר קִדְּשָׁנוּ בְּמִצְוֹתָיו. וְצִוָּנוּ לְהַדְלִיק נֵר שֶׁל־שַׁבָּת:

Baruch ata Adonai Eloheynu Melech Ha-olam asher kid'shanu b'mitzvotav vitzivanu l'hadlik ner shel Shabbat.

Holy One of Blessing, Your Presence Fills Creation
Making us holy with Your commandments and calling us to light the lights of Shabbat.[17]

At least two candles are lit, symbolizing the great dualities of life: female and male, light and darkness. The rabbis declared that the two candles stand for the two forms of the commandment to "remember" and "observe" *Shabbat*.[18] But while two is the minimum, there is no maximum. Bella Chagall's mother lit seven candles because she added a flame for each of her five children. Among some Sephardic Jews, candles are lit for family members who have died.[19] If guests are present at candlelighting, they can be invited to light candles for their families as well. A great blaze of candles is always festive.

According to tradition, the *mitzvah* of lighting candles is assigned to women, though incumbent upon men in their absence. While some women prefer to reserve this custom to themselves, there is a wide range of practice on this count. In many homes, all women and girls light a pair of candles, though in some families, the honor rotates and includes everyone regardless of gender.

Candlelighting is a wonderful moment for children, and blowing out the *Shabbat* match is a special treat in liberal homes.[20] A gift of small candlesticks on a birthday or Hannukah confers a new, more grown-up Jewish status on a child, and the first time he or she uses them can be a family event. Long fireplace matches are a good idea, and fun.

Generally, the candles are the short, white, kosher (no animal fat) tapers that are sold for Sabbath use in many supermarkets as well as Jewish food and specialty stores. Some people substitute colored or rainbow candles for a special occasion *Shabbat,* such as a child's birthday.

The only regulation regarding candlesticks or other ritual objects for *Shabbat* is the rabbinic principle of *hiddur mitzvah,* which states that when a physical object is needed to fulfill a commandment, it should be beautiful. Candlesticks handed down from one generation to the next are especially precious, but any object reserved for *Shabbat* use only quickly becomes a family treasure. Candlesticks with Jewish symbols may be purchased at Judaica shops, but for something that already has the patina of age and experience, a secondhand store or antique shop may yield an "instant" heirloom.

After the candles are lit, someone or everyone says *"Shabbat Shalom"* ("Sabbath peace") or *"Gut Shabbes"* (Yiddish for "a good Sabbath"). In some families, everyone exchanges kisses.

Blessings for a spouse. According to ancient custom, a husband reads or (chants) to his wife from the book of Proverbs (31:10–31). *Eshet Chayil,* "a woman of valor," is the phrase that begins this section, which lists her many virtues, including generosity, industry, business acumen, beauty, wisdom, cheerfulness, and loving-kindness. Verses from the Song of Songs can be substituted and read aloud.

In some households, this tradition is honored by spouses taking a moment to look into each other's eyes and say, *"Eshet chayil"* (to a woman) or *"Ish chayil"* (to a man). Others simply take a moment to kiss and say "I love you." Any such gesture makes it very difficult to allow leftover quarrels to compromise the peace and harmony of *Shabbat.*

Blessings for children. The Bible records several parental blessings, which are echoed in the custom of blessing children on Friday. There are three traditional blessings. The blessing for sons refers to Joseph's sons, Ephraim and Menashe, whose mother, Osenath, was an Egyptian-born noblewoman. The Midrash says that these two were singled out for praise because they held fast to their Jewish identity. The blessing for daughters names the matriarchs: Sarah, whose response to adversity was laughter; Rebecca, the model of hospitality; Rachel and Leah, who personify sisterhood in the most difficult circumstances. Last, there is the threefold benediction, also called the "priestly blessing" (*birkat kohanim*), so called because it is traditionally recited over the entire congregation by the members of the priestly caste, *kohanim*, or the rabbi.

Some parents add or substitute a more personal message for each child—praise for something that happened during the week, or just a whispered "I love you."

For boys:

יְשִׂימְךָ אֱלֹהִים כְּאֶפְרַיִם וְכִמְנַשֶּׁה:

Y'simcha Elohim k'Efrayim v'ch'M'nashe.

May God make you as Ephraim and Menasheh.

For girls:

יְשִׂימֵךְ אֱלֹהִים כְּשָׂרָה רִבְקָה רָחֵל וְלֵאָה:

Y'simeych Elohim k'Sara, Rivka, Rachel, v'Leah.

Make God make you as Sarah, Rebecca, Rachel, and Leah.

For either or both:

יְבָרֶכְךָ יְיָ וְיִשְׁמְרֶךָ:
יָאֵר יְיָ פָּנָיו אֵלֶיךָ וִיחֻנֶּךָ:
יִשָּׂא יְיָ פָּנָיו אֵלֶיךָ. וְיָשֵׂם לְךָ שָׁלוֹם:

Y'varech-ch'cha Adonai v'yish-m'recha.
Ya'er Adonai panav eylecha vichuneka.
Yisa Adonai panav eylecha v'yasem l'cha shalom.

May Adonai bless you and keep you.
May Adonai shine the Countenance upon you and be gracious
to you.
May Adonai favor you and grant you peace.

In her prayer book, *The Book of Blessings,* poet Marcia Falk re-
wrote the traditional blessings in language that speaks to the individuality of each child.

Blessing of the Children
BY MARCIA FALK

To a girl:

הֲיִי אֲשֶׁר תִּהְיִי—
וַהֲיִי בְּרוּכָה
בַּאֲשֶׁר תִּהְיִי.

_____ (her name)
Hayi asher tihyi—
vahayi b'rukhah
ba'asher tihyi.

_____ (her name)
Be who you are—
and may you be blessed
in all that you are.

To a boy:

הֱיֵה אֲשֶׁר תִּהְיֶה—
וֶהֱיֵה בָּרוּךְ
בַּאֲשֶׁר תִּהְיֶה.

_____ (his name)
Heyeyh asher tihyeh—
veheyeyh barukh
ba'asher tihyeh.

_____ (his name)
Be who you are—
and may you be blessed
in all that you are.[21]

Blessing for wine (**kiddush**). The word *kiddush* comes from the
Hebrew *kadosh*, which means "holy." The term refers to all blessings
made over wine, all of which contain this line:

בָּרוּךְ אַתָּה יְיָ. אֱלֹהֵינוּ מֶלֶךְ הָעוֹלָם. בּוֹרֵא פְּרִי הַגָּפֶן:

*Baruch ata Adonai Eloheynu Melech Ha-olam boray pree
hagafen.*

Holy One of Blessing, Your Presence fills Creation, forming
the fruit of the vine.

On Friday night, this blessing is sandwiched between two longer
passages. The first, from the Torah, recounts the creation of the world.
The second sounds three of the great themes of *Shabbat*: Creation, the
exodus from Egypt, and the sanctity of the Sabbath.

וַיְהִי־עֶרֶב וַיְהִי־בֹקֶר
יוֹם הַשִּׁשִּׁי: וַיְכֻלּוּ הַשָּׁמַיִם וְהָאָרֶץ. וְכָל־צְבָאָם: וַיְכַל אֱלֹהִים בַּיּוֹם הַשְּׁבִיעִי
מְלַאכְתּוֹ אֲשֶׁר עָשָׂה. וַיִּשְׁבֹּת בַּיּוֹם הַשְּׁבִיעִי מִכָּל־מְלַאכְתּוֹ אֲשֶׁר עָשָׂה: וַיְבָרֶךְ
אֱלֹהִים אֶת־יוֹם הַשְּׁבִיעִי וַיְקַדֵּשׁ אֹתוֹ. כִּי בוֹ שָׁבַת מִכָּל־מְלַאכְתּוֹ. אֲשֶׁר־בָּרָא
אֱלֹהִים לַעֲשׂוֹת:

*Vayehi erev vayehi voker yom hashishi. Vayechulu ha-
shamayim veha'aretz vechol tzeva'am vayechal Elohim bayom
hashevi'i melachto asher asa, vayushbot bayom hashevi'i
mikol melachto asher asa. Vayevarech Elohim et yom
hashevi'i vayekadesh oto, ki vo shavat mikol melachto asher
bara Elohim la'asot.*

There was evening and there was morning the sixth day. And
the heavens and the earth and all that they contain were completed. And on the seventh day God completed the work that
God had made. And God rested on the seventh day from all
the work that God had made. And God blessed the seventh
day and made it holy, because on it God rested from all the
work that God created and made.[22]

בָּרוּךְ אַתָּה יְיָ. אֱלֹהֵינוּ מֶלֶךְ הָעוֹלָם. בּוֹרֵא פְּרִי הַגָּפֶן:

בָּרוּךְ אַתָּה יְיָ. אֱלֹהֵינוּ מֶלֶךְ הָעוֹלָם. אֲשֶׁר קִדְּשָׁנוּ בְּמִצְוֹתָיו. וְרָצָה בָנוּ.
וְשַׁבַּת קָדְשׁוֹ בְּאַהֲבָה וּבְרָצוֹן הִנְחִילָנוּ. זִכָּרוֹן לְמַעֲשֵׂה בְרֵאשִׁית: כִּי הוּא יוֹם
תְּחִלָּה לְמִקְרָאֵי קֹדֶשׁ. זֵכֶר לִיצִיאַת מִצְרָיִם: כִּי בָנוּ בָחַרְתָּ. וְאוֹתָנוּ קִדַּשְׁתָּ
מִכָּל־הָעַמִּים. וְשַׁבַּת קָדְשְׁךָ בְּאַהֲבָה וּבְרָצוֹן הִנְחַלְתָּנוּ. בָּרוּךְ אַתָּה יְיָ. מְקַדֵּשׁ
הַשַּׁבָּת:

*Baruch ata Adonai Eloheynu Melech Ha-olam Boray pree
hagafen.*

   *Baruch ata Adonai Eloheynu Melech Ha-olam asher
kid'shanu be-mitzvotav v'ratza vanu, veShabbat kodsho
be'ahava uveratzon hinchilanu, zikaron lema'asei vereishit;
ki hu yom techila lemikra'ei kodesh, zecher litziyat mitz-
rayim; ki vanu vacharta ve'otanu kidashta mikol ha'amim
veShabbat kodshecha be'ahava uveratzon hinchaltanu. Baruch ata Adonai mekadesh haShabbat.*

Holy One of Blessing, Your Presence fills Creation, forming
the fruit of the vine.

   Holy One of blessing, Your Presence fills Creation, You have
made us holy with Your commandments and delighted in us. In
love You have favored us with the gift of Your holy Shabbat, a
heritage that recalls the work of creation. It is the first day
among holy days, reminding us of our going out from Egypt. You
gave us Your holy Shabbat as a treasure to grace all our generations. Holy One of Blessing, You make Shabbat holy.

There are many customs for how to give voice to *kiddush*. Some simply say the *"boray pree hagafen"* part of the prayer; others sing the entire *kiddush* aloud in Hebrew. In some families, it is the custom for everyone to stand, but in other households, everyone stays seated. Some make the blessing over a single cup, which is then passed or poured into other cups. Elsewhere, everyone drinks from his or her own glass.

It is also traditional to hold the cup so as to demonstrate that this cup of wine is not simply for drinking or even toasting. According to the Zohar, a medieval book of mystical Bible interpretation, the glass is held in the palm of the right hand, with the fingers facing upward and curled around the base to represent a five-petaled rose, an ancient symbol of perfection and of longing for God. Any glass can be used for *kiddush,* but again, it is considered preferable to use a special glass or goblet to fulfill the precept of *hiddur mitzvah,* or beautifying the commandment. *Kiddush* cups are common gifts for *bar* and *bat mitzvah* kids, but there is no reason to wait until a child is 12 or 13. Younger children treasure their own special *Shabbat* cups, as well.

Jewish law calls for kosher wine to be used whenever a blessing is recited. (For a full explanation of kosher wine and food, see "What Jews Eat.") For some, *kiddush* isn't *kiddush* unless the wine in the cup is the thick, sweet, red, and indisputably kosher liquid produced by companies like Mogen David and Manischewitz; however, there is a great selection of fine kosher vintages, produced in Israel, the United States, France, Italy, among others. Some parents substitute watered wine or grape juice reserved for *Shabbat* for children.

Rabbi Hanina wrote, He who prays on the eve of the Sabbath and recites the verses that begin, ". . . and the heaven and the earth were finished," the scriptures speak of him as though he been a partner in creation with the Holy One.

TALMUD: SHABBAT 119B

Hand washing: This ritual has nothing to do with hygiene, but is a symbolic reminder of the ceremonies in the ancient Temple, a gesture that reminds us that our tables are, in fact, altars. By saying a prayer over the washing of hands, we are prompted to discover the sacred within even the most mundane acts.

While any glass or cup can be used, two-handled cups or lavers are made especially for this purpose, some of which bear the accompanying blessing:

בָּרוּךְ אַתָּה יְיָ. אֱלֹהֵינוּ מֶלֶךְ הָעוֹלָם. אֲשֶׁר קִדְּשָׁנוּ בְּמִצְוֹתָיו. וְצִוָּנוּ עַל־נְטִילַת יָדֵים:

Baruch ata Adonai Eloheynu Melech Ha-olam asher kid'shanu b'mitzvotav vitzivanu al netilat yadayim.

Holy One of Blessing, Your Presence Fills Creation, making us holy with your commandments and calling us to wash our hands.

There is a custom of remaining silent after saying this blessing until reciting the blessing for *challah,* making a connection between the two rituals. Some people hum during this pause, which not only enhances the moment but also makes it easier (and more fun) to keep from speaking.

Blessing the challah. In many languages, the word "bread" is synonymous with "food." A blessing for bread is thus a blessing over food, sustenance, life. Jews make a blessing called *motzi* ("brings") over *challah,* a word that comes from a biblical reference to a sacrificial Temple offering of dough.[23] According to tradition, *challah* is any bread prepared for the purpose of making a *motzi,* a process that requires breaking off and burning a small piece of dough and reciting a blessing. Today, *challah* generally refers to a braided egg-rich loaf with a soft, almost cakelike texture. It is available in Jewish bakeries, and happens to be one of the easiest yeast breads to bake at home. Good recipes abound, children love braiding the dough, and the aroma of fresh bread is certainly an example of heaven on earth.

בָּרוּךְ אַתָּה יְיָ. אֱלֹהֵינוּ מֶלֶךְ הָעוֹלָם. הַמּוֹצִיא לֶחֶם מִן הָאָרֶץ:

Baruch ata Adonai Eloheynu Melech Ha-olam hamotzi lechem min ha-aretz.

Holy One of Blessing, Your Presence Fills Creation, bringing forth bread from the earth.

It is traditional to have two loaves on the table, recalling the double portion of manna the Israelites gathered on the sixth day so they would not have to collect food on *Shabbat*. The double portion of bread also symbolizes bounty, and some use a small *challah* roll to symbolize a second loaf. The bread is often covered with an embroidered or woven cloth, which, like special *challah* plates and knives, adds to the beauty of the *Shabbat* table.

There are many customs for saying the blessing. Some hold two loaves together; others invite everyone at the table to touch the bread or make a connection with someone else who has a hand on the *challah*. Some sprinkle the bread with salt, the traditional reminder of tears and of the destruction of the Temple. Because metal is considered a reminder of war, some people keep sharp knives off the table, which is why, in some households, no knife is put to the *challah* at all and it is ripped apart by hand instead.

When the world was created, God made everything a little bit incomplete. Rather than making bread grow right out of the earth, God made wheat grow so that we might bake it into bread. In this way, we could become partners in completing the work of creation.

MIDRASH

The meal. The very act of eating and sharing meals on *Shabbat* is considered a *mitzvah*, which is why there are so many rabbinic stories and folktales about the importance of feeding beggars and bringing strangers home on the Sabbath. Judaism has always been respectful of the fact that basic needs must be satisfied and that holiness and hunger are, in some fundamental sense, mutually exclusive. As the Talmud says, "Without flour [food] there is no Torah."[24]

The *Shabbat* table is considered a place to nourish mind and spirit, as well as the body. In the words of *Pirke Avot,* a much-quoted section of the Mishna, "If three have eaten at the table and speak words of Torah, it is as if they have eaten from the table of God."[25]

In some families, a real attempt is made to avoid "shop talk" or gossip. People might take turns talking about the important events of the previous week: good news, blessings, accomplishments, something newly learned. It is a *mitzvah* to host guests for *Shabbat* dinner, but the guests also do a *mitzvah* in that they enrich and enliven the conversation.

Blessings after the meal (**birkat hamazon**). The *birkat hamazon* (blessings for food) is a series of blessings and prayers filled with thanks and praise and set to a string of melodies. Praying the *birkat hamazon* is also called *benching,* from the Yiddish word for prayer, and is found in most daily prayerbooks, or *siddurim.* On *Shabbat, birkat hamazon* begins with Psalm 126, which begins with the joyful words, "When God brought Israel back to Zion/We were as in a dream/Our mouths were filled with laughter/Our tongues with joyous song."

The following paragraph of *birkat hamazon* is sometimes used as an abbreviated version of the longer blessing.

> Holy One of Blessing, Your Presence fills creation, You nourish the world with goodness and sustain it with grace, loving-kindness, and mercy. You provide food for every living thing because You are merciful. Because of Your great goodness, the earth yields its fruit. For Your sake we pray that we shall always have enough to eat, for You sustain and strengthen all that lives and provide food for the life that You created. Holy One of Blessing, You nourish all that lives.[26]

After dinner, the candles create a kind of hearth for lingering or reading. *Shabbat* candles are lit not merely for decoration, but for use, so studying by their light is considered an added *mitzvah*. Relax. Listen to music. Go outside and watch the night sky. Read *Shabbat* stories aloud to your children. Read love poems to your beloved.

Synagogue. The cycle of formal *Shabbat* worship begins on Friday evening with a service known as *Kabbalat Shabbat* (welcoming or receiving the Sabbath), which was developed by a group of Jewish mystics who lived in the city of Safed in the 16th century. Although there are variations on the Friday evening service, virtually all of them contain some version of *"L'cha Dodi,"* a poem from that community set to music. Today, in many congregations, when the final stanza is sung, everyone rises to face the door to symbolically welcome the Sabbath bride.

The Friday night service is held at different times in different synagogues; some just before sunset so people can get home to *Shabbat* dinner; others are scheduled to follow the evening meal. Some synagogues host *Shabbat* dinners on a regular or occasional basis.

Many liberal congregations include candle lighting and *kiddush* on Friday night and some share *challah* as well. When services are held later in the evening, they are followed by a gathering called *Oneg Shabbat* ("joy of the Sabbath"), a communal celebration of schmoozing (conversation) and noshing (eating).

Making love. The imagery of marriage abounds in Jewish texts; *Shabbat* is often described as a bride. God and the people Israel are like groom and bride, with the Torah as their *ketubah*, their marriage contract. The Kabbalists imagined God's unity to have been shattered by the expulsion of humanity from Eden. The feminine side of God— called *Shechinah*—would wander the earth in exile until the redemption of the world was complete. On *Shabbat,* however, God's two halves were reconciled and united in an act of love.

In Yiddish literature of the late 19th and early 20th century, there is a keen sense that on Friday night, husbands and wives looked at each other with different eyes. On a purely practical level, the men and women of the *shtetl* and ghetto looked their best. The quarrels and conflicts of the week were put aside as well since another reason for all the smiling was the rather public secret that Friday night was the time for sex. Indeed, Jewish folklore held that *erev Shabbat* was the most auspicious time for conceiving a child.

"*Y'did Nefesh*," a traditional song for Friday night, makes the connection between spiritual and physical union quite explicit.

> *Draw me to You with the breath of love,*
> *Swiftly shall I come to stand within your radiance*
> *That I may attain that sweetest of all intimacies.*
> *My soul aches to receive your love.*
> *Only by the tenderness of Your light can she be healed.*
> *Engage my soul that she may taste your ecstasy.*[27]

Shabbat Morning

With the morning, the focus shifts from family to community, from home to synagogue. For some, Saturday morning services are a weekly event, while others attend only rarely or, on special occasions, such as when invited to attend a *bar* or *bat mitzvah* (literally, "son or daughter of the commandment," a rite of passage for 13-year-old boys and girls). (See pages 225-233.)

For those unfamiliar with Hebrew and synagogue customs, *Shabbat* morning services can seem daunting. The best way to explore and enjoy them is to try to relax. No one in the synagogue is there to judge you. No one will know if it is your first time ever inside a temple, or the first time you have been to synagogue in decades. Some of the most important elements of *Shabbat* are available for newcomers as well as for regulars; voices raised in song, being part of a community gathered in peace, the opportunity to sit still and simply be. If you feel strange about just showing up at a temple, you can call the rabbi, introduce yourself, and tell him/her that you are planning to attend services. This is also a good way to gauge the warmth of a congregation.

What follows is a general outline of Sabbath worship services. While variety is one of the hallmarks of liberal observance, the essential elements that appear here are as close to "standard" as possible.

The Sabbath morning service (Shacharit). Commonly, there are five sections in the *Shabbat* morning service. The first two—morning blessings, and hymns and psalms—are introductory. *Shacharit* proper begins with a call to worship *(Barchu)*, and continues with the

Shema and its blessings, and the standing prayer (called *Amida* or *Tefila*). This is followed by the Torah reading.

The Torah, which is also called the Five Books of Moses and the Pentateuch, consists of the first five books of the Hebrew Bible: Genesis, Exodus, Leviticus, Numbers, and Deuteronomy. The Torah is divided into 54 sections, each of which is called a *parasha* or *sedra,* and which are read in an annual or, in many congregations, a triennial cycle.

Every portion is further divided into seven parts, each of which is called an *aliyah,* and on *Shabbat* morning all seven are read or chanted. (Only one *aliyah* is read during the Torah service on Monday and Thursday morning, and Saturday afternoon.) Special blessings are recited before and after each reading, and it is a special honor, also called an *aliyah,* to be called up to read from the Torah and/or to say these blessings.

The Torah is read from a scroll that contains no vowels or punctuation of any kind, so its reading requires training and skill. There are special books that contain the Torah text *with* vowels, punctuation, and cantillation (called trope)—markings that dictate the melody used for chanting. The designated Torah reader, called a *Baal Kriyah* (or *Baal Korey*), which means "master of the reading," prepares the reading in advance using such a book, which is called a *Tikkun.* A *bar* or *bat mitzvah* spends months learning to read a few verses, but even a skilled reader reviews the weekly portion before attempting it at services.

The Torah reading itself can vary from one congregation to the next. In some synagogues, the entire portion is chanted in Hebrew, while in others only a few sections are read. Some congregations do some or all of the Torah portion in English, and some have adopted the custom of a triennial or three-year cycle for Torah reading, so only a third of each *parasha* is read every week.

The Torah reading is the emotional and intellectual center of the service. The Torah is read as communal study and offered as an ever-renewing challenge to discover fresh meanings in its words, stories, characters, and ideas. Rabbis often base their sermons on the portion being read, and in some synagogues the rabbi or a congregant will lead a discussion of it. This kind of Torah reading can range far and wide, into politics and psychology as well as theology.

In most congregations, the Torah service includes a *haftarah* reading. *Haftarah,* which means "conclusion" or "completion," refers to selections from the biblical books of the Prophets, which are arranged in readings that thematically correspond to Torah portions. This part of the service probably dates from the second century B.C.E., when the Syrian Greeks prohibited reading from the Torah and Jews substituted selections from the Prophets that contained themes reminiscent of the forbidden *parasha.*

After the Torah portion has been read, there are concluding prayers and a familiar hymn. Some congregations have an additional service (*Musaf*).

Children at services. Taking children to *Shabbat* morning services can be wonderful or awful, depending both on parental attitudes and synagogue policies. Some parents feel that attending services is an important part of their children's Jewish education; that just being in the synagogue, hearing the sounds of worship, and seeing adults engaged in prayer is vital. To keep very young children occupied, a *Shabbat* backpack is part of the morning, filled with quiet playthings (books, crayons, puzzles, etc.) for use in the synagogue.

Others believe that worship services are basically an adult activity and that forcing children to sit for hours will do nothing but make them hate Judaism. They either arrange for a sitter, or take turns coming to services.

Actually, both of these approaches can be accommodated by good synagogue programming for children. Such activities might include age-appropriate services for schoolchildren, *Shabbat*-centered arts-and-crafts projects and singing for little ones, and even child care for babies. Sometimes, children join their parents during the pageantry of the Torah service as the scrolls are paraded around the sanctuary with singing, and at the end of the service for a final song. Some synagogues plan family services that feature singing, movement, and even puppet shows to tell the story in the week's Torah portion. Most congregations are very supportive of parents who want to help organize such activities, if they don't already exist.

Shabbat Afternoon

The first order of business after services is lunch, the second official meal for *Shabbat*. (Traditionally, breakfast does not count as one of the three Sabbath meals.) The *kiddush* over wine at this meal is called "the great *kiddush*" (*kiddush rabbah*). According to legend, the fancy name was supposed to compensate for the longer, more impressive Friday night *kiddush*. The second loaf of *challah* from the Friday night meal is often eaten at lunch.

The "great *kiddush*" and the blessing for bread (*motzi*) are often said in the synagogue after services, with everyone gathered around a table of wine (or spirits) and *challah*. If there is a *bar* or *bat mitzvah* celebration, the blessings may precede and kick off the *simcha*, which literally means "joy," and is also the name for a Jewish party.

In general, however, most people have lunch at home, which is where they spend the remainder of *Shabbat*. Again, it is always a *mitzvah* to invite guests home on *Shabbat*, especially anyone who might not otherwise have a warm, friendly place to eat. Encouraging children to invite friends over to eat and play helps make *Shabbat* a joyful time, and gives them the chance to extend hospitality of their own.

While lunch is seldom as elaborate as Friday night's meal, the noon meal is often festive or in some way different from weekday lunches. The whole notion of *Shabbat* rest discourages fancy cooking in favor of leftovers, casseroles prepared in advance, or a selection of salads and sandwich fixings. But in some families, Saturday means lunch *rabbah* (the great lunch) because it always features chocolate pudding or soda or chips. *Shabbat* can be a day of rest from saying "No" to children's insatiable passion for otherwise-forbidden treats.

A whole culinary history could be written about *Shabbat* lunch. In order to fulfill the *mitzvah* of eating a full meal without lighting fires or doing any real cooking, hearty casseroles were kept warm either at the back of the family stove or in a community oven. In Eastern Europe, for example, lunch was *cholent*, a heavy meat stew. In Morocco, the midday *Shabbat* meal was *dafina*, a concoction of chickpeas, potatoes, wheat, and meat, warmed all night in Arab bakery ovens. In Iraq, lunch was *tbeet,* a pot filled with rice and stuffed chicken, on top of which eggs were baked for breakfast.

After lunch, the afternoon stretches lazily on. The goal for *Shabbat* afternoon is to achieve the same level of relaxation one feels on the last afternoon of a two-week vacation. However, since many people find it difficult to face hours of uninterrupted leisure—especially at a time when the rest of the world is busy doing errands and cleaning out the garage—it can be helpful to make specific plans.

---

a rest of love freely given
a rest of truth and sincerity
a rest in peace and tranquility, in quiet and safety
a perfect rest in which You find favor.

FROM THE *SHABBAT MINCHA* SERVICE

Traditional *Shabbat* afternoon activities include napping, visiting the sick, and walking without a particular destination in mind. Some people reserve these hours for activities and pastimes such as bicycle riding, swimming, writing letters, baking cookies, puttering in the garden, reading poetry, sitting still and really listening to music, and going for nature walks. *Shabbat* is a wonderful time for spouses to talk, and for parents and children to play. And the more any activity is saved only for *Shabbat,* the more *Shabbat*-like it becomes.

Perhaps the most time-honored *Shabbat* afternoon activity is study. Some people meet monthly with a group of friends to discuss a book or the week's Torah section, a project that truly requires no knowledge of Hebrew or academic background in Judaism. The first five books of the Bible have been studied for more than two thousand years, in part for the sheer pleasure of trying to comprehend their meanings. There are no correct or ultimate answers—just new levels of understanding.

One way to proceed is by reading the week's portion out loud. This not only lifts the activity out of the weekday practice of reading for information; it also means that no one will have failed to do the "homework."

Nor does a *Shabbat* study circle have to be limited to the Bible. Indeed, the phrase "studying Torah" is traditionally applied to all Jewish learning, which includes the Hebrew language, a Jewish novel, a book of history or commentary, even last Sunday's editorial about Israeli politics. The caveat is that sad topics are avoided to preserve the joy of *Shabbat*.

Shabbat *ends*: Havdalah. According to the Talmud, *Shabbat* ends when three stars are visible in the sky, or on overcast evenings, when a blue thread is indistinguishable from a white thread held at arm's length. In other words, it should be dark.

Even so, there is almost no limit to how late *havdalah* can begin. The ritual that ends the Sabbath, *havdalah,* which means "separation" or "division," dates back to Talmudic times. It is a brief, enchanting ceremony that recalls the intimate power of the Friday night home ritual, though it is far more melancholy because it marks *Shabbat*'s passing. While some congregations hold *havdalah* services, this is, by and large, a home celebration. It consists of four blessings: over wine, over fragrant spices, over fire, and over distinctions between sacred and profane.

The lighting of a candle announces the *end* of the Sabbath, when making fire is no longer prohibited. The candle used for *havdalah* has at least two wicks, because the blessing refers to the "lights of the fire." *Havdalah* candles, which are available in Judaica shops and online, contain several braided wicks and are often elaborate, multicolored, and beautiful.

Although the candle is lit first, the first blessing does not mention light or fire; it is *kiddush,* although the wine is not drunk at that moment.

בָּרוּךְ אַתָּה יְיָ. אֱלֹהֵינוּ מֶלֶךְ הָעוֹלָם. בּוֹרֵא פְּרִי הַגָּפֶן:

Baruch ata Adonai Eloheynu Melech Ha-olam boray pree hagafen.

Holy One of Blessing, Your Presence Fills Creation, forming the fruit of the vine.

Next comes a blessing over fragrant spices. The sense of smell has been put to religious use since ancient times; indeed, incense was part of the service in the Temple in Jerusalem. There are a number of imaginative explanations for the presence of spices at *havdalah*. The sweetness of the spices symbolizes both the sweetness of paradise and also the wish for a sweet week to come. And according to one legend, during *Shabbat* people are given an additional soul, and when the Sabbath ends and this soul departs, the spices revive us and keep us from fainting.

בָּרוּךְ אַתָּה יְיָ. אֱלֹהֵינוּ מֶלֶךְ הָעוֹלָם. בּוֹרֵא מִינֵי בְשָׂמִים:

Baruch ata Adonai Eloheynu Melech Ha-olam boray minai v'samim.

Holy One of Blessing, Your Presence Fills Creation, making fragrant spices.

After this blessing, it is common to pass a spice box filled with cloves and spices. Flowers or freshly cut fruit can be used as well, but the spice box is a lovely ritual object. The oldest date from 16th century Germany, when they were made to resemble architecturally ornate towers or turrets. Today, spice boxes come in all shapes and sizes, made out of everything from tin to wood to porcelain, often as part of a *havdalah* set that includes a candleholder, *kiddush* cup, and tray.

Next comes the blessing over the fire of the candle, which has been burning during the blessings over wine and spices.

בָּרוּךְ אַתָּה יְיָ. אֱלֹהֵינוּ מֶלֶךְ הָעוֹלָם. בּוֹרֵא מְאוֹרֵי הָאֵשׁ:

Baruch ata Adonai Eloheynu Melech Ha-olam boray m'orai ha'eysh.

Holy One of Blessing, Your Presence Fills Creation, forming the lights of fire.

Since all Jewish blessings require some form of action, it is traditional to hold the hands up in order to feel the warmth of the flame
and to use the light to distinguish between the nails and fingers.
This custom probably derives from folk beliefs that fingernails revealed omens of the future. However, since there was great rabbinic
opposition to such forms of divination, the rabbis devised alternative
interpretations. They reasoned that since God started the first week
with light, it was fitting to begin every week with a prayer of thanks
for light. Then there's the legend that Adam and Even were covered
by a protective shell, like the fingernails, before their expulsion from
Eden, so looking at the nails is a way to recall the perfection of paradise.

The final blessing thanks God for creation and for the distinctions
(*havdalah*) that differentiate the universe into the place we inhabit and
sanctify.

בָּרוּךְ אַתָּה יְיָ. אֱלֹהֵינוּ מֶלֶךְ הָעוֹלָם. הַמַּבְדִיל בֵּין־קֹדֶשׁ לְחֹל. בֵּין־אוֹר
לְחֹשֶׁךְ. בֵּין־יִשְׂרָאֵל לָעַמִּים. בֵּין־יוֹם הַשְּׁבִיעִי לְשֵׁשֶׁת יְמֵי־הַמַּעֲשֶׂה. בָּרוּךְ אַתָּה
יְיָ. הַמַּבְדִיל בֵּין־קֹדֶשׁ לְחֹל:

Baruch ata Adonai Eloheynu Melech Ha-olam hamavidil
bayn kodesh l'chol, bayn l'hosheh or l'choshech, bayn Yisrael
l'amim, bayn yom hashvi-i leshaishet y'may hama'aseh.
Baruch ata Adonai hamavdil bayn kodesh l'hol.

Holy One of Blessing, Your Presence Fills Creation.
You separate the holy from the not-yet-holy, light from darkness, Israel from the other peoples, Shabbat from the six other
days.
Holy One of Blessing, You separate the holy from the ordinary.

The wine is drunk after this blessing, but only after a few drops
are spilled into a plate or tray. This is a gesture of sadness and loss; as
Shabbat ends, so ends its glimpse of redemption, of a world made

whole. *Havdalah* expresses a longing for a never-ending *Shabbat*, which for Jews is embodied in the idea of *moshiach*, Messiah. Because the prophet Elijah (*Eliyahu*) is the legendary harbinger of Messiah and since Talmudic legend has it that Elijah will come after *havdalah,* it is traditional to sing a song about him at the end of *havdalah*.

אֵלִיָּהוּ הַנָּבִיא אֵלִיָּהוּ הַתִּשְׁבִּי אֵלִיָּהוּ הַגִּלְעָדִי:
בִּמְהֵרָה בְיָמֵינוּ יָבֹא אֵלֵינוּ עִם מָשִׁיחַ בֶּן דָּוִד:

Eliyahu Hanavi
Eliyahu Hatishbi
Eliyahu, Eliyahu
Eliyahu ha-Giladi
Bimheira v'yameinu
yavo eilenu
Im Maschiach ben David
Im Maschiach ben David.

Elijah the prophet
Elijah the Tishbite
Elijah from Gilad
Come to us soon
in our days
with Messiah
child of David.

For a dramatic flourish, the burning candle is lowered into the wine while singing "*Eliyah HaNavi,*" timing it so that the light sizzles out with the very last word. Russian Jews, who used schnapps instead of wine for *havdalah,* would thus set fire to the liquor, and the smoke was thought to represent departing Sabbath angels. Hasidic Jews would dip their fingers into the wine and touch their pockets and foreheads as invocations for a successful, wise, and sweet week.

Havdalah is a treat for children as well as adults. The ceremony is short, dramatic, and full of ways for everyone to participate with all the senses. Children can be given most if not all the honors of touching, carrying, and passing the ritual objects. Indeed, it is traditional for a child to hold the candle up during the ceremony.

At the conclusion of *havdalah,* everyone says "*Shavua tov.* A good week." In some families, everyone kisses, or takes a moment to make a wish for the coming week. "*Shavua Tov*" is also the name of a simple, well-known song.

> *A good week*
> *A week of peace*
> *May gladness reign*
> *And joy increase . . .*

With *havdalah* over, a new week begins and a different spirit prevails almost immediately. Some people try to make the feeling last by making a little ritual of cleaning and setting aside their *Shabbat* candlesticks and other ritual objects until the next week, or planning whom to invite for the following Friday night *Shabbat* dinner.

Havdalah can segue into a party called a *Melavah Malkah,* literally "escorting the queen." This happens most often during the weekend of a major life-cycle event. So a Saturday evening party after a *bar* or *bat mitzvah* concludes a full day of celebration; Sunday wedding festivities may begin right after *havdalah.*

Shabbat in the Real World

Few recipes come out looking like the illustration in the cookbook. After all, those dishes were not only prepared by a professional chef; they were also arranged for the camera by a food stylist and perhaps even digitially enhanced. In real life, the same dish may taste great, but it invariably looks messier.

The same goes for *Shabbat.* Despite plans and good intentions, kids will balk about coming to the table on Friday night, and your spouse will be late or unable to get home at all. Or Friday night will be delightfully peaceful but Saturday will be filled with chores and errands and e-mails that can't wait; the kids will want to play soccer on Saturday morning along with the rest of their friends, Jews as well as non-Jews.

In the past, the world was divided into people who observed all the laws of *Shabbat* and those who observed none of them. The choice was either/or. Even today, the *Shabbat*-versus-work/errands/soccer question is rarely an issue if the entire family spends most of Saturday in synagogue, and shares lunch with others within a supportive community doing much the same. But for most American Jews, *Shabbat* is a work-in-progress, a goal. In other words, a "practice," in every sense of the word.

Almost everyone begins experimenting with *Shabbat* observance by trying on Friday night home rituals. For some, that remains the extent of their *Shabbat* observance. Others create a regular Saturday lunch group. Some try to avoid errands on Saturday but, when something important intrudes, put it off until the last minute to extend *Shabbat* as long as possible. And even on a Saturday filled with chores and soccer, some families try to have everyone regroup for *havdalah* so that *Shabbat* can at least end as peacefully as it began.

Starting any *Shabbat* observance may engender some family conflict, and it is true that many Jewish choices—including *Shabbat*—do impose limits that other kids do not face.

With older children, it is important to talk about your reasons for choosing to make *Shabbat* and to answer their questions: Why do we have to be home on Friday nights? Why do we go to synagogue? Why do we do this stuff when even Grandma thinks it's weird? Parents need to be able to answer honestly, even if that includes occasionally acknowledging your own doubts and fears and talking about what it means to make Jewish choices.

It is also important to let older children and especially teenagers decide about *Shabbat* observance for themselves—even if you disagree with their decisions. Later you can ask, "How did you feel about going to Jan's slumber party instead of staying home for *Shabbat* dinner?" For parents who want their children to grow up to identify as Jews and cherish their Judaism, one of the tasks of parenting is to give kids practice at making their own Jewish choices.

Of course, being a good parent also means making unpopular decisions about all sorts of things, from breakfast menus to bedtimes. Being a Jewish parent entails making Jewish parenting decisions. Say, for example, your son is invited to a friend's *bar mitzvah* on the morning of a very important soccer game. He tells you that he wants to play in the game and then go to the big party, after the *bar mitzvah* ceremony is over. If you give permission for him to go to the party and miss the religious service, you are letting him know that as far as you are concerned, Judaism is not as important as either soccer or ice cream and cake. Which probably does not further your goals as a Jewish parent.

But most of all, children learn from their parents' example. When adults make a heartfelt commitment to *Shabbat,* when Jewish family rituals seem as natural and dependable as the tides and the seasons, when the Jewish parts of family life are fun, arguments about soccer games and slumber parties take their place as minor disturbances in a broader context that has been defined in positive Jewish terms.

GOOD DEEDS

When a Jewish baby is born, there is a traditional prayer that the child will grow into a life that includes Torah, *huppah*, and *ma'asim tovim*. Torah stands for learning, especially Jewish learning. *Huppah*, the wedding canopy, symbolizes love, commitment, and family. *Ma'asim tovim* means good deeds, because for Jews doing good is what defines a *mensch*—a human being.

Because one of Judaism's primary goals is the transformation of people into *menschen* (the plural of *mensch*), good deeds are not left to the regrettably unreliable human impulse to do good. Feeding the hungry, clothing the naked, housing the homeless; for Jews, these are not voluntary acts of charity, a word that derives from the Latin *caritas,* and means "Christian love." Jews are commanded to feed, clothe, and shelter those who lack the basic necessities through *mitzvot*.

The general concept of good deeds—*ma'asim tovim*—may be divided into three categories: *tzedakah, gemilut hassadim,* and *tikkun olam. Tzedakah,* the giving of money to the poor, is commonly explained as charity, although a more accurate translation is "righteous giving." *Gemilut hassadim,* "acts of loving-kindness," refers to the kinds of activities Americans tend to associate with voluntarism: donating time and energy to help those in need. *Tzedakah* and *gemilut hassadim* are ancient Jewish concepts, discussed in the Talmud and recognized by all Jews as fundamental to Jewish observance. *Tikkun olam,* "the repair of the world," is a 20th century notion (based on a 400-year-old mystical story) that elevates the biblical prophets' demands for social justice to the status of a *mitzvah. Tikkun olam* is the religious obligation to work for peace, freedom, and justice for all people.

These three categories are all expressions of *ma'asim tovim.*

Tzedakah, tikkun olam and *gemilut hassadim* are described separately in this chapter not only for the sake of organization, but also to reflect the fact that people tend to "specialize" in one or another aspect of *ma'asim tovim*. The man who volunteers at a soup kitchen every Sunday is not always the person who collects vast sums for that operation. The woman who lobbies tirelessly on behalf of universal health care is not necessarily the person who visits nursing homes.

The obligation to do *tzedakah, gemilut hassadim,* and *tikkun olam* is, first and foremost, incumbent upon individuals and families. That said, no one is expected to repair the world by him or herself. The Jewish community as a whole is considered responsible for the performance of good deeds and is obligated to organize on behalf of the poor and the needy. "The Organizational World" contains information about communal organizations concerned with *ma'asim tovim.*

The Talmud states, "Though it is not your duty to complete the work, neither are you free to desist from it."[28] This chapter contains many practical suggestions for ways of incorporating good deeds—*ma'asim tovim*—into everyday life.

Righteous Giving—*Tzedakah*

The word *tzedakah* is related to several other Hebrew words, including *tzadik*, "righteous person," and *tzodek*, "correct." In the Bible, the word generally denotes righteousness. The much-quoted passage from Deuteronomy, usually translated, "Justice, justice shall you pursue," actually calls for *tzedek, tzedek.*[29] The Talmud is full of references, parables, and teachings on the *mitzvah* of *tzedakah* and goes so far as to say, "*Tzedakah* is as important as all the other commandments put together."[30]

Giving *tzedakah* is not viewed as an expression of individual goodness or goodwill, but as a response to an obligation based upon biblical imperatives and the belief that all needy humans deserve help. While it has always been considered preferable to give *tzedakah* cheerfully and willingly, the important thing is the gift itself, not the spirit in which it is given.

The story is told about two women on a fund-raising tour of a hospital's pediatric ward. At the end of the visit, one woman is in tears, deeply moved by the care and compassion of the place. She pulls out her checkbook and offers a check for $100. The other woman is visibly annoyed throughout the tour, and even complains about having her time wasted; why didn't they just send her a letter. As she walks out, she calls her attorney and asks him to direct $100,000 from her foundation to the hospital. For Jewish tradition, the tears are nice but essentially irrelevant.

Which is not to say that the rabbis did not recognize the intrinsic value of *tzedakah* to the donor as well as to the recipient. *Tzedakah* was never looked upon as a burden or a tax, but as a privilege: a way of expressing dignity, affirming self-respect, and participating in an activity that defines a *mensch*. Doing good feels good, which is partly why Jewish law requires that even the very poor give something to those less fortunate than themselves, even if their gift comes directly from someone else's *tzedakah* to them.[31]

Rabbi Chayim of Sanz said: "The merit of charity is so great that I am happy to give to one hundred beggars even if only one might actually be needy. Some people, however, act as if they are exempt from giving to one hundred beggars in the event that one might be a fraud."

DARKAI CHAYIM, 16TH CENTURY BOOK OF
MORAL TEACHINGS

The most important commentary on *tzedakah* in Jewish history was written by Rabbi Moses Maimonides in the 12th century. Known as "Maimonides' Ladder of *Tzedakah*," it lists ways of giving in order of their worthiness, a ranking organized according to what would spare the poor embarrassment. The ladder's highest rung is reserved for that which is given anonymously and enables another to become self-sufficient. Maimonides was also quite specific about how much *tzeda-*

kah is enough, and considered 10 percent of income an average and proper budget.

Maimonides' Ladder of Tzedakah

1. To help someone else to become self-sufficient
2. To give so that neither the person giving nor the receiver knows each other's identity
3. To give anonymously (donor knows the recipient, but the recipient doesn't know the donor)
4. To give without knowing who is receiving (recipient knows the donor, but the donor doesn't know the recipient)
5. To give without being asked to give
6. To give what is needed, but only after being asked
7. To give less than one should, but with compassion and in a friendly manner
8. To give grudgingly, reluctantly, or without wanting to give and not in a friendly manner

MISHNEH TORAH, MAT'NOT ANIYIM 10:7–14

Tzedakah does not just happen by accident. Although Jewish tradition supports spontaneous giving—such as responding to beggars on the street or neighbors asking for a donation to cancer research—taking on the *mitzvah* of *tzedakah* requires finding ways to incorporate it into the rhythm of daily life.

Many Jews make this happen through the time-honored tradition of making regular donations on Jewish holidays and personal milestones. Some put aside money for *tzedakah* before lighting *Shabbat* candles every week and on holidays. For small gifts like these, the *pushke*—a coin box reserved for *tzedakah,* a kind of Jewish piggy bank—is used. *Pushkes* range from works of art made of brass or silver, to blue-and-white aluminum cans. Making a family *pushke* is a favorite arts-and-crafts project and whether the result is a glazed clay masterpiece or an old coffee can covered with children's handprints, the result can become a family heirloom.

The custom of remembering the poor at moments of celebration is a way to add even more meaning to life's sweetest moments. In the small, tight-knit Jewish communities of the past, local beggars were invited to wedding feasts, and at Passover the community ensured that even the poorest family could afford a proper *seder*. In that spirit, many families, synagogues, and other Jewish organizations now regularly set aside a voluntary *tzedakah* gift of 3 percent of the food costs at weddings, *b'nai mitzvah*, and other banquets for an organization called MAZON, A Jewish Response to Hunger. MAZON allocates donations from the Jewish community to prevent and alleviate hunger among people of all faiths and backgrounds. For more information, go to www.mazon.org.

It is also traditional to give *tzedakah* in honor of a rite of passage. Indeed, some wedding invitations, *bar* and *bat mitzvah* invitations, and birth announcements request that donations be sent to a specified charity, sometimes in lieu of a gift. Indeed, *tzedakah* has become a focus for many synagogue *bar* and *bat mitzvah* programs; children may study and volunteer at a local agency, teach others about what they learned, and give some of their cash gifts to that organization. Twelve- and 13-year-old children are old enough to understand that the world is filled with inequities and *tzedakah* becomes a way for them to make a difference. Indeed, in Jewish schools of all kinds raising money and volunteering are part of the curriculum.

There are many ways to make *tzedakah* a family project. Putting coins into a *pushke* every Friday night is the simplest, and is also a way to begin talking to children about poverty and hunger, and how they can help. School-age children can help decide where the *pushke* money should go, and some parents talk candidly about the family's *tzedakah* budget, explaining how much money they give and to whom. Another easy way to add *tzedakah* to everyday life is at the supermarket. Let children pick out a can of food for donation to your synagogue or school food drive, and then volunteer for a family outing to help stock a local food pantry.

In some families, children are expected to designate some portion of their allowance for *tzedakah*. Parents and grandparents might want to open a *tzedakah* endowment fund for children, either at birth or on the occasion of a *bar* or *bat mitzvah*. Using the word *tzedakah* and linking your giving with Jewish settings and values reinforces the lesson.

Deciding where to give money is difficult because there are so many worthy causes. Traditionally, *tzedakah* was allocated in concentric circles, beginning with family and extending to the poor of the local community, and then to the poor who live at a distance, especially in Israel. Although Jews have always been enjoined to help the non-Jewish poor as well, the primary goal of *tzedakah* was seen as helping fellow Jews, who could not rely on others. This argument remains compelling. If Jews don't support services for the Jewish elderly, or Jewish educational and cultural institutions, there is no reason to expect non-Jews to do so. Many Jews also feel strongly that nondenominational organizations deserve their support as well, and divide their giving accordingly.

Much Jewish giving is done through federations, umbrella fundraising organizations that allocate monies to local and national Jewish agencies and to Israel. Family foundations are an increasingly common conduit, and some individuals pool their resources in *tzedakah* collectives, leveraging individual giving by joining with others to research, discuss, and select beneficiaries.

As tiny scales join to form a strong coat of mail, so little donations combine to form a large total of good.

TALMUD: BABA BATHRA 9B

Deciding how much to give is another sort of challenge. Maimonides' questions still challenge us to consider "How much is enough?" One oft-cited rule of thumb is: If the total of all charitable contributions makes absolutely no dent in your lifestyle, if you don't have to give up so much as one dinner in a nice restaurant, you're probably not giving enough.

Acts of Loving-kindness

According to many Jewish sources, *gemilut hassadim* is the highest form of doing good in the world. Raising money and writing checks to Jewish institutions and other worthy causes is an essential *mitzvah,* but there is also a sense that money alone does not meet the biblical demand for righteousness. Especially in America, where it can be relatively easy to remain insulated from hunger, poverty, and pain, *gemilut hassadim* calls for face-to-face encounter with real needs.

Gemilut hassadim is not, strictly speaking, a *mitzvah.* Because it is a feeling, loving-kindness cannot be required or commanded. But like a *mitzvah,* loving-kindness is not only about feelings but about rolling up your sleeves, giving up an evening a week, and working for the benefit of strangers. For American Jews, this notion dovetails with the national tradition of voluntarism.

There are six traditional forms of *gemilut hassadim:* providing clothes for the naked, visiting the sick, comforting mourners, accompanying the dead to the grave, providing for brides, and offering hospitality to strangers. These acts are considered especially holy because, according to Midrash, God performed them for human beings: attending Eve at her wedding to Adam, comforting Isaac as he mourned for Abraham, his father, and burying Moses.[32]

In the Talmud, *gemilut hassadim* is described as more spiritually powerful than *tzedakah* in three ways. First, *tzedakah* involves only money, but *gemilut hassadim* requires personal involvement. Second, *tzedakah* is given only to the poor, but *gemilut hassadim* can be done for anyone, regardless of his or her station in life. And third, while *tzedakah* can only be given to the living, *gemilut hassadim* can even extend to the dead.

The definition of *gemilut hassadim* has been extended over time to include such activities as feeding the hungry, helping people find jobs, visiting the elderly, teaching people to read, providing shelter for the homeless, saving animals from suffering, planting trees, lifting the spirits of the depressed, caring for orphans, and perpetuating the memory of someone who has died.

Nearly one-third of all Americans do some kind of volunteer work on a weekly basis, the highest percentage among developed nations. Thus, urban synagogue soup kitchens and shelters are staffed by congregants, and Jewish religious schools require high school students to perform some kind of community service.

Rabbi Isaac said: "He who gives a coin to a poor man is rewarded with six blessings. But he who encourages him with friendly words is rewarded with eleven."

TALMUD: BABA BATHRA 9A

Families can participate in *gemilut hassadim* in a number of ways. Parents who are involved in volunteer work can explain exactly what they are doing and why to their children. And while it may not be appropriate to take children to a battered women's shelter or soup kitchen, there are other ways to involve kids, such as collecting outgrown and unused clothes and making a family trip to deliver them to a local shelter; baking Hannukah cookies and bringing them to a Jewish nursing home; or "adopting" an isolated Jewish elder and visiting him or her regularly.

Jewish organizations are always in need of volunteers. So are community hospitals, nursing homes, legal aid societies, and literacy programs. The list is endless, and so are opportunities for acts of loving-kindness.

Repairing the World

During the 16th century, in the town of Safed in the land of Israel, Isaac Luria[33] described the creation of the world in terms that have captured the imaginations of Jews ever since.

Before creation, said Luria, there was nothing but God. God was in all time and space, and God's light filled the cosmos. In order to make room for creation, God had to make some space where there was no God. So God took a deep breath to make room for the universe.

In the space from which God had withdrawn, the heavens and the earth were formed. But that meant God was nowhere in creation. So God exhaled some of God's light into the world.

But this light was too strong, too bright, too much for the vessels that were meant to hold it, so they shattered. And the world was filled with tiny sparks of God's light.

The world is filled with these divine sparks. They are hidden, lost, everywhere, and it is the responsibility of each Jew to gather some of these sparks and to restore them to their place. By doing this, creation can be restored to its original, perfect state. The task of restoring or repairing the world is called *tikkun olam*.

According to Luria's intent and traditional interpretations, *tikkun olam* is accomplished by performing the *mitzvot*: from the commandments for keeping kosher and lighting *Shabbat* candles to those that mandate caring for the elderly or working for world peace. In modern times, Jews have come to understand *tikkun olam* in somewhat different and broader terms. The repair of the world is associated with tackling problems in macrocosmic rather than in interpersonal or even communal terms. *Tikkun olam* is identified with working for social justice, peace, freedom, equality, and the restoration of the environment.

This definition is not an exclusively modern formulation, however. Judaism has always blurred distinctions between religious duties and social obligations. Indeed, the Jewish notion of redemption is political in the sense that it calls not for the perfection of individual souls but for the liberation of the entire world. The prophets demanded an end to poverty, bigotry, and all forms of oppression. The words of Isaiah, which are repeated at services every Yom Kippur, have never been more powerful in their insistence upon action than they are today.

Behold on the day of your fast you pursue business as usual and oppress your workers. Behold you fast only to quarrel and fight, to deal wicked blows. Such fasting will not make your voice audible on high.

This is my chosen fast: to loosen all the bonds that bind men unfairly, to let the oppressed go free, to break every yoke. Share your bread with the hungry, take the homeless into your home. Clothe the naked when you see him, do not turn away from people in need . . .

If you remove from your midst the yoke of oppression, the finger of scorn, the tongue of malice, if you put yourself out for the hungry and relieve the wretched, then shall your light shine in the darkness, and your gloom shall be as noonday.[34]

Since the opening of the ghettos in the 19th century, Jews have been involved in virtually all attempts to improve human life. Sometimes, *tikkun olam* takes a specifically Jewish form, as in the search for a just and secure peace for Israel and her neighbors. However, a commitment to *tikkun olam* also requires, almost by definition, attention to many issues that are not strictly limited to Jewish interests, among them, the environment and ecology, nuclear disarmament and international peace, and equal protection for all, regardless of race, sex, sexual orientation, or national origin. Jews are prominent among the supporters, activists, and leaders in all of these causes.

Doing *tikkun olam* includes everything from writing letters to Congress about toxic waste, to attending rallies in support of funding for health care. *Tikkun olam* means supporting candidates and voting with a self-consciously Jewish perspective. Even recycling waste paper, bottles, and cans responds to the call to repair the world.

This formulation of *tikkun olam* claims political commitment as a specifically Jewish endeavor. And it helps blur the tendency to segregate Jewishness to those things that are done at home, or in a synagogue, or among other Jews. In a sense, *tikkun olam* demands that Jews act as Jews in every arena of life.

THE PEOPLE OF THE LIBRARY

Jews are often called "the people of the book," and for good reason. The legacy of universal literacy—for women and men, for poor and rich—has set Jews apart from their neighbors throughout history.

It would be more accurate to refer to Jews as "the people of the library." First of all, "The Book," the Jewish Bible, is itself a library, a collection of books, and the foundation and cornerstone of a 3,000-year-old tradition of intellectual inquiry, writing, and publishing. But the basic texts of Judaism include much more than the Bible. Jewish literacy requires familiarity with some of the classical sources and genres as well: Torah, Talmud, Midrash, Kabbalah, *siddur.*

The presence of books, especially books dealing with Jewish subjects, is a hallmark of virtually all Jewish homes. Reading and study, discussion and writing, are part of the social as well as intellectual glue that has kept Judaism and the Jewish people alive. The secret ingredient of this glue, taught to children by their parents, is the pleasure of study for its own sake, in Hebrew, *Torah lishma.*

Jewish Texts: Some Definitions

Bible. There is no Hebrew word for "bible." The English word probably comes from the Greek *biblia,* meaning books and reflecting the fact that the Bible is itself an anthology. When Jews talk about the Bible, the reference is shorthand for "the Jewish Bible" or "the Hebrew Bible." (It is only the "Old Testament" to Christians, who believe that there is a "New Testament," which describes a new covenant between God and humanity that was announced by Jesus.)

The Hebrew term for the Bible is *tanakh,* which is an acronym for the three Hebrew letters that correspond to its three major divisions:

Torah—The five books of Moses, Pentateuch
Ne'vi'im—Prophets
Ketuvim—Writings

Arguments about the authorship of the Bible cut right to the heart of religious belief. Traditionalists attribute the writing of the Torah to Moses, Psalm 92 to Adam, and Song of Songs to King Solomon. Modern biblical scholars generally agree that the Bible, as we know it, was codified sometime during the first or second century C.E.

The Hebrew Bible—*Tanakh*

Torah:
Genesis—Beresheet
Exodus—Shemot
Leviticus—Vayikra
Numbers—Bemidbar
Deuteronomy—Devarim

Prophets: Nevi'im
Joshua—Yehoshua
Judges—Shoftim
I Samuel—Shmuel Alef
II Samuel—Shmuel Bet
I Kings—Melakhim Alef
II Kings—Melakhim Bet
Isaiah—Yishayahu
Jeremiah—Yirmiyahu
Ezekiel—Yekhezkel

The 12 Minor Prophets
Hosea—Hoshea
Joel—Yoel

Amos—Ahmos
Obadiah—Ovadya
Jonah—Yona
Micah—Meekhah
Nahum—Nakhum
Habakkuk—Khbakuk
Zephania—Tzafania
Haggai—Haggai
Zakariah—Zekharya
Malachi—Malakhi

Writings: Ketuvim
Psalms—Tehilim
Proverbs—Mishlei
Job—Eyov
Song of Songs—Shir Hashirim
Ruth—Root
Lamentations—Eikha
Ecclesiastes—Kohelet
Esther—Ester
Daniel—Daniel
Ezra—Ezra
Nehemiah—Nekhemya
I Chronicles—Divray Yamim Alef
II Chronicles—Divray Yamim Bet

Torah. A word with multiple meanings, the Torah is also called the Pentateuch and the five books of Moses. It consists of the first five volumes of the Bible: Genesis, Exodus, Leviticus, Numbers, and Deuteronomy. *The Torah* also refers to the scroll on which this part of the Bible is written.

But "Torah," without the definite article, refers to much larger concepts. "Torah" can be used to mean revelation—God's word as understood by human beings. To further complicate things, Torah also refers to all Jewish study, and all of Jewish literature.[35]

Talmud. The Talmud (Hebrew for "study") is an encyclopedia of commentaries on Jewish law, and of commentaries upon commentaries on Jewish law. Written in Hebrew and Aramaic, which was the *lingua franca* of the ancient Near East, the Talmud comprises two major sections called *Mishna* and *Gemara*.

According to tradition, Moses received two forms of revelation on Mount Sinai: written and oral. The written law, the Torah, was much shorter and less specific than the oral law, which was transmitted through the generations, first from Moses to Joshua, then to the elders of the Hebrew people, to the prophets, and on to successive leaders until it reached the men who were, in effect, the earliest rabbis. These scholars of the first and second century C.E. began putting the oral law into writing in what came to be called the *Mishna*.

The *Mishna* (Hebrew for "recitation" or "recapitulation") was completed by the third century C.E. in an attempt to put the commands contained in the written Torah into practical terms. Its authors sought to convey the idea that the laws found in the Bible did not apply just in their original context, but embraced all aspects of life throughout time. The six sections of the *Mishna* are called Orders, which are further divided into 63 smaller sections called tractates (literally, "webbings"). The *Mishna* deals with holiday observance, family life, agriculture, the rituals of the Temple, and much more.

The most famous section of the *Mishna* is the tractate known as *Avot*, or "fathers," which contains many famous proverbs, axioms, and sayings, such as, "If I am not for myself, who will be for me? If I am for myself alone, what am I? And if not now, when?"[36] This tractate has long been published as a book of practical wisdom entitled *Pirke Avot*, usually translated as "Ethics of the Fathers."

Who is wise? One who learns from all men.
Who is wealthy? One who is happy with is portion.
Who is mighty? One who subdues his passions.
Who is honored? One who honors all creation.

PIRKE AVOT 4:1

Over succeeding generations, the study of *Mishna* inspired a literature of explanation and commentary, which became an object of study
in its own right. This body of writing was called *Gemara,* Aramaic for
"study." The *Gemara,* which is an unstructured, almost stream-of-
consciousness transcript of discussions, arguments, and stories, examines a broad range of questions from daily life. Sometimes the sublime
and the ridiculous share a single paragraph:

> *Who is to be considered truly wealthy?*
>
> *In the opinion of Rabbi Meir: He who derives peace of mind*
> *from his wealth.*
>
> *Rabbi Tarfon says: He who has a hundred vineyards, a hun-*
> *dred fields, and a hundred workers working in them.*
>
> *Rabbi Akiva says: He who has a spouse who does exquisite*
> *deeds.*
>
> *Rabbi Yossi says: He who has a bathroom near his dining*
> *room table.*[37]

Midrash. *Midrash,* which means "search," or "investigation," refers
not to a single book but to a genre of biblical commentary. Using every
kind of imaginative and literary device, Midrash embroiders upon the
biblical text. Explaining Midrash requires metaphoric language; it has
been described as something "between commentary and fantasy . . .
that sprouts up in the spaces between the consecrated words of Scripture."[38] If the compressed images of the Bible are like photographs, a
midrash is the story about what happened or what might have happened before and after the flash went off.

There are several collections of *midrashim* (plural of *midrash*), most
them produced between 400 and 1200 C.E. One of the most famous
of these is *Midrash Rabbah,* the "Great Midrash." Here is an example
of how *Midrash Rabbah* explicates the line in Genesis that says, "And
God said, Let us make man."

> *When the Holy One came to create the first man, the angels took*
> *sides. Mercy said, "Let him be created, for he will be merciful."*
> *But Truth said, "Do not let him be created because he will lie."*

Righteousness said, "Let him be created for he will do righteous deeds." But Peace said, "Do not let him be created because he is full of strife."

The Holy One took Truth and flung him to earth, and the angels argued with God, and asked God to raise truth up again from the earth.

While the angels were arguing, The Holy One created man. And then God said to the angels, "Why do you argue? Man is already made."[39]

Codes. The whole of Jewish law is called *halachah,* probably from the verb for "going," as in, the way one should go. *Halachah* is often used to refer to the laws and rules that govern and inform Jewish life. The Talmud is not a set of laws but a discussion of the law, and has been compared with the *Congressional Record,* which provides a verbatim account of what is said on the floor of the U.S. Congress; not only the formal speeches, but the jokes and side comments as well. To find out what the law says, people turn not to the Talmud but to the codes, which are practical, accessible guides to action based upon the debates in the Talmud.

The two classic codes are the *Mishna Torah,* written by Moses Maimonides, the great 12th century Mediterranean rabbi and philosopher, and the *Shulchan Aruch* ("The Prepared Table") by Joseph Karo, a 16th century rabbi who lived in the town of Safed, Palestine. Maimonides and Karo based their guides on careful reading of Talmud, consideration of contemporary rabbis' decisions (known as *responsa* literature), and the Jewish practice of their times. These books remain cornerstones of *halachic* discussion and debate, which continues unabated today.

Kabbalah. The rationalist tradition in Jewish thought has been dominant, but there has also been a long and illustrious history of Jewish mysticism, which is called Kabbalah. Like Midrash, Kabbalah is not a book but a way of looking at the world and understanding Jewish tradition. Kabbalistic literature includes several books of biblical commentary, including *Sefer Yetzirah* ("The Book of Creation") and the *Bahir* ("Brilliance"). The most influential of all mystical texts, however, is the Zohar ("The Book of Splendor"). Typified by evocative, lyrical language and concepts, the Zohar was a commentary on the Torah, probably written by the Spanish rabbi Moses de Leon (1230–1305).

The contemporary fad for Kabbalah, among non-Jews as well as Jews, minimizes the ways that this subject is rooted in Jewish tradition and law, stressing an esoteric mysticism divorced from *mitzvot, halachah,* and Jewish life.

Siddur. The daily book of prayer—used both in the synagogue and at home—is called the *siddur,* from the Hebrew root for "order." The prayer book used for festivals and the High Holidays is called the *machzor,* from the Hebrew root for "cycle."

Prayer books have been the most commonly owned of all Jewish books. Over time, the content and order of the prayer book has evolved and changed. Modern prayer books tend to contain readings that reflect Jewish history and theology from many periods, including our own.

Creating a Home Library

No two Jewish homes have identical Jewish libraries. People select books as idiosyncratically as they choose art for their walls and food for their tables. Books reflect the character, curiosity, and impulses of their owners. Jewish literature expands exponentially every few years with the publication of important new works in virtually every discipline, so that any listing is bound to be outdated almost before the ink dries. And of course the Internet will continue to enlarge the limits of the Jewish home library, with ever-growing connections to books, periodicals, institutions, blogs. What follows is a short list of classics, offered as a guide to assembling the foundation for a Jewish home library.

Bible

The Jewish Publication Society (www.jewishpub.org) produces an accurate, readable translation of the Bible, available in either one or three volumes.

The Jerusalem Bible, published by Koren Publishers of Jerusalem (www.judaism.com) contains very accurate Hebrew and English versions in a single volume, although the English is not as readable as the JPS version.

Torah

As a rule, Jews do not read the first five books of the Bible without some form of commentary. For close study of the Torah as it is read in its weekly portions during services, people use what is called a *chumash*. A *chumash* (from the Hebrew word for "five") includes both Hebrew and English versions of each week's portion, the weekly Haftarah section (readings from the Prophets), and English commentaries and notes. Two of the best known of these are: *The Torah: A Modern Commentary*, edited by Rabbi Gunther Plaut (www.ccarpress.org), and *Etz Hayim: Torah and Commentary* (www.uscj.org).

Siddurim / Prayer Books

Generally produced by the movements, prayer books offer more than just the rubric for synagogue services. Most provide essays and commentaries on prayer as well as sections covering home observances, such as the prayers for the Sabbath and holidays.

Conservative: *Sim Shalom* (www.uscj.org)
Reconstructionist: *Kol Haneshamah* (www.jrf.org)
Reform: *Mishkan Tefila* (www.ccarpress.org)

Talmud

The Essential Talmud by Adin Steinsaltz (Basic Books, 1984) is a brief and lucid introduction to Talmud.

The Talmud: The Steinsaltz Edition (Random House) gives unprecedented English access to the original text by one of the 20th century's most erudite and prolific Jewish scholars.

The Mishna is available in English in several editions of one or two volumes. The section of Mishna known as *Pirke Avot* is available in many versions, including some with explanatory notes and commentaries.

Also recommended are *Back to the Sources* by Barry Holtz (Summit Books, 1986), a single volume with eight essays about the major Jewish texts, including the Bible, Talmud, Midrash, Hasidic writings, and the prayer book; and *The Zohar, Annotated and Explained* by Daniel Chanan Matt (Skylight Paths Publishing, 2003), a good introduction to the classic book of Jewish mystical commentary.

General Reference

The Encyclopedia Judaica (Macmillan Library Reference, 2006). The "EJ," as it is known, is the *Britannica* of Judaism, and there is little it does not cover. The 18-volume set, newly updated, includes contributions by thousands of scholars. A CD version is available from www.jewishsoftware.com.

A Guide to Jewish Religious Practice by Isaac Klein (Ktav Publishing House, 1979) is the standard reference book of *halachah* published by the Conservative movement; this is where you go to look up the law on just about anything.

The New Joys of Yiddish by Leo Rosten and Lawrence Bush (Three Rivers Press, 2003). More than just a funny dictionary of English, Yiddish, and "Yinglish" words, this is a useful guide for exploring *Yiddishkeit*—"Jewishness."

Jewish Literacy: The Most Important Things to Know About the Jewish Religion, Its People and Its History by Rabbi Joseph Telushkin (William Morrow, 1991). An excellent overview.

History

A History of the Jewish People, edited by H. H. Ben-Sasson (Harvard University Press, 1985). A definitive volume of 1,000 pages that covers Jewish history to the modern period.

The Gifts of the Jews: How a Tribe of Desert Nomads Changed the Way Everyone Thinks and Feels by Thomas Cahill (Anchor, 1999). A light-handed, modern perspective.

American Judaism: A History, by Jonathan Sarna (Yale University Press, 2005). Concise and readable, it covers 350 years, from colonial beginnings in 1654.

Jewish People, Jewish Thought: The Jewish Experience in History by Robert M. Seltzer (Prentice-Hall, 2003). A survey of Jewish thought, beginning with the ancients and running through the 20th century.

Israel

The Zionist Idea, edited by Arthur Hertzberg (Jewish Publication Society, 1997). A collection of essays providing an intellectual history of Zionism, with brief biographies of the leaders of the early movement.

In the Land of Israel, by Amos Oz (Harvest Books,1993). A series of interviews conducted by the well-known Israeli novelist.

One Palestine Complete: Jews and Arabs Under the British Mandate, by Tom Segev (Owl Books, 2003). An Israeli journalist and historian explores the early history of the state.

Philosophy

God in Search of Man: A Philosophy of Judaism, by Abraham Joshua Heschel (Farrar, Straus and Giroux, 1976), is a contemporary attempt to describe the relationship between human beings and God.

After Auschwitz, by Richard Rubenstein (The Johns Hopkins University Press, 1992), articulates a radical post-Holocaust Jewish theology.

A Maimonides Reader, by Isador Twersky (Behrman House, 1976), is an introduction to one of Judaism's great minds, written by a master.

Spirituality

The Way of Man According to the Teachings of Hasidism, by Martin Buber (Citadel Press, 1995). A modern interpretation of six Hasidic tales that explain some of Judaism's basic tenets.

The Sabbath, by Rabbi Abraham Joshua Heschel (Farrar, Straus and Giroux, 2005), is the classic text for understanding the theological and spiritual importance of *Shabbat.*

God Was in This Place and I, i Did Not Know: Finding Self, Spirituality and Ultimate Meaning, by Lawrence Kushner (Jewish Lights Publishing, 1993). A spiritual journey into a single biblical verse (Genesis 28:16).

Major Trends in Jewish Mysticism, by Gershom Scholem (Schocken Books, 1995). A historical consideration of the mystical "counterhistory" that includes Kabbalah and Hasidism.

Holocaust

The War Against the Jews: 1933–1945, by Lucy Dawidowicz (Bantam, 1986), is an exhaustively researched historical anthology of the Holocaust.

Fiction and memoir provide some of the most powerful commentaries on those years. A few of the best include *Night* by Elie Wiesel, *Survival in Auschwitz* by Primo Levi, and *The Last of the Just* by André Schwarz-Bart.

Holy One of Blessing, Your Presence Fills Creation, You make us holy with Your commandments and call us to occupy ourselves with words of Torah.

THE BLESSING RECITED BEFORE JEWISH STUDY

WHAT JEWS EAT

The philosopher Martin Buber described Judaism as a system for living without distinctions between the secular and the spiritual. He wrote, "Basically the holy in our world is what is open to God, as the profane is what is closed off from Him . . . hallowing is the event of opening out . . ."[40] *Kashrut*, the system of rules and laws regulating what Jews eat and how Jews prepare food, can be understood as a way of hallowing the very mundane act of eating, as a way of "opening out" to God with every meal.

For over two thousand years, *kashrut* has been a defining element of Jewish life, part of the cultural glue that kept Jewish communities interdependent and united, and also a constant affirmation of Jewish differentness in the most fundamental aspects of life. Because the laws of *kashrut* so clearly set Jews apart, food often became a focus of anti-Semitism. There are countless stories about Jews being forced to eat pork—or dying rather than comply.[41]

Although many Jews think of *kashrut* as an essential aspect of Jewish identity and observance, most American Jews do not "keep kosher." Nonetheless, there is increasing interest in the dietary laws among liberal Jews who are willing to learn from all aspects of tradition. And given that so many people are eating more self-consciously for reasons of health, fitness, and even in response to political and ecological concerns, Judaism's approach to spiritual eating takes on new possibilities for meaning. (Of course, Jews are not the only ones with religious dietary laws. Muslims share the stricture against pork and almost all of India—as many as 20 percent of the world's population—eat no meat whatsoever, and many do not touch eggs or milk either.)

What's Kosher, What's Trafe

The laws of *kashrut* divide all edibles into two categories: kosher and *trafe*. The word "kosher" means "fit" or "proper." *Trafe*, which comes from the Hebrew for "torn" or "damaged," designates things that are unfit or improper to eat.

Kashrut further divides all kosher foods into three categories: dairy (*milchig*), meat (*flayshig*), and neutral (*pareve*). *Kashrut* demands a complete separation of dairy and meat. *Pareve* foods, which include all fruits, vegetables, many fish, and eggs, can be prepared and eaten with either dairy or meat products.

The primary source for the dietary laws is the Torah, which lists the animals, birds, fish, and insects that may and may not be consumed by the people of Israel.[42] However, the laws that regulate food preparation were laid out in the Talmud and subsequent codes of law. For example, the biblical injunction against boiling a kid in its mother's milk,[43] was elaborated by the rabbis into the total separation of milk and meat, which then calls for different sets of dishes and utensils. Although the laws of *kashrut* are specific, food presents too many individual issues for any written code to address them all, which is why one of the major tasks assigned to rabbis throughout history has been to answer questions about *kashrut*. That said, here are the fundamentals:

Fruits and vegetables. Everything that grows is both kosher and neutral or *pareve*. Every kind of plant, herb, weed, grain, tree, shrub, moss, fungi, fern, and bush is kosher. Every fruit, flower, vegetable, seed, root, and nut is permitted.

Fish. Any fish that has both fins and scales is kosher. This encompasses a great many varieties, including (but not limited to): anchovies, bluefish, carp, flounder, grouper, halibut, lake trout, mackerel, perch, rainbow trout, salmon, tuna, whitefish, and yellowtail. Kosher fish are also *pareve*, and can be served with either dairy or meat.

Nonkosher fish include: shellfish (crustaceans such as crab, lobster, mussels, and shrimp), eels, porpoise, shark, whale, and all other sea mammals. Frog, turtle, and octopus are also *trafe*.

Meat. All animals that both chew their cud and have a split hoof are kosher. This includes: antelope, buffalo, cattle, deer, eland, hart, gazelle, goat, moose, sheep, and yak. *Trafe* animals include: camels, donkeys, pigs, horses, and rodents.

However, for meat to be considered kosher, the permitted animals must be ritually slaughtered according to the laws of *sh'chitah* by a butcher called a *shochet,* a person who is conversant with both the relevant religious teachings and has hands-on skills. Furthermore, since meat may have no trace of blood on it, after ritual slaughter and inspection, it is soaked in water, salted, and soaked again.

Fowl. Most domestic birds are kosher, including: chicken, turkey, duck, and geese. Domesticated pigeon, dove, and songbirds are also permitted. Fowl are considered meat, and must be slaughtered, inspected, and soaked and salted as described above.

Wild birds and birds of prey are forbidden. *Trafe* birds include: eagle, heron, ostrich, owl, pelican, swan, and vulture. Eggs from non-kosher birds are prohibited.

Eggs from kosher birds are kosher and *pareve;* however, a single spot of blood renders an egg *trafe.*

Dairy products. Generally, all dairy products are permitted.

Liquor and wine. All beers, and grain and fruit liquors, are kosher and *pareve.* Some cream liquors are dairy.

Because wine falls into the category of things used for sacramental purposes—specifically, for making *kiddush*—the Talmud outlawed the use of any wine made by non-Jews for fear it might have been used for idol worship. "Kosher wine" is a designation given to wine made under rabbinical supervision, with the intent of being used for *kiddush.*

There are many excellent kosher vintages and some people make a point of buying kosher wine from Israel as a way of supporting the nation and people.

High-tech trafe. BHT, MSG, mono- and diglycerides, food colorings, preservatives, growth hormones: while none of these things are technically *trafe,* some Jews treat them as such. Since Judaism places great value on protecting health, careful reading of labels and the avoidance of potentially harmful additives and ingredients can be seen as a religious act as well as prudent shopping.

The Meaning of *Kashrut*

The most common assumption about *kashrut* is that it was implemented to protect health and life. While rationales based on health have been offered for centuries, there is little evidence to support the argument that God wants Jews to forgo spaghetti carbonara because ham mixed with cream does bodily harm.[44] Jews who keep strictly kosher have managed to clog their arteries with chicken fat while assiduously avoiding bacon grease.

Actually, the health argument has been widely dismissed since the time of the Talmud. Rabbis have always "explained" *kashrut* as something Jews do because God demands it in the Torah. The act of obeying the commandment—of performing the *mitzvah*—is its own reward. However, since rabbinic Judaism also encourages Jews to discern God's intent in the Torah and to find personal meaning and fulfillment in the laws, *kashrut* has been given many interpretations.

Perhaps the most compelling explanation is the idea, restated in modern times by Martin Buber, that *kashrut* hallows the everyday. The intent of *kashrut* is not to deny the body's needs or pleasures, but to turn a natural function into a holy act.

According to another ancient line of thought, *kashrut* has been interpreted as a way of instilling reverence for life, especially animal life. There is evidence that boiling a kid in its mother's milk was a pagan ritual the Hebrews rejected, perhaps simply as a way of distinguishing themselves from their neighbors. But the injunction against boiling or slaughtering a kid in front of its mother has long been interpreted as a way of preventing cruelty to animals. The biblical mandate not to "cause pain to any living creature," *tsa'ar ba'alei chayim*, has been cited as an explanation for the rules of ritual slaughter and as the justification for Jewish vegetarianism.

According to many interpreters, God's original plan did not include meat eating at all. The description of Eden includes a completely herbivorous and vegetarian world: "I give you every seed-bearing plant that is upon the earth, and every tree that has seed-bearing fruit, they shall be yours for food."[45] It is only in the story of Noah that humanity was given permission to eat meat, and then as a concession to the post-Edenic state of the species. Later in the Bible, Isaiah's vision of a redeemed world is entirely vegetarian. "And the lion shall eat straw like the ox."[46]

To the rabbis who wrote the Talmud, it seemed clear that since only God could give life, only God was permitted to take it. While they were disturbed by any killing, even for food, the fact remained that people eat meat. Thus they instituted the elaborate laws regarding animal slaughter, which reinforced the idea that Jews kill only by divine sanction. Specific prayers were prescribed, and quick, relatively pain-free (for the era) methods were mandated. Jews were thus effectively prevented from hunting.

Choosing *Kashrut*

For people who grew up in kosher homes, there is nothing strange or difficult about using two sets of dishes, buying meat from kosher butchers, or forgoing cheeseburgers. *Kashrut* is as normal as apple pie; kosher food is comfort food. But for those who have no family or gustatory memories of special meals and special recipes, *kashrut* may seem daunting.

Jews take on the *mitzvah* of *kashrut* for a variety of reasons: as something that connects us to countless generations of Jews; as a daily reminder of our Jewishness; as part and parcel of the overall discipline of being Jewish that we choose to practice. But for many Jews who keep kosher, the decision does not lend itself to rational explanation; it just feels right.

While *kashrut* may be a system for cultivating a holier approach to life, it is not always easy. It entails a certain amount of self-denial that will be far more difficult for meat-and-potatoes people than folks who prefer fish and salad for dinner. Choosing to keep kosher can be a difficult decision on many levels. For one thing, it is not easy to explain to others. Keeping kosher means embracing a basically non-Western system of self-discipline that runs counter to a culture of consumerism and instant gratification. It means making a very fundamental distinction between yourself and others—and that includes not only non-

Jews, but also Jews who do not keep kosher, and Jews who keep kosher differently than you do.

Besides, any major change in eating habits can be a deeply unsettling experience. Unlike animals, human beings do not eat simply to sustain life. For people, eating, like sex, is not simply a physical act. Eating is arguably life's first sensual pleasure and the table is an important setting for social as well as physical sustenance. Furthermore, food places us within historical, ethnic, and familial contexts, even as it expresses idiosyncrasies and individuality.

The following list describes some of the ways that contemporary Jews choose to keep kosher, arranged in levels of increasing complexity and challenge.

Biblical kosher. Basically, this means avoiding all animals and fish prohibited in the Torah. At a Chinese restaurant, it means passing up the spring rolls unless you determine they contain no shrimp or pork. Some people also read labels in order to avoid foods prepared with lard and other nonkosher meat products.

Biblical kosher plus separation of meat and milk. As above, plus not mixing meat and milk at the same meal. This means not cooking chicken breasts in butter and avoiding meats served with cream sauces at restaurants.

Kosher meat. This represents a quantum leap. Fresh meat is purchased only at a kosher butcher shop, and frozen meat must display a *hechsher,* a symbol of rabbinic supervision (explained below). Dining at nonkosher restaurants means vegetarian or *pareve* meals only.

Further separation of meat and milk. At home, this entails two separate sets of dishes, cutlery, and pots and pans. Some people institute a waiting period (one to six hours) after eating meat before dairy is served. Traditionally, there is no waiting period for serving meat after eating dairy products.

Rabbinic supervision. Eating prepared foods that have been produced under rabbinic supervision and bear a symbol *(hechsher)* attesting to their *kashrut.* This reflects concern not only about kosher ingredients, but also about the status of the utensils and environment in which food is prepared. In order to maintain this level of *kashrut,* dining out would be limited to kosher restaurants and to kosher homes.

However, some people who require *hechshers* at home eat vegetarian meals elsewhere.

Vegetarian/Vegan diets. Vegetarianism certainly simplifies *kashrut,* since it does away with the need to find kosher meat and resolve issues around mixing meat and dairy. In addition to the biblical and religious justifications for this practice, there are also political, ecological, and ethical rationales for avoiding meat altogether. Given that meat is such a resource-intensive food and since so many other sources of high-quality protein are now available, a vegetarian lifestyle can be seen as a way of helping to repair the world.[47]

Dining out. Many Jews who keep kosher eat at nonkosher restaurants and in nonkosher homes—making selections that reflect their level of observance. Practice varies from individual to individual, from family to family. Some who are kosher at home will eat only vegetarian meals at other people's homes and in restaurants while others make a fairly complete separation between what goes on at home and what they do in public; there may be nothing but kosher meat in the freezer, but when at McDonald's, it's cheeseburgers all around. While this may seem like a double standard, practicing different levels of *kashrut* at home and on the road may be seen as a way of making a distinction between what goes on inside a Jewish home and what happens in the rest of the world.

Kashrut *and children.* The idea of turning into "*kashrut* cops" repels some people and discourages them from instituting any observance of Jewish dietary laws. However, children raised in kosher homes generally do not feel deprived. If home cooking is kosher cooking, the idea of drinking milk with a roast beef sandwich will seem as foreign and unappetizing as roasted bugs (which also happen to be *trafe*). Reading labels can be made into a game, and so can keeping meat and milk dishes separate.

It is, of course, far more difficult for an older child to understand a decision to suddenly outlaw cheeseburgers from the backyard grill if she's been eating them for as long as she can remember. Transitions should be slow, methodical, and fully explained. As in every other aspect of observance, if a parent's attitude is positive, and the approach flexible and open, children will learn by example.

A Kosher Home

Traditionally, a kosher home is one in which only kosher meat is prepared and eaten, where the separation of dairy and meat products includes separate dishes, cutlery, pots, pans, and cooking utensils. Some kosher households may have separate dish towels, dishrags, sponges, and cutting boards. Glassware is exempt from this division and may be used on all occasions.

However, since there are so many styles and levels of *kashrut,* everyday decisions about how to keep kosher vary. Some families that do not cook or eat meat and milk at the same meal use a single set of dishes and utensils. Others keep dishes and utensils strictly separated, but use the same cleanup gear for all meals. However it is defined, a kosher home is one in which family members respect, understand, and follow the same rules.

People who choose to keep kosher usually do it in a series of incremental steps rather than one leap. Kashering—making kosher—a home is a big step. Rabbis and friends who keep kosher are a good source of practical advice about the "how-tos" of setting up a kosher home.

No matter how *kashrut* is defined or observed, mistakes will happen: a dairy pot gets used for reheating chicken soup; halfway through the soup that the waitress promised was strictly vegetarian, you discover a big chunk of beef.

Ever realistic about human foibles, Jewish law is very explicit about how to correct errors. According to *halachah,* certain things that are "*trafed*" are boiled, others buried in the ground, and still others thrown away. Some Jews correct errors simply by washing the offending item, and trying not to make the same mistake again.

The bottom line on accidents is that they do not invalidate anything. It has been suggested that the way people handle mistakes says a great deal about their understanding of *kashrut* as a *mitzvah.* Screaming at a spouse or a child, or making a guest feel terrible, about mixing up the spoons seems way out of line with a discipline intended to keep you in touch with holiness. If mix-ups become an everyday occurrence and *kashrut* is the source of tension, it might be time to reexamine why and how you are keeping kosher, and to recall the old story about a great rabbi who arrived in a strange town, where he was invited to spend the night in the mayor's home. As the mayor escorted the sage to his house, he boasted, "Rabbi, you should know that we adhere to the highest standards of *kashrut*. No one has ever made a mistake in my house." To which the rabbi replied, "Well then, I couldn't possibly eat in your house."

Shopping kosher. Shopping for kosher food is not difficult. Regular supermarkets and specialty shops can supply virtually everything except perhaps meat, though some supermarkets do stock frozen kosher poultry. Cities of any size support at least one kosher butcher, and people living in smaller communities may commute to larger Jewish centers to buy meat. Kosher food is also available online.

Shopping kosher does require a fair amount of label reading, first to see that products are free of lard—animal fat that renders them nonkosher. Foods designated "kosher" are thus sought not only by Jews, but also by Muslims and vegetarians who want to avoid pork or meat products. Another reason for reading labels is to determine whether a product contains any milk products, which would make it incompatible with a kosher meat meal.

When buying packaged and prepared food, some people buy only foods that bear a symbol called a *hechsher,* which is a validation that the product is kosher and prepared under rabbinical supervision. *Hechshers* appear on a wide variety of products, from cheeses to cake mixes to canned fish. The FDA permits use of the K (for kosher) wherever there is rabbinic supervision. There are many *hechshers,* some granted by regional or local rabbinic boards. A few of the better-known symbols include:

 THE UNION OF ORTHODOX JEWISH CONGREGATIONS (OU)

 THE ORGANIZED KASHRUS LABORATORIES (OK)

 KOSHER SUPERVISION

Jewish cooking. *"Vesti da Turco e mangia da Ebreo."* The ancient Italian adage advises, "Dress like a Turk and eat like a Jew."[48] Jewish culinary tradition is rich and diverse, reflecting the fact that Jews have lived all over the world and absorbed the best of many cuisines.

Jewish cooking in America has been associated mostly with a limited number of gastronomic clichés: bagel, lox, and chicken soup. The tendency toward starchy, heavy food comes from Central and Eastern Europe, where German and Russian peasant foods were adapted to lives of heavy manual work in cold climates. However, American Jews have embraced other Jewish culinary traditions. Sephardic Jews cook with dates, raisins, leeks, plum sauces, and exotic spices. Israeli foods—falafel (fried chickpea patties), shwarma (roasted meat), and various fresh salads—are now staples for American Jews as well.[49]

Around the world and throughout history, Jewish cooks have found ways to prove the Talmudic dictum that every forbidden food, even ham, has an exact, kosher taste-equivalent.[50] Today, there are hundreds of Jewish and kosher cookbooks that prove the point. While specifically kosher cookbooks are a good source for special holiday menus and recipes, most books (except maybe *The Wonderful World of Pork*) may be adapted to kosher cooking. Vegetarian cookbooks are an obvious choice, but cuisines based on oil rather than butter— Italian, Middle Eastern, and most Asian culinary traditions—are also a great resource. It is also easy to adapt and change nonkosher recipes. In many cases, using nondairy margarine instead of butter will not affect the flavor of a dish, and meat-based soups can become *pareve* with the substitution of vegetable stock for beef or chicken.

Kosher for Passover. *Kashrut* takes a new dimension during the holiday of Passover when, in memory of the exodus from Egypt, Jews eat no leavened foods. In order to be "kosher for Passover," all food must be absolutely free of any leavening agent, such as yeast. Thus all breads are forbidden, as is beer.

However, the prohibition against leaven extends not only to things made with yeast but any foodstuff likely to ferment, which includes anything made with flour, including pastas and most cereals. These restrictions are challenging, especially in baking, but potato starch and matzo meal are substituted for flour. Passover cookbooks are a big help in planning interesting leaven-free meals, and all kinds of prepared food may be purchased with a "Kosher for Passover" *hechsher,* which means the product was prepared in a leaven-free as well as a kosher environment. (See "Passover.")

As in all things, Jews observe Passover *kashrut* in a wide variety of ways. Keeping kosher for Passover traditionally requires an intensive housecleaning to free the house of even a trace of leavening, or *hametz.* Some people have a closet of special dishes, pots and pans, utensils, and cutlery that have never touched *hametz* and are used only at Passover. Other families, which do not keep kosher the rest of the year, simply clean the house of *hametz* and avoid bread and other foods made with flour.

Kosher etiquette. As dietary needs, allergies, and health-related restrictions have become more widespread, people tend to be vocal about what they can and cannot eat, which has made it easier to keep kosher. A kosher-observant guest invited to dinner in a nonkosher home should volunteer information about what he or she can and cannot eat. Likewise, kosher-observant hosts can help by tactfully explaining their practice to guests who offer to bring food or drink. At Passover in particular, a basket of fruit or a a box of "kosher for Passover" candy are among the safest edible "hostess gifts."

The most important rule of thumb is always "When in doubt, ask." If everyone is relaxed and tolerant, questions can lead to an interesting conversation about the hows and whys of *kashrut.*

COMMUNITY

According to a Yiddish proverb, "The best synagogue is the heart." Many people have attributed Judaism's survival to its focus on the family. But there is a necessary counterpoint to Judaism's emphasis on hearth and home. "Do not separate yourself from the community," says the Talmud.[1] In other words, Judaism's vitality does not reside solely within individuals, but also depends upon the energy and momentum generated by groups of people working together in all kinds of settings: synagogues, schools, charitable agencies, cultural activities, social clubs, political groups.

In a sense, the organized Jewish community exists to support individual Jews in their decision to live as Jews. Because the truth is, no one can be a Jew by him or herself. Lighting candles every Friday night, reading sophisticated Jewish books, celebrating the holidays at home with friends and family, and never eating shrimp again may all be deeply meaningful, but there is a limit to a totally insular, personal Judaism.

There is a limit to how much anyone can learn without teachers or other students to challenge their assumptions. There is a limit to how fully anyone can explore his or her Jewish commitment without exercising it in a public forum. Without a community, energy is bound to ebb and inspiration wane.

Another Yiddish proverb says, "Life is with people." Jewish life can only be fully experienced in the company of other Jews. Especially in the absence of extended family, which is the norm for many Americans, the Jewish community creates a larger context for all aspects of life, an indispensable source of identity, growth, recognition, and support, especially at times of transition. Births are greeted with resounding congratulations; illness and deaths are surrounded by healing concern.

The relationship between public and private, personal and communal, clearly benefits the individual, but it is also necessary for the survival of Judaism. Individuals do not educate rabbis, cantors, and Jewish teachers. Nor can individuals provide for the needs of all the Jewish elderly, or advocate for Jews who are persecuted or attacked. These functions, and many others, require work and financial support from everyone in a community that cares about the continuation of its culture, faith, ideas, and dreams.

Continuity is, in fact, one of Judaism's most compelling demands. The Talmud tells the tale of a man named Honi, who one day saw an old man planting a carob tree.

Honi asked, "How long will it take for that tree to bear fruit?"

"Seventy years," replied the old man.

"But you are already old; you will never live that long," said Honi.

"I know," said the man, "but my parents and grandparents planted fruit trees for me, so I am planting fruit trees for my children and my grandchildren."[2]

As long as there have been Jews, there have been Jewish communal groups. At first these were called tribes, and membership was all-inclusive, automatic, and permanent. Today, membership is largely voluntary. Becoming a part of the community requires filling out application forms and writing checks—in other words, making choices and connections with other Jews. Joining a synagogue, attending a lecture or a class, volunteering to serve on a committee or a board of directors, organizing a discussion group, even joining a virtual community for study and connection: any and all of these are opportunities to establish Jewish roots.

Of course, all human contact entails friction, and Jews are a notoriously contentious bunch. Fortunately, the American Jewish community is large and diverse, with countless places and ways to fit in. And, in the great Jewish tradition of dissent, if you do not like the institutions that you find, you can always start your own.

The doors to the Jewish community are wide open. Browsers are always welcome.

SYNAGOGUES

A synagogue is a *beit k'nesset,* a house of gathering or assembly. A place to find lifelong friends, a place where teenagers forge Jewish identities over pizza, and where families go to laugh at the annual Purim play and to organize canned food drives for the hungry.

A synagogue is a *beit midrash,* a house of study, a house of stories. A place with a library and classrooms, with teachers and students of all ages. A place of argument and enlightenment.

A synagogue is a *beit tefilah,* a house of prayer. A place to say words of praise that are older than memory, a place to sing about the birth of a child, a place to sit in sorrow, a place to search for peace.

Judaism purposefully mixes and confuses these categories: community, prayer, and learning. Among Jews, prayer services require the presence of the community, represented by a quorum of 10 called a *minyan.* The study of Jewish texts is considered a form of prayer.

People go to synagogues for all kinds of reasons: human contact, intellectual stimulation, spiritual fulfillment. People rarely find precisely what they are looking for in any one synagogue, in part because their criteria are impossibly high, and in part because synagogues rarely live up to their own goals. Still, over the course of their lifetimes, most American Jews join and belong to synagogues in search of a communal and spiritual home.

An individual who prays alone must hope that the time of prayer is an acceptable one; for the prayer of a congregation there is never an unpropitious time.

DEUTERONOMY RABBAH 2:12

History

The first building associated with Jewish worship was built in Jerusalem by King Solomon during the 10th century B.C.E. The complicated rituals described in the book of Leviticus—including animal sacrifices, instrumental music, and burning incense—took place in this temple, The Temple. The ancient Israelites traveled from all over the land for the festivals and holidays celebrated there and only there.

This centralized form of worship, performed by the priestly castes of Kohanes and Levites, was interrupted in 586 B.C.E. when the Babylonians conquered Jerusalem and took the Jews into captivity. Scholars do not agree about the precise beginnings of what we would recognize as synagogues, but groups of Jews probably began meeting for the purpose of prayer and Torah study during the Babylonian captivity.

When the Babylonians were defeated by the Persians in the 586 B.C.E., the Jews were permitted to return to Jerusalem, which is when public readings of the Torah on *Shabbat,* Mondays, and Thursdays began. By the time of the destruction of the Second Temple by the Romans in 70 C.E., synagogues and regular patterns of worship were part of Jewish life, both in and outside of Israel.

By the second century of the Common Era, the synagogue was so much a fact of Jewish life that it was considered incumbent upon any community that could muster a *minyan*—10 adult Jewish men at the time—to build one. Synagogues were eventually built in every corner of the earth—Alexandria and Rome, Worms and Barcelona, Singapore and New Delhi—with architecture that reflected the styles of their time and host cultures. There are Byzantine, Romanesque, Gothic,

Renaissance, Baroque, and Moorish synagogues. In Kai Feng, China, one was built after the pattern of the region's Taoist temples.

Actually, "synagogue" is not a Hebrew word. The term appeared in the Christian Bible as the Greek translation of the term *beit k'nesset,* "house of assembly." Until the 18th century, Jews used the word "temple" only to refer to the Temple of Jerusalem, which would, according to tradition, be rebuilt only by divine command. But the Reform movement (described below) rejected the notion of a rebuilt Temple and reclaimed the word as a synonym for synagogue. *Shul,* the Yiddish word for synagogue, comes from the German *shule,* or "school."

The Movements

Despite the universal tendency to romanticize the past as a period of unanimity and universal piety, sectarianism has permeated Jewish history from the ancient days of the Pharisees and the Sadducees until today. But the Enlightenment introduced a whole new dimension to the divisions within the Jewish world. The subsequent political emancipation, which unlocked the ghettos and opened the great universities of Europe, permitted Jews to step outside their communal identity and act as individuals. For the first time, Jews had the option of becoming citizens of the wider world without having to convert to Christianity.

In response to this revolutionary change, the precursors of the modern Jewish movements—Reform, Conservative, and Orthodox—made their debuts. Despite their differences, all three schools of thought faced the same challenge: reconciling the traditions and beliefs of Judaism with modern intellectual and political realities. Out of that dilemma, liberal Judaism—the process of reconsidering and wrestling with tradition, and then self-consciously choosing how to be Jewish—was born.

Liberal Judaism in America has three major denominations or movements: Reform, Conservative, and Reconstructionist, described below. Each of these has a central organization with which most individual congregations are affiliated, and all of them train educators and rabbis; publish books, magazines, and teaching materials; run summer camps and youth programs; and more.

Although the three movements differ in their approach to theology and practice, all ordain women as rabbis, engage in interfaith and inter-movement dialogues, and actively support the state of Israel. Although there are differences, these three also share the basic assumption that Jewish law, *halachah,* is an historical collection of human responses to the divine.

In addition to the movements, there are unaffiliated synagogues as well, some of which avoid all labels, or describe themselves as postde-nominational or "renewal." The hallmark of American Judaism is its diversity. Because each congregation is autonomous, official movement statements or position papers do not necessarily describe the practice of each affiliated synagogue. And every synagogue changes over time, reflecting changes in membership and leadership. Indeed, movement affiliation may describe little more than the rabbi's alma mater and even that is not a given, since some congregations do hire rabbis trained in the seminaries of other movements.

Worship differs from one temple to the next in many ways—congregational singing versus formal cantorial singing, the amount of Hebrew in the service, the introduction of creative prayers and new ser-vices. Programmatically, congregations have unique strengths and weak-nesses, sometimes based on a rabbi's interests, sometimes reflecting congregants' passions. Thus, some synagogues are known for their social action programs, while others focus more energy on worship and spiritu-ality. You can learn about what's going inside any given *shul* by looking at its Web site and reading its membership materials and mailings. Ulti-mately, you have to walk through the doors and talk to the people.

Reform

The Reform movement (it's Reform, not Reformed) was the first orga-nized attempt at a systematic liberal Jewish theory and practice. While it began in Germany, Reform matured and flourished in the United States. The early Reform movement was characterized by rationalist philosophy and a "light unto the nations" theology, which saw the Jews as special heirs to the biblical prophetic tradition of social justice. The movement also instituted many radical changes in synagogue observance, including the use of vernacular languages, musical instruments, and mixed seating for men and women. Reform leaders eased restrictions on Sabbath activities and rejected the dietary laws, in some measure as an effort to attract Jews who were abandoning Judaism altogether.

Classical Reform Judaism was often charged with being assimilationist, and more concerned with Christian approval than with Judaism's integrity. However, the Reform movement began an era of Jewish political and social activism that helped redefine Judaism's place in the world. Reform Judaism has changed a great deal since its beginnings, and continues to change, citing the truism "Reform is a verb." Practices, symbols, and rituals once dismissed by the movement—everything from prayer shawls and head coverings, to immersion in a *mikveh*—have been embraced by many in the movement.

Reform Judaism affirms the ability of every Jew to choose, on the basis of study and experimentation, the observances and rituals that bring him or her closer to God. *Halachah,* Jewish law, serves as a resource but does not determine these choices. For Reform Jews, the Talmud and its subsequent elaborations are part of Judaism's evolving insight as to how individuals and communities make God available in their lives. For more information about the Reform movement, see www.urj.org.

Conservative

Conservative Judaism, which also had its roots in early 19th century Germany, was formulated in the late 19th and early 20th century in the United States. It was conceived as a middle ground between Reform, which was viewed with alarm as having gone too far, and traditionalists, who were seen as unrealistic in their rejection of modern opportunities and insights.

While Conservative Judaism shares with Reform the idea that Jewish law is historical and therefore changing, it supports a commitment to the workings of the law. According to the Conservative view, while the law itself changes in every era in response to social, economic and political realities, individuals are nonetheless expected and encouraged to conform to certain classical behaviors, such as keeping kosher, Sabbath and holiday observance, and daily prayer. The authority of these behaviors and of the laws contained in the Torah and later commentaries derives from the belief that they were inspired by God.

While Conservative Judaism counts certain ritual behaviors as necessary and even mandatory, the range of practice among Conservative Jews is extremely varied. Indeed, the religious practice of many Conservative Jews does not differ from that of many Reform and Reconstructionist Jews; on the other hand, there are members of Conservative congregations who embrace a lifestyle essentially indistinguishable from that of many Orthodox Jews.

Conservative Judaism has always responded to important changes in modern life, as when the ban on *Shabbat* driving was modified to enable suburban Jews to get to their synagogues. The Jewish Theological Seminary began ordaining women in the mid-1980s in response to lay support for the change, and the tension of holding the middle ground continues to challenge the movement on theological and social issues. For more information about the Conservative movement, see www.uscj.org.

Reconstructionist

The Reconstructionist movement began as Mordecai Kaplan's vision of a new direction for Conservative Judaism. A longtime faculty member of the Conservative rabbinical seminary, Kaplan was eventually convinced by his students to lend his support to the founding of the Reconstructionist Rabbinical College in Philadelphia. The seminary, which opened in 1968, trains leaders for the synagogues and *havurot* (fellowships, described below) that were formed in response to Kaplan's teachings.

Kaplan conceived of Judaism not simply as a religion but as an evolving, changing civilization with a religious basis. Kaplan believed that Jews in every generation had an obligation to keep Judaism alive through the process of reconstructing it; reinterpreting ancient rituals and practices and discovering new meanings in them.

According to Reconstructionism, the rabbi is not an authority but a facilitator and resource who teaches and guides congregants in their own process of creating Jewish community. Kaplan's ideas have had an enormous impact on many Reform and Conservative Jews. For more information about Reconstructionist Judaism, see www.jrf.org.

Nondenominational Communities

In addition to the three formal branches of liberal Judaism, alternative Jewish institutions exist to fulfill the functions of synagogues for their members. Some unaffiliated congregations have rabbis, dues, boards of directors, and buildings with mortgages. Other groups meet in rented spaces or living rooms, and while some pay a teacher, rabbi, or "guide," others are entirely run by volunteers. Less-formal groups require more of a commitment of time and work from their members and usually do not offer the full range of synagogue "services," such as a religious school. However, they can provide a kind of intimate, hands-on Judaism—a fact that has led large congregations to foster small groups within their membership.

Havurot, usually translated as "fellowships," are autonomous groups that choose their own activities and set their own calendar of events, services, and meetings. Because they often concentrate on home- and family-based celebrations, members sometimes describe *havurot* as their extended families. A *havurah* might meet to break the Yom Kippur fast, build a communal *sukkah* and eat in it, enjoy a Hanukkah party, and celebrate a Passover *seder* together. Some *havurot* schedule regular book discussions, and some attend Jewish cultural events, such as plays and films, as a group. An annual summer institute, sponsored by the National Havurah Committee, gathers groups and individuals from around North America for study, worship, and community networking. For more information, see www.havurah.org.

Many synagogues now encourage members to form *havurot* as part of congregational life—a way to foster the warmth and intimacy of a small group within a larger institution. Synagogue-based *havurot* meet for study or family-centered holiday observance, and often function as extended families for their members.

A *minyan* is the name for the quorum of 10 adult Jews traditionally required for certain prayers to be said, and for a full worship service to be held. Although *minyanim* (the plural) run many of the same kind of family- and holiday-focused activities as *havurot,* they tend to be worship-focused. Many were formed as a way to permit women's full participation in otherwise traditional services and their members tend to be more observant of dietary and Sabbath laws. Some individual *minyanim* have Web sites.

The Jewish Renewal movement is a network of individuals, synagogues, and *havurot,* some of which have formal affiliations with ALEPH the Alliance for Jewish Renewal, which runs workshops and publishes books and other materials. Based in large measure upon the philosophy and teachings of Reb Zalman Schachter-Shalomi, Jewish Renewal combines an emphasis on Jewish mysticism and a commitment to *tikkun olam,* "the repair of the world." For more information search "Jewish Renewal" on the Web, and see www.aleph.org.

Joining a Synagogue

Although some Jews join a synagogue strictly on the basis of geography, becoming members of the closest and most convenient congregation, most people shop around before making such an important commitment. While it may seem a little crass to talk about "shopping" for a spiritual home, it is actually far less so than selecting a synagogue based on commuting time.

The criteria for what makes a "good" synagogue are very personal, which makes selecting a synagogue rarely a simple or straightforward process. Expectations may be vague or confused; past experiences may create anxiety.

To begin the process, ask people who already belong to a congregation what they like about their synagogue, and ask if you can go to services or a class with them.

In general, it is not a good idea to go synagogue shopping during the High Holidays. Rosh Hashanah and Yom Kippur services are not representative of what goes on the rest of the year, and the rabbi and staff will probably be extremely busy and not as free to chat or schedule meetings with prospective members.

A good first step is to attend a regular *Shabbat* service. Call the synagogue office and find out when services are held. The call can be anonymous, or you can say that you are thinking of joining the synagogue, in which case you may be referred to the rabbi or another staff member. A membership committee person may call you back, to tell you something about the congregation and to offer brochures, a copy of the temple newsletter, or membership materials. Some congregations hold regular open houses for prospective members, and in some temples, potential members are invited for *Shabbat* dinner.

On a first visit to any synagogue, it can be helpful to remember that few people feel altogether comfortable their first time anywhere. Customs vary from one congregation to the next, so newcomers always feel somewhat awkward, especially when everyone else seems to know all the words to all the songs. Try to relax. Hum along with the melodies. Look around you at the faces in the sanctuary. Is there a wide range of ages in the room? Are there single people? Are there children around and/or is there special programming for them? Do you see people you would like to meet?

Regarding the service, is the amount of Hebrew used intimidating or inadequate for you? Are supplemental readings meaningful? Who leads the service? Are laypeople helping or does the rabbi (and/or cantor) do it all? Are people smiling? Do they seem engrossed in the prayers or are they dozing?

Do you like the way music is used in the service? Does the cantor perform or do people sing along? If the rabbi gives a sermon, does it challenge or bore you? Does he or she seem to have a rapport with the congregants? As the service progressed, did you get more relaxed or more tense?

If a house was built just as a house, and then afterward it was dedicated as a synagogue, it is considered a synagogue. However, it is not considered holy until people have prayed in it.

SHULCHAN ARUCH, ORACH CHAIM 153:8

In addition to your reaction to the synagogue, consider the synagogue's reaction to you. Does anyone greet you or say *"Shabbat Shalom"*?

Unless your first impression is totally negative, go a second time, and a third. Are you starting to strike up conversations with people? Has the rabbi greeted you? If your first visit is on a Friday night, remember that the congregants who attend Saturday morning services may be an altogether different group of people. It might be worthwhile to attend a whole *Shabbat*'s worth of services as well as a lecture or adult education class. Explore the range of programs the synagogue offers to see how and where you might fit in. Ask yourself whether this particular *shul* can meet your needs and those of your family, not only now but in five years or ten.

There are many things to consider when exploring a prospective congregation: Does the schedule of adult education classes or lectures appeal to you? Does the synagogue ever run retreats? How good is the religious school for children? (See "Education.") Is there a synagogue youth group? Does the synagogue stress family education and family programming? Are there special events on the holidays where children and parents participate together? Does the synagogue help organize and foster *havurot*, small groups that function as extended families within the larger community? Does the temple have special programs for empty-nesters and elders? Is there a nursery school? A women's group? A men's group? Does it provide a clear welcome to Jews of color, and to gay and lesbian Jews? Is the building accessible to the handicapped?

Does the congregation participate in local interfaith programs? Is there an active social action committee, and what are its priorities? How does the synagogue relate to its intermarried members and to the children of intermarried couples? If this question is relevant to you, it should be asked immediately. While many synagogues welcome non-Jews as full members of the congregation, some limit the participation of non-Jewish spouses and the children of non-Jewish mothers.

Although any temple is much more than the rabbi(s) on its staff, the personality and skills of the clergy do shape the congregation, and your response to him/her/them is worth taking into account. Rabbis' job descriptions are almost dizzying. Congregational rabbis are spiritual leaders who teach and preach. They also officiate at religious ceremonies and rituals, visit the sick, and provide family, marriage, and spiritual counseling. They act as representatives of the Jewish community at interfaith meetings and secular events, and some rabbis function as business administrators of their congregations and as principals of their religious schools.

Not surprisingly, few rabbis are good at all these tasks. A superb pastoral counselor may be a mediocre preacher; an inspired leader of prayer may be a terrible administrator. Despite the improbability of finding one human being who can excel at everything, most people bring impossible expectations to their relationship with the rabbi, who is also inevitably viewed as a symbolic parent.

In the past few decades, there has been slow movement away from the model of the authoritarian rabbi: the one with all the answers, the one who "does" Judaism on behalf of his or her congregation. In much the same way that the physician's role as the ultimate, unquestioned medical authority has been challenged by more sophisticated patient-consumers, laypeople are taking more responsibility for their own Jewish lives. This is actually less a break from tradition than an acknowledgment of the rabbi's true status: not priest, but teacher.

Despite the move toward greater lay participation, rabbis still shape their synagogues in fundamental ways. The rabbi generally sets the tone of worship services, leads in policy decisions regarding Sabbath observance within the synagogue, and provides leadership in his or her own areas of interest and strength.

Before joining a congregation, it is a good idea to schedule a private meeting with the rabbi—preferably not during the late summer or early autumn, when rabbis are preparing for the High Holidays and the beginning of the school year. In synagogues where there is a senior and a junior or associate rabbi, try to speak with both. While you may have more contact with the associate rabbi, the senior rabbi sets the tone for the congregation. Besides, junior rabbis often leave for their own pulpits after two or three years.

Go to the meeting with the rabbi prepared to answer a few questions. You might be asked about your Jewish background, and what you and your family want from the congregation. You should feel free to ask questions of your own, for example: What makes this congregation unique? What do you do best here? In the rabbi's opinion, what are the congregation's failings? What needs to be improved? What is expected from congregants and how important is lay participation?

Parents may have many questions about religious education at the temple, and rabbis should be able to talk about the school's philosophy and direct you to the educator or a teacher. But don't let your children's needs trump all others, and ask yourself, how can this synagogue help me grow as a Jew?

Finally, before meeting with a rabbi, it is also useful to examine your own feelings about the rabbinate. Interviewing a rabbi is not unlike a first meeting with a physician or a therapist, someone with whom you are going to have an intimate but professional relationship. It is best to try to leave expectations and grudges at home.

Concerning other staff, if the rabbi doesn't suggest it, feel free to ask for meetings with the synagogue's other professional staff: the cantor and, if applicable, the director of education or religious school principal.

The job of the cantor is to lead the congregation in prayer and song. The title of cantor (in Hebrew *hazzan, hazzanit* for female cantors) is given to people trained in liturgical music. The Reform and Conservative movements both run cantorial schools, which operate as graduate programs in Jewish liturgical music. Cantors frequently lead services and officiate at funerals in the absence of the rabbi, and are usually licensed by the state to perform weddings.

Cantors have very different approaches to their musical and congregational roles. Some perform and are listened to, while others invite the congregation to sing along. Some cantors lead services quite often, and in some synagogues they are in charge of *bar* and *bat mitzvah* preparation. There are congregations where the cantor teaches children and adults.

If the synagogue runs a religious school, the director of education or principal and school committee chair helps set educational policy. A meeting with them is in order if you plan to enroll a child in the congregational school. Like cantors, directors of education can be a major force in the congregation, shaping programs for adults as well as children, and generally contributing to the educational and spiritual life of the community.

Membership

There are as many ways to belong to a congregation as there are reasons to join. Some people see synagogue membership as a necessary evil, like life insurance. They pay their dues as a bet against future needs (for a *bar* or *bat mitzvah*, wedding, or funeral) or as a way of ensuring children's Jewish identity. Their monthly checks are the total extent of their commitment.

If, however, you join a synagogue with hopes of exploring your own spirituality, or of expanding your sense of community, or of delving into Jewish thought, signing the membership form is just the beginning. The next step is finding a niche. Attending services and classes, and volunteering on a committee or for a project, are among the best ways to explore possibilities and to begin feeling like someone who belongs.

Synagogues are complex organizations, and it is a good idea to know how they function. While there are enormous variations, most are governed by an elected volunteer board of directors. In some congregations, prestige is attached to officerholders, with positions of leadership going to people who support the institution with substantial financial gifts. Elsewhere, people rise through the ranks of committees, and become community leaders as a result of commitment and ability.

As with most nonprofit organizations, committees do much of the work. Joining a committee is one way to get immersed in synagogue life and lore, and its feuds and politics, too. Synagogue committees may include: membership, which recruits and meets with new members; finance, which may prepare budgets or raise money; ritual/worship, which helps plan religious services and works closely with the rabbi and cantor; adult education, which plans courses, lectures, and events such as weekend retreats; school, which oversees the religious school and may be broken down in various ways (preschool, high school, family education, youth group, etc.); social action, which advocates for justice, with social and political concerns ranging from helping resettle Jewish immigrants to running soup kitchens and shelters for the homeless. And caring community committees organize assistance for members who need help due to the birth of a new baby, illness, or death.

Obviously, all activities require financial support. Synagogues run like businesses, with fixed expenses for mortgage, staff, utilities, and movement dues, which support seminaries, youth programs, and summer camps. Synagogue expenses are met, in part, by annual membership dues. Some congregations have sliding scales; others charge a fixed amount, which may be reduced or waived by special arrangement. No synagogue turns people away because of an inability to pay dues, but each congregation handles financial need in its own way, some with more sensitivity than others. In addition to dues, there may be other financial expectations of members, such as pledges to a building fund, school fees, and charges for attending adult education courses and lectures.

Perhaps the oldest joke in the long history of Jewish humor is the one about the Jew who was stranded on a desert island. When a ship happens across him years later, his rescuers find three huts.

"Why three?" he is asked.

"I live in one," he says. "The other two are synagogues."

"Why on earth would you need two synagogues?" asks the rescue party.

"One I pray in. The other I wouldn't be caught dead in."

No two Jews can agree on much of anything, especially when it comes to religious practice. Many a large, venerable synagogue began as a renegade splinter group from another even more venerable congregation. If there is no synagogue that provides you with reasonable levels of comfort and fulfillment, you can always begin your own congregation or *havurah*.

Starting a synagogue or *havurah* means focusing religious and communal goals, usually in agreement with several other families. It also requires a huge investment of time, work, and money. Then again, creating an authentic communal spiritual home is its own priceless reward.

THE ORGANIZATIONAL WORLD

Nothing demonstrates the vitality of Jewish life as well as its array of organizations, agencies, federations, committees, associations, and councils. The alphabet soup of the organized Jewish world represents every conceivable area of Jewish concern, and provides leadership and assistance at every level, from feeding the Jewish elderly in America, to supporting various strategies for peace in the Middle East.

For the first centuries of Jewish life in North America, communal groups focused strictly on the basic needs of newcomers and founding community institutions, including synagogues. But as each new wave of Jewish immigration expanded the needs of the community, the organizational mandate expanded as well.

For a time, many social and cultural needs were met by *landsmanschaften*, organized groups of people from the same town in the old country. These groups pooled their resources to provide such services as death benefits for widows and orphans. Hebrew Free Loan societies were established to make low-cost credit available to immigrants, and the traditional Jewish commitment to *tzedakah*, "righteous giving," supported thousands of small relief efforts and local projects. For example, Jews saw to it that poor members of their community could buy kosher food for Passover.

Religious Movements

Most American Jews belong to one of the three major liberal religious Jewish denominations—Conservative, Reconstructionist, and Reform—with a smaller number affiliated with Renewal or Havurah groups.

Although expressly not religious, the Society for Humanistic Judaism and the Workmen's Circle provide members with the kind of fellowship and learning opportunities generally associated with synagogues. Traditional or Orthodox Judaism is not monolithic either: Hasidic sects and independent synagogues fall under this rubric; however, the Orthodox Union is the umbrella organization for what is called Modern Orthodoxy. For more information about the Orthodox Union, see www.ounetwork.org.

In addition to providing a wide array of services to their constituent congregations and *havurot*—everything from educational materials for adults and children to synagogue management consultation—the denominations ordain clergy, run youth programs and adult retreats, publish books and magazines, lobby Congress on issues of concern; the list goes on and on. You can learn more about each on their respective Web sites.

United Synagogue of Conservative Judaism—www.uscj.org
Reconstructionist Federation—www.jrf.org
Union for Reform Judaism—www.urj.org
The National Havurah Committee—www.havurah.org
Renewal—www.aleph.org

Federations

Communal efforts became larger and more sophisticated in the 19th century, when Jewish communities built hospitals and supported a growing social work network. As the Jewish community grew and diversified, the need for a more integrated, centralized way to raise and allocate funds became increasingly apparent. By the beginning of the 20th century, the "federations" became a force in American Jewish life.

Federations began as loose associations of community service groups and agencies that pooled fund-raising efforts to avoid competition and to enhance effectiveness. Today, Jewish federations (which have different names in different cities) support a vast array of programs, which can be divided into three broad categories: social service (Jewish Big Brother/Big Sister, family and children's agencies, services for the elderly, etc.), education (support for local schools, vocational counseling, etc.), and community relations (community relations councils, and the Anti-Defamation League). The federations provide significant support to Israeli agencies, and also contribute to secular and non-Jewish relief efforts.

The longest road in the world is the one that leads from your pocket.

YIDDISH PROVERB

Federations are the primary philanthropic and grant-making bodies for local Jewish communities. They raise funds, assess and plan for the needs of the community, setting programmatic goals and directions and channeling dollars accordingly. Federations work to develop leadership by running programs that include study, social action programs, Israel trips, and purely social gatherings. While they employ professional administrators, federations depend upon volunteers to do the hard work of fund-raising and staffing committees.

Volunteering in any Jewish organization—including your synagogue—is one of the surest and fastest routes to a sense of belonging. Opportunities to make a difference are virtually unlimited, from serving juice to children in synagogue preschool classrooms, to participating on the committees that make important decisions about the future of American Judaism. Every organization represents a doorway into Jewish communal life and to a sense of belonging and of making a difference. Local federation Web sites can direct you to a volunteer clearinghouse. For more information about federations and to locate the one in your community, see www.ujc.org.

Alphabet Soup

The national and international Jewish scene is fluid, ever-changing, and potentially confusing. Organizations are born, die, redefine their missions, or split in response to the times. The Jewish National Fund, for example, which began in 1901 to buy land for Jewish settlement in Palestine, now supports land development and the forestation of Israel. B'nai B'rith, which began as a fraternal and social group for German Jews, grew to become an international organization, and in 1989, B'nai B'rith's women's division split off to form an independent organization. The American Jewish World Service was incorporated in 1985 to provide a Jewish presence in the realm of international assistance.

New agencies and organizations open every year to meet the changing needs of the Jewish community. There are programs, support groups, and Web sites for every kind of Jew and any Jewish concern you can imagine. This makes it impossible to compile an up-to-date listing of Jewish organizations, agencies, and advocacy groups, which makes the Internet an invaluable tool for finding the resources you need: from camps for special needs children to trips to Israel for seniors, from local organizations that fight anti-Semitism to reviews of Jewish-themed films. One good portal for exploring the Jewish Web is www.shamash. org. The "Jewish Finder" listing on www.ujc.org also provides a current listing of organizations.

EDUCATION

Study may be the only undisputed and shared value upon which all Jews, regardless of affiliation or belief, can agree. Study is seen as its own reward and is considered one of life's great pleasures.

Historically, Jewish learning was valued above wealth or fame, and community standing was based upon erudition. Having a scholar in the family was such a source of pride that, in the days of arranged marriages, promising students were preferred even over wealthy young men as matches for daughters. Knowledge of Torah and Talmud was considered a virtue second to none. Well, almost none. The Talmud says, "An animal is better than a sage who lacks sensitivity to people's feelings."[3]

The sweetness of learning is a common theme in traditional writings: "Anyone who teaches Torah in public and does not make the words as pleasant as honey from the honeycomb for those who are listening, it were better that he not teach the words at all."[4] On the first day of school in some Eastern European communities, children were given sweet cakes in the shapes of the Hebrew letters.

But study is not considered a virtue for children only; education is considered a lifelong obligation and joy for Jews of every age and status. A common Yiddish greeting is *"Sog mir ein possock,"* "Tell me a verse," or "Teach me something." In the Torah, the Israelites were challenged to become a "nation of priests." The Jews became a nation of students.

In the 20th century, the Jewish passion for learning was applied to secular studies with impressive results. The overwhelming majority of American Jews attend college, and although less than 3 percent of the population, account for more than 20 percent of students in elite college.

But while Jews were entering the arts and sciences, the quality of

Jewish education languished. Today, many Jews recall their religious school as boring, or worse: a kind of unpleasant but necessary rite of passage meant as an inoculation against assimilation—momentarily painful but good for you in the long run. For most, it was over after *bar* or *bat mitzvah,* which is how it came to be that several generations of American Jews knew more about Milton and Newton than Maimonides.

Today, however, there is greater support and demand for excellence in Jewish education for people of all ages, from preschool through retirement. There has also been a broadening of the definition of Jewish education to include the informal learning that takes place outside of the classroom. While there are many ways to define excellence or success, the goal of a Jewish education is to impart the skills, concepts, vocabulary, curiosity, and commitment that will motivate a lifetime of Jewish study.

Day Care and Preschool

Although most Jewish learning for very young children happens at home (setting the table for *Shabbat,* preparing for holidays, listening to the grown-ups talk, reading bedtime stories), an early education program can help reinforce and supplement family lessons. The Jewish communal world provides a variety of options for the littlest Jews. Jewish community centers, YM/YWHAs, and synagogues offer everything from half-day nursery schools to full-time day care for infants and toddlers.

Jewish preschool is not a place where children sit at tables memorizing Hebrew letters. Most early-childhood specialists today feel that formal "study" is not appropriate for preschoolers at all. The guiding philosophy is that learning is a developmental process, which means that children are encouraged to learn through stimulating play.

In many ways, there is little difference between a day at a Jewish preschool and a day at a secular program. Children enrolled at Jewish preschools sing songs, do art projects, play outside, visit the fire station, take naps, eat snacks, and sit down to listen to stories during "circle time." What is different at Jewish early education programs is the content of the story, the names of the songs, and the subjects of the art projects.

Jewish programming varies a great deal from one preschool setting to the next, but generally, art projects will follow the Jewish calendar, making menorahs in December and Purim masks in March. The weekly cycle is also important, with Friday as a highlight, as children pour grape juice, eat *challah,* and sing *Shabbat* songs.

The primary consideration in choosing day care or a preschool is that children have a happy, safe, and warm experience. If their first memories of "school" are fond ones that include pleasant associations with things Jewish, they will have made a wonderful discovery. Apart from Jewish content, the same criteria that apply to all early education programs apply to Jewish day care and preschool: the operation should be licensed, clean, and cheerful; the ratio of staff to children should be low and at least in compliance with state law; parental visits should be welcome at all times.

Elementary Education

Most Jewish Americans enroll their children in some kind of formal program either in full-time private day schools or in a supplementary religious school, which is usually, though not always, part of a synagogue and held after school and/or on weekends. With parental support and participation, either choice can result in a successful Jewish education, which is to say one that instills a love of Judaism and a passion for lifelong Jewish commitment and learning.

From what age should a parent begin to teach his child?
From the moment he begins to speak.

SHULCHAN ARUCH

Whether you are considering day school or supplementary school, take the time to visit, attend classes, look at the art projects hanging on the walls, examine the textbooks and other materials in use, and talk to other parents and to the principal or director. It's important to think about the curriculum as more than just a listing of courses and books, too; consider the school's approach toward Judaism, its goals for students, and the role of parents. It's helpful to draw up a list of questions when considering a step as important as enrolling a child in school; that list can be used to pose questions or just to clarify your own values and goals. For example:

Are subject areas developed from year to year for continuity? Do teachers stress dialogue and discussion? Are lessons taught through lectures, worksheets, or games? Is there a regular music program or song-leader? How much time is devoted to the arts?

What is the body of Jewish knowledge that the school hopes to teach? What kind of Jew does the school hope to "produce"? Is religious observance expected of children, and how is that expectation expressed? Is prayer a part of the classroom experience? In the more advanced grades, is a single theology or approach to *halachah* (Jewish law) taught, or are different points of view presented?

How long do teachers tend to stay employed in this school? Are they offered in-service training? What is the student absentee and dropout rate? How many students continue their Jewish education through high school?

Supplementary school. The majority of Jewish parents choose a supplementary program for Jewish learning, offered after school or on weekends. Called Hebrew school, or religious school, these are usually run by synagogues, although there are some free standing, transdenominational programs as well. Also, the Workmen's Circle runs secular programs that stress Yiddish rather than Hebrew.

It is extremely difficult to generalize about religious schools since they vary in almost every way, beginning with their hours of instruction. Time requirements range from one to eight hours per week, with variations between grades. And despite published criteria and goals generated by the denominations, religious school faculties, administrations and curricula are dependent upon the culture and resources of each synagogue or school. In some synagogues, the rabbi or cantor runs the school; in others there is a paid school administrator or principal. The principal might hold a graduate degree in Jewish education, and teachers might be well trained and well paid. However, some schools are entirely run and taught by volunteers.

Paid or volunteer, teachers may be extremely knowledgeable and motivated. But because of the chronic shortage of Jewish teachers, professional standards are not always observed. College students often serve as religious school teachers, with varying results. Efforts to train and maintain talented teachers are ongoing, but the range of quality in religious school runs the gamut from excellent to abysmal.

Measuring the academic achievement in supplementary schools is difficult, in part because expectations are all over the map. Many parents expect religious schools to produce Jewish identity and Hebrew literacy in a few hours a week. Then again, others expect little, considering it merely "better than nothing."

The world is only maintained by the breath of school-children.

MAIMONIDES, MISHNEH TORAH

However, there are many excellent supplementary programs, proving that it is possible to devise demanding and reasonable goals for supplemental Jewish schooling. Some of these might include: a working Jewish vocabulary (*mitzvot, tzedakah, Shabbat, kiddush,* Torah, Maimonides, Herzl, Kristallnacht, Tel Aviv, etc.); the ability to read prayer book Hebrew; familiarity with the Jewish calendar of holidays and life-cycle rituals. It is also reasonable to expect children graduating from religious school to know more about the Torah and the Bible than a few stories. Most important, a religious school should nurture children's natural curiosity and enthusiasm for learning within a friendly, warm, and positive environment. While the formal curriculum is crucial, the way it feels to learn there—to be there—will ultimately determine whether religious school becomes a good or a bad memory.

Many religious schools now feature off-site programs that bolster children's sense of belonging. *Shabbat* retreat weekends can be a vital and invigorating teaching tool. These nights or weekends away from home with classmates and teachers are part summer camp, part spiritual retreat, part slumber party, and create an instant Jewish community and are often the high point of the school year. The presence of retreats for schoolchildren of various ages is a sign of a lively religious school.

People choose religious school programs for several reasons. Jewish parents, as a group, continue to support public education and feel that a supplementary education can provide what they want for their children in terms of developing a positive Jewish identity and community. Indeed, religious school can not only introduce the child to new friends but help integrate the entire family into congregational life. Cost is also a factor.

There are, however, some inherent problems with even the best supplemental Jewish education. Afternoon programs put tired, restless kids into classrooms precisely when they want and need to play. Also, religious school is invariably in competition with other after-school and weekend programs.

Another major dilemma for religious schools is the fact that many parents enroll their children for only a few years, in preparation for *bar* or *bat mitzvah*. Children attend classes, study with tutors, and then disappear after the big day. The *bar/bat mitzvah* "mill" approach offends many people, and religious schools and synagogues deal with this issue differently. Some congregations do not permit *bar* or *bat mitzvah* for students who have not been enrolled in the school for several years. Others will enroll students at any point, hoping that the experience at religious school will make children want to return for high school classes. One clue to the vitality of a religious school—and probably its best measure—is the number of students who stay past *bar* and *bat mitzvah*, get involved in the youth group, and/or graduate from the high school program.

However, one of the biggest problems for religious schools has less to do with students than with parents. If Mom permits virtually any other activity (skiing or shopping or cramming for a math test) to take precedence, if Dad never sets foot in the synagogue, if the adults do not even ask about what happened in religious school today—a child will start to treat the whole experience as the parents do: as an afterthought. But if parents make religious school a priority, if they volunteer for committees and fields trips, if they are taking classes at the temple, then religious school can be an important part of learning how to make Jewish choices for a lifetime.

Many communities support a local board of Jewish education as part of the local federation, which may provide an overview of the local community's resources for supplementary education, and indeed, all forms of Jewish learning.

Day school. A growing segment of the liberal Jewish community is choosing full-time day school education for their children. Once associated solely with Orthodox Jews, who still account for about 80 percent of all day school students, liberal day schools are proliferating across North America. The most established and numerous of these are sponsored by the Conservative movement, many of whose schools are named for Solomon Schechter, a founder of the Conservative movement. A smaller number of Reform-sponsored schools have opened, and there are also a number of community day schools, unaffiliated with any particular movement, that serve children from a wide range of Jewish backgrounds.

As with other private schools, Jewish day schools vary in curriculum and pedagogic approach, which can range from creative to traditional, from very competitive to noncompetitive. Every school has its strengths and weaknesses, and the principal or headmaster tends to set the tone and the agenda. Jewish day schools are typically run by people who hold advanced degrees in Jewish studies and/or education.

Some schools divide the day between Jewish studies (including Hebrew language and literature, classic Jewish texts, the Jewish calendar, Jewish history, Israel) and a full complement of secular studies (math, science, history, English language and literature). Many day schools emphasize Hebrew, which is not only taught but used as a language of instruction, which means graduates may become fluent or near-fluent

Hebrew speakers and readers. Secular academics tend to be excellent in all Jewish day schools, which typically pride themselves on the success of their students after graduation.

Socially, day schools offer a totally integrated Jewish experience and a full-time immersion in unconflicted Jewish identity. Many schools begin the day with a morning prayer service. Cafeteria food is kosher. The school year is arranged around the Jewish calendar; obviously there are no Christmas carols and no Easter break. Nor is there any division between sports and Jewishness, or math and Jewishness. School friends will be Jewish friends, and while some members of the faculty may be non-Jews, the majority of adult role models will be knowledgeable, committed Jews.

An added advantage noted by many parents is the fact that attendance at a Jewish school means more free time for kids who might otherwise be enrolled in afternoon or weekend religious school. Day school can also provide a communal focus—a place where parents can meet other like-minded adults.

There are issues and drawbacks connected with day school, the chief problem being the expense; while most schools provide tuition assistance and scholarships, private education can be as costly as college. Other issues include a lack of racial, religious, and social diversity, and the fact that day school attendance can make commuting a constant fact of life for parents. With school friends scattered all over town, after-school and weekend play dates require more driving. Also, children with special needs are often at a disadvantage at day schools, which tend to have extremely high academic expectations and requirements and may not be able to provide the support staff needed.

If there is no private Jewish high school option for graduates from elementary day schools (after sixth grade or eighth grade), students must negotiate the transition to secular settings. Teachers and administrators help children and parents make the switch, which most take in stride. Principals and headmasters can put you in touch with families who have traveled this path before.

It is not a good idea to select a Jewish day school strictly on the basis of its reputation for secular academics and its success rates, or only because the public schools are not an option. Parents need to feel comfortable with a school's mission and goals, which should be clearly stated in its promotional materials.

Some organizations that can provide more information about day schools include:

PEJE Partnership for Excellence in Jewish Education; a national initiative to strengthen the quality of Jewish day school education in North America—www.peje.org

PARDES: Progressive Association of Reform Day Schools—www.pardesschool.org

RAVSAK: Reshet Batei Sefer Kehillatim, The Jewish Community Day School Network—www.ravsak.org

The Solomon Schechter Day School Association: Conservative movement—www.ssdsa.org

Special education. Jewish communities strive to provide special education programs for the physically and mentally challenged, and for those with learning disabilities. There are a variety of programs for children with special needs, including *bar* and *bat mitzvah* tutoring and camping opportunities, as well as in-class support for all kinds of education settings.

To find out what is available, check out the local Jewish family agency (Jewish Family and Children's Services) or the education department at your local federation. Rabbis, day school principals, and religious school principals will be aware of other resources as well.

Some of the organizations committed to providing access for all include:

The Association of Jewish Family and Children's Agencies—www.ajfca.org

The Jewish Braille Institute of America—www.jewishbraille.org

Tikvah: A camping program for children who are learning disabled or who are emotionally or mentally challenged, run by the Conservative movement's Ramah camps—www.campramah.org/tikvah

P'TACH: Parents for Torah for All Children; a resource for parents of children with learning disabilities—www.ptach.org

---

The parent should teach the child on the level of the child's understanding.

TALMUD: PESAHIM 116A

High School

The vast majority of Jewish children in America do not continue their Jewish education after *bar* or *bat mitzvah*. This is a great shame since, by high school, students are developmentally ready and eager for meaningful conversations about personal responsibility, ethics, God and spirituality, the problem of evil in the world, anti-Semitism, and the Holocaust. Hebrew high school programs can address these subjects, explore the real-world moral choices facing adolescents, and also engage teenagers' passions for social justice in Jewish settings.

Supplementary programs for teens are run by some synagogues, consortia of congregations, or nondenominational community organizations. Many programs meet weekly, others more often. Some stop after 8th grade while others go through 11th or 12th grade, ending with a confirmation or graduation ceremony.[5]

Teenagers are savvy consumers and they will reject programs that do not challenge and excite them. Given the distractions and competing interests of adolescence, a well-attended Hebrew high school indicates a good program and excellent teachers. Finally, the social aspects of Hebrew high schools are also important. Since they provide a place to meet other Jews of similar ages and interests, Jewish high school programs are a venue for young adults to start making Jewish choices of their own.

While Orthodox day schools generally continue through high school, in recent years, a growing number of liberal, nondenominational Jewish high schools have been founded. Some of these offer a dual-track program to accommodate students who did not attend an elementary Jewish day school.

Most of the information regarding elementary day schools above applies to Jewish high schools as well. On the whole, Jewish secondary schools are academically strong institutions with arts and sports programming to meet the needs of the students. Religious pluralism is generally addressed head-on, with opportunities for respectful discussion and debate unavailable elsewhere in the Jewish world. Graduates tend to be accepted by the colleges and universities of their choice. Socially, a Jewish high school tends to limit conflicts with parents about dating non-Jews, or participating in events on *Shabbat* or holidays.

Informal Jewish Education

Experiential or informal Jewish education is a category that includes the learning that takes place outside the classroom, in settings where young and not-so-young Jews learn how to make Jewish choices through a shared experience of Jewish living. Although not as structured as classroom learning, informal education doesn't "just happen." It involves a serious, planned effort to build a strong Jewish identity.

Settings for this kind of learning include Jewish summer camps, youth groups, family education, JCC cultural and sports events, Hillel events, and trips to Israel. For all their differences, these experiences teach through direct experience.

Jewish camping. American Jews have been sending their children to Jewish summer camps since the early 20th century. At its inception, camping was an extension of Jewish day school—a way to create a year-round Jewish learning experience while getting the kids away from the hot city. Over time, Jewish camps added the full complement of American camping experiences: softball, hiking, canoeing, swimming, arts and crafts, and the like.

Jewish camping has grown and diversified, and parents now choose Jewish camps for a wide variety of reasons. Some simply want their children to play with other Jews while others seek a total immersion in Jewish practice for their kids, complete with Hebrew study. Zionist camps focus on Israel in song, dance, language, and in just about every other imaginable way. There are camps for the religious and camps for secularists, camps for children of all ages, and specialized summer programs in Jewish arts, leadership, and social justice.

There are some camps where the only obviously Jewish element is the campers' last names; these tend to be privately owned for-profit camps. However, most Jewish camps are nonprofit programs run by large organizations, such as local federations or their agencies. The Conservative, Reform, and Reconstructionist movement all sponsor summer camps.

The best way to select any summer camp is to start a year early and, if possible, visit several, but there are other ways to explore what different camps have to offer. Synagogues and Jewish community centers run summer camp fairs, at which representatives set up booths and talk to prospective campers and their parents. Camp directors often spend the winter months on the road recruiting campers. Some questions to ask camp directors might include: What are your qualifications? How old are the counselors and on what basis are they hired? What is the staff-camper ratio? Most important, how many campers return from one summer to the next?

The best source of information about Jewish camping is word of mouth. Both parents and kids should do some research, and the child's opinion deserves serious consideration, since he or she is the one who literally lives with this decision.

Summer camp is expensive. But if money is keeping you from sending your child to a Jewish camp, be sure to ask whether scholarships are available. Local federations may provide financial aid, and some synagogues have automatic scholarships for kids going to camps run by their movement.

Many parents—especially those who remember their own Jewish camping experiences fondly—see summer camp as an educational and Jewish priority. Jewish camping allows a child to try on ideas and practices on his or her own. To spend time in a beautiful place where the rhythms of daily life are set according to a Jewish clock, where there are no distractions or competing pressures from the secular world. Camp is a place where being Jewish is easy and fun, and where peer pressure is generally on the side of doing more rather than less Jewish stuff. The staff—especially high-school- and college-age counselors—are very special role models. Perhaps most important of all, Jewish camp memories belong wholly to the child as an individual, not as a member of a family.

As children grow and discover their talents and passions, you might want to explore alternative Jewish summer programs, some of which are run by the denominations, some of which are held on college campuses.

To find a local Jewish day camp, check out your Jewish Community Center or YM/YWHA.

For more about overnight or resident camping, contact the following organizations.

The Foundation for Jewish Camping: A nondenominational agency and the central address for information about and advocacy for nonprofit Jewish overnight camps.—www.jewishcamping.org
Reform Camps—www.urjcamps.org
Conservative Camps—www.ramahcamps.org
Reconstructionist Camps—www.campjrf.org
JCC Resident Camps—www.jcca.org/find_camp

Youth groups. For many adolescents, youth groups provide an independent forum for developing a Jewish identity. A youth group creates a local community of friends who may attend different high schools and would not otherwise meet. Since youth groups are part of regional and national organizations, which run conferences, retreats, and summer camps, the chance to travel and meet Jewish kids from all over a city, a state, and the country, is both a great attraction and a wonderful informal Jewish learning experience. For those who get involved, the social events, religious services, conferences, first loves, and late-night bull sessions that are the mainstay of youth grouping, are the source of strong, positive, and entirely personal (rather than family-oriented) Jewish memories.

There are three large national youth organizations, which operate on regional, local, and chapter levels. NFTY, the North American Federation of Temple Youth, is the youth program of the Reform movement (www.nfty.org). USY, United Synagogue Youth, is run by the Conservative movement (www.usy.org). Unlike the NFTY and USY chapters, which are usually run by synagogues, BBYO, B'nai B'rith Youth Organization, is sponsored by local B'nai B'rith chapters (www. bbyo.org). No'ar Hadash is the Reconstructionist federation youth program (www.noarhadash.org). All of these organizations run a variety of programs, including summer camps, youth leadership training programs, social justice and *tzedakah* projects, and tours of Israel.

There are also Zionist youth organizations that promote interest in and support for Israel through summer camps, year-round youth group activities, and programs in Israel. These include: Hashomer Hatzair (www.hashomerhatzair.org), Habonim Dror (www.habonimdror.org), and Young Judea (www.youngjudea.org), which is run under the auspices of Hadassah.

Synagogues that sponsor youth groups provide an adult adviser, and the national organizations are run by professional staffs. However, youth grouping seeks to give kids a major say in decisions about programs, conferences, and social events. The structure of committees, officers, and boards of directors on chapter, regional and national levels, mirrors the world of adult Jewish organizations, which makes youth grouping a hands-on leadership training program. It is common for youth group *machers* (Yiddish for "big shots") to assume leadership roles in the adult Jewish community later in life.

Youth group programming varies a great deal and includes everything from dances to seminars with rabbis to leading *Shabbat* and holiday worship services to working in food pantries. While Zionist groups are focused on Israel, all Jewish youth organizations run tours that bring thousands of Jewish American teens to Israel every summer. (See "Israel trips," below.)

Family education. Synagogues and JCCs offer all kinds of programs that involve parents and children learning together. Some of these are part of religious school curricula, some are freestanding annual events. But they also respond to the fact that the most important

Jewish learning takes place within the family. Activities are geared to interest children of various ages, and may include things like baking *challah,* creating a mural about Passover, learning Hebrew songs and dances, or building a *sukkah.* For families with older children, there may be fewer arts and crafts and more discussion and study.

Family education is not only for children but can be a relaxed way for adults to begin or renew their own Jewish education. Indeed, one of the goals of family education is to teach and empower parents to act as Jewish teachers to their children.

One of the most memorable kinds of family education experiences is family camp or a family retreat—time spent at a conference center or summer camp. Away from familiar contexts and removed from the usual chores and expectations, studying and playing in an entirely Jewish context, parents and children have the chance to be students together—a rare and precious opportunity. Similarly, a family trip to Israel—either as part of a group or on your own—is a way to share a powerful experience of cultural and religious connection, identity, and education.

Israel trips. There are all kinds of tours available for teens, for families, for young adults, and for professionals. Youth group tours offer various combinations of sightseeing with meeting Israeli teens, working on a kibbutz or at an archaeological site, or volunteering with the poor, the ill, and the elderly in Israel. Family trips seek to balance the needs of children for play and rest, with their parents' desire to tour and see the sights. (For more about Israel, see below.)

College

For some young adults, the college years are a time for putting distance between themselves and Jewish life; for others, it's a time of forging a new connection to their religious heritage. If you want your adolescent to choose a college or university where it is possible to make meaningful Jewish choices, it's important to introduce Jewish criteria to the selection and application process.

Opportunities for formal and informal Jewish learning abound on many campuses. Jewish learning in college has become increasingly easy as hundreds of private and public colleges and universities offer a variety of relevant courses. Jewish Studies departments have proliferated, but many schools that do not have an entire department frequently offer classes with Jewish content. A look at the course catalog may reveal, for example, Hebrew language courses, "The Literature of the Holocaust" (in the English department), and classes in Jewish philosophy.

For many, Jewish academics are less important than a Jewish social life on campus, which requires a critical mass of fellow Jews and a place for them to meet. While the denominations run programs for college students and some local federations sponsor events and services for students, most Jewish college programming is run under the auspices of Hillel: The Foundation for Jewish Life on Campus (www.hillel.org).[6] Hillel is a national nondenominational organization with a presence on more than 500 campuses in North America. The Web site includes a "Guide to Jewish Life on Campus," with information about hundreds of colleges and universities, including the size of the Jewish population, Jewish studies, religious life, student interest groups, and kosher dining.

Every campus program provides a different combination of services, depending both on the student body and on the staff. Some Hillels have several full-time staff members, including one or more rabbis. Hillels also serve graduate students and faculty, and sometimes attract participation from the surrounding community.

Many Hillels run kosher kitchens and sponsor as many as five separate worship services every *Shabbat,* with different liturgies for Reform, Conservative, egalitarian-traditional, Reconstructionist, and Orthodox students. Some Hillels are renowned for lecture series and Israeli folk dance evenings, and most run social action or community service programs. Hillel offices can also help students arrange Israel trips.

Adult Education

On one level, all any adult Jewish student needs to continue his or her Jewish education is access to a good bookstore or a decent Jewish library, an Internet connection, and perhaps subscriptions to some Jewish magazines. However, Jewish tradition encourages communal learning in the strongest terms. In the Talmud, Rabbi Eliezer spoke of a student who studied silently, but after three years forgot all he had learned.[7]

The classroom is a cornerstone of the Jewish community, one of the raisons d'être of the synagogue. Torah study—examining the weekly portion—is a *Shabbat* tradition that fulfills both intellectual and communal needs. Indeed, studying with partners or in a *hevrah*— a circle of friends—is a time-honored Jewish tradition. And Judaism teaches that there is no greater honor or pleasure than studying with a great teacher. Taking a course is one of the best ways to transform feelings of Jewish inadequacy and illiteracy into a sense of engagement, empowerment, mastery, and even wonder.

The range of courses and lectures for the adult learner is virtually limitless, and in larger communities there is something for nearly everyone: lectures by visiting scholars, weekly conversations about the Torah, college courses with demanding reading lists, weekend Sabbath retreats, beginning prayer book Hebrew and advanced modern Hebrew conversation, classes in basic Judaism, close readings of mystical texts, introductions to the Torah service, Talmud study, workshops for intermarried couples, holiday cooking classes, film series, panel discussions on Israeli life and politics.

Adult education opportunities are provided by all sorts of organizations, including Jewish community centers, YM/YWHAs, and local chapters of national organizations such as Hadassah. Colleges and universities sometimes offer evening courses in Judaica for part-time students or auditors. Local Jewish newspapers invariably contain advertisements and listings for lectures and courses that are either free or low cost. Upon request, organizations that sponsor adult education programs will gladly add you to their regular mailing list.

Virtually all synagogues sponsor a panel of adult education programs. Usually, the rabbi(s), cantor, and director of education will teach some courses, with others offered by members of the religious school faculty, congregants, as well as guest teachers and lecturers.

If you have studied with one teacher, do not say, "It is enough." Go study with another, too

AVOT DE RABBI NATAN A:3

ISRAEL

The relationship between the Jewish people and the land of Israel begins with the biblical promise that the children of Abraham would inherit the land and that it would be theirs forever. Jewish identification with and longing for the ancestral land in the Middle East has been a dream kept alive in literature and liturgy for centuries. In many ways, that dream of a homeland unified and sustained a wandering, homeless, often hunted people.

Although a small number of Jews have lived in the land of Israel from the Babylonian exile (which began in 586 B.C.E.) until 1948, when the modern state of Israel was established, the overwhelming majority lived in the Diaspora, in a self-described state of exile. Throughout those centuries, Jews have always faced toward Jerusalem in prayer, acknowledging the sacred geography of the Jewish imagination. This faithful orientation and a committed familiarity with the biblical names and places that define our earliest history and identity express a deep longing for *home* and everything that word means: rest, welcome, unconditional belonging.

Since 1948, this metaphysical and metaphorical relationship to the land of Israel (*Eretz Yisrael*) has coexisted with the new metaphors and realities of the modern nation-state of Israel (*Medinat Yisrael*). Although the state is officially secular, the very first law it passed—granting the right to citizenship for any Jew who wished to move there—honored the ancient, fundamental, and essentially religious centrality of this particular place as home. Whether or not Jews in Canada or Cancún chose to move to Israel, the "right of return" was tangible proof of their membership in a worldwide peoplehood.

Israel was founded in the shadow of the Holocaust, its acceptance

and approval by the international community a response, in large measure, to its guilt over the genocide of six million Jews. From its birth,
the state of Israel inspired pride in Jews around the world as it welcomed hundreds of thousands of immigrants that no other country
wanted, and then quite literally, caused the desert to bloom through
hard labor, ingenuity, and the support of worldwide Jewry.

The emotional impact of Israel's founding has faded somewhat
for Jews living abroad; for most people alive today, the state has always been a fact on the ground. And while the overwhelming majority of Jews around the world continue to provide support to Israel,
Diaspora Jews are no longer universally deferential when it comes to
Israeli politics and policies on subjects ranging from the struggle
over recognition and resources for liberal Jews in Israel, to the relationship between Israeli Arabs and Israeli Jews, to the questions surrounding Palestinian statehood.

But disagreements over such matters remain dinner-table debates,
family differences that, however heated, cannot threaten the passionate and practical connections and commitments among Jews, wherever
they live. North American Jews send vast sums of money to Israel,
making choices about contributions that reflect their interests and
concerns: environmental causes, peace fellowships for teens, support
for people wounded by terror attacks, universities, the arts.

Visiting Israel is a milestone in Jewish life for those who make the
trip.[8] For a tiny country, no bigger than New Jersey, there are a stag-
gering number of sights to see and experiences to savor. The countryside includes mountains, valleys, deserts, seashores, as well as countless
historical sites sacred to the histories of Judaism, Christianity, and Is-
lam. Of course, Israel is anything but a museum, with a vibrant contemporary arts scene flourishing in Tel Aviv, and the challenges of a
nation still absorbing immigrants of all ages, races, and national backgrounds.

Although many individuals travel to Israel on their own, the majority of first-timers go on tours organized by local federations, synagogues, or youth groups. High school and college students can attend
summer-long, semester-long, or yearlong programs for touring and
study, which provide contact with young Israelis.

Trips to Israel can be exhausting, confusing, exalting, inspiring, and frustrating. There are too many sights to see, too many stories to hear. But for Jews, travel to Israel is different from a trip to Costa Rica or Corsica, or any other international adventure. As Rabbi Lawrence Hoffman has written, "Jews visit Israel not just as tourists but as pilgrims."[9] Indeed, a great many people make the trip in groups called "missions."

"They pack tour guides but also Bibles and prayer books that they haven't looked at in years . . . They can't get enough [of Hebrew and] stare in awe at Coca-Cola written in Hebrew letters."[10]

Israel exerts a gravitational pull on Jewish hearts and minds. Some are so drawn to the integrity of living in a place where everything slows down on *Shabbat,* where the language of the marketplace and the Internet is Jewish, that they "make *aliyah*" (the word means "to go up") and move to Israel. But even for those who live elsewhere, Israel is one of the gifts of being a Jew in the 21st century, one of its challenges, one of its choices.

Here are a few of the hundreds of Web resources about Israel.

American Israel Public Affairs Committee: AIPAC is a registered lobby that meets with members of Congress on legislation affecting Israel—www.aipac.org

ARZA: The Association of Reform Zionists of America—www.rza.org

Israel Ministry of Tourism—www.goisrael.com

Hadassah: The Women's Zionist Organization of America, which sponsors Zionist youth programs and supports many social welfare and medical programs in Israel—www.hadassah.org

JNF: Jewish National Fund, which works for forestation, land reclamation, and environmental causes in Israel—www.jnf.org

MERCAZ: The Zionist organization of the Conservative movement —www.mercazusa.org

The New Israel Fund: Supports social justice projects in Israel, including women's rights and Arab-Jewish cooperation—www.nif.org

The World Zionist Organization: Promotes immigration to Israel—www.wizo.org.il

TRAVELING JEWISH

If making Jewish choices happens only at home or in the synagogue, then traveling for pleasure or on business means leaving Judaism behind along with the cat and the television set. But if Jewishness is an authentic part of self and life, it does not get shelved when the newspaper delivery is suspended.

Traveling Jewish can be a special delight; a unique opportunity for learning about Judaism, and about the world and your place in it. Celebrating *Shabbat* in a hotel room can be a way of calming down and of finding peace and balance during an otherwise dreadful business trip. Attending services at an ancient European synagogue or in Anytown, USA, can transform your experience of the city and even your perception of an entire culture. Giving money to a begging child in a poverty-stricken land can move you to reconsider your budget for *tzedakah*.

Making Jewish choices on the road takes two forms, the first of which involves re-creating personal Jewish routines. Lighting candles and saying blessings in a vacation cottage by the sea or in a tent on a mountainside can become a treasured family memory. Packing and shopping for a vacation *Shabbat* focuses the trip in a particular way, and Judaica vendors sell traveling candleholders, *kiddush* cups, and *hannukiot* that fold up to easily packable proportions.

Jews who keep kosher find it relatively easy to maintain their practice on the road. Airplanes and ocean liners generally offer kosher as well as vegetarian alternatives for travelers. Kosher meals are available in the most unlikely places—such as the Air Lanka flight from Colombo, Sri Lanka, to Bangkok, Thailand.

While there are kosher cruises and kosher resorts—in the Caribbean and in Mexico as well as in Miami Beach—people have managed kosher trips in far less hospitable places simply by keeping to a vegetarian diet. All major airlines and cruise lines offer kosher food on request and do not charge extra for it. In cities and countries where there are Jewish communities, seeking out kosher restaurants can lead to very special travel experiences and a sense of belonging to a global family.

Traveling Jewish means seeking out new Jewish experiences: finding a Jewish neighborhood, eating in a kosher restaurant, or visiting the local Jewish museum. Once you have seen all the landmarks that every tourist visits, you have the opportunity to make a far more personal connection with a foreign culture. Attending a service in Rome or New Delhi can make you feel at home even in a place where you had felt like a complete stranger. If you find yourself very far from home during a Jewish holiday, consider exploring the local customs: imagine Hannukah in Hong Kong, Passover in Paris, or Sukkot in Singapore. But even on business trips in North America, attending services at a synagogue near the hotel can forever alter your feelings about trips to Cleveland, Houston, or Toronto.

Of course, not all Jews are hospitable or effusive, and it would be naive to expect to be treated like a long-lost sibling just because you are in what seems an exotically non-Jewish place. Nevertheless, there are countless stories about unexpectedly warm welcomes for total strangers simply because they identified themselves as Jews. Travelers have been invited to people's homes and given tours of the city.

For a worldwide synagogue directory see Maven Search (www.maven.co.il).

May it be your will, Adonai, God of our parents, to lead us in peace and guide our steps in safety, so that we arrive at our destination alive, happy, and in peace. Deliver us from enemies and danger along the way. May we find favor, kindness and compassion in your eyes and in the eyes of all we meet. Hear our prayers, for You are a God who listens to prayers. Holy One of blessings, hear our prayer.

THE TRAVELER'S PRAYER

THE CYCLE OF THE YEAR

Rabbi Abraham Joshua Heschel wrote, "Jewish ritual may be characterized as the art of significant forms in time, as architecture of time."[1] Heschel, one of the great teachers of the 20th century, thought of *Shabbat* as the essential expression of Judaism's "architecture of time," and referred to the Sabbaths as "our great cathedrals." Judaism provides other ritual structures, too, in the annual cycle of holidays and in the ceremonies that mark rites of passage.

There is another, more personal metaphor that may be applied to the Jewish cycles of observance. Tradition—made up of history and custom, memory and song—is like a mirror, a tool for considering life and self in the context of Judaism. Looking into it, every person calls forth something new. Not answers. Mirrors do not supply answers. Yet there is something special about a mirror that can change the way people see themselves. The source of the transforming power of this mirror is time. Possessing context, connection, and continuity, time is both why and how Jewish holidays and life cycle observances "work."

Time seems tender and almost palpable at the holidays because every celebration is a window on the past: when parents were children lighting their first Hannukah candles, when the light from the candles was the brightest light in the house, or when the Maccabees lit a lamp in a rededicated Temple. Every Hannukah distills the present, like a snapshot. Every Hannukah is a "first": the first year the baby is allowed to light the candles, the first year without Grandpa.

Every time a couple meets under the *huppah,* the Jewish wedding canopy, it is as if time collapses. The details of the day—the style of the bride's dress, the music, the menu—are forgotten. Suddenly and forever, it is the first wedding, when according to one legend, God braided Eve's hair. And it is the ultimate wedding, the culmination of four thousand years of Jewish weddings.

JEWISH TIME

The holidays are islands in time where people can stop to reflect on the meaning of their days, to consider the distance between who they are and who they wish to be, the distance between today and the day when the world will be what we wish it to be. Like *Shabbat,* the holidays are about providing a glimpse into what life and time will be like when those wishes are realized. These islands in time are not abstract ideas but ritual structures built of customs, prayers, food, songs, family gatherings, and memories. They are embedded in the Jewish calendar, which expresses a particular understanding of time and eternity.

The calendar. For more than two thousand years, Jews have juggled two time zones, straddled two calendars. According to the secular calendar, the date changes at midnight, the week begins on Monday, and the year starts in the winter. According to the Jewish calendar, the day begins at sunset, the week begins on Saturday night, and the new year is celebrated in the autumn.

The secular or Gregorian calendar is a solar calendar, based on the fact that it takes 365.25 days for the earth to circle the sun.[2] With only 365 days in a year, after four years an extra day is added to February and there is a leap year. The Jewish calendar is both solar and lunar. The months are lunar, made up of either 29 or 30 days, which add up to a 354-day year, 11.25 days short of a solar year. The discrepancy is corrected with the occasional addition of a leap month tucked between the spring months of Adar and Nisan.

The Jewish month begins with the new moon, when no moon is visible in the sky, so the moon is full on the 15th of every month whose names (starting with the autumn month when the year begins) are: Tishrei, Heshvan, Kislev, Tevet, Shvat, Adar (and seven times every 19 years Adar II), Nisan, Iyar, Sivan, Tammuz, Av, and Elul. The year changes on Rosh Hashanah, on the first day of Tishrei, when according to the traditional Jewish reckoning of time, the world was created.

The Gregorian and Jewish calendars are never quite in sync, thus the inevitable grumbling about how the Jewish holidays are never "on time"—somehow either too late or too early in relation to the secular date. But since their purposes are so different, the two calendars are rarely in conflict. The Gregorian calendar is the calendar of the workweek, the school year, and the mundane needs of daily life. The Jewish calendar has exclusively religious purposes: it is for keeping track of holidays, and is used for writing Jewish marriage contracts and for determining the anniversary of a death. The secular calendar is a tool for keeping track of time, for managing time, unlike the Jewish calendar, which is not used for civil purposes anywhere—not even in Israel.

The secular calendar stretches endlessly into the future. The Jewish calendar is a tool for cherishing time, and for sanctifying it. The Jewish calendar moves forward toward redemption in a dance with the past, choreographed by the holidays.

The Jewish holidays have two main sources: biblical and historical.[3] The Torah established the observance of Rosh Hashanah, Yom Kippur, Sukkot, Shmini Atzeret, Pesach (Passover), and Shavuot. They are called "holy convocations," or "a Sabbath unto the Lord," and the Torah contains specific instructions for celebrating these days and for refraining from work on them.

The Torah also assigns reason and meaning to the holidays as well: Rosh Hashanah is for sounding the ram's horn and for the new year; Yom Kippur is the day for asking forgiveness; Sukkot is about the harvest; Passover is for remembering slavery and the exodus from Egypt; Shavuot is about the harvest of the first fruits.

The historical holidays developed in response to transforming events in the experience of the Jewish people: Purim reacts to the dangers of living in exile; the day of mourning called Tisha B'Av became part of the calendar after the destruction of the Temple in Jerusalem; in the second century B.C.E., after the Maccabees fought and won the right to Jewish self-rule in the land of Israel, Hannukah became an annual celebration of rededication. The historical development of the calendar continues in modern times with the addition of Yom HaAtzmaut and Yom Hashoah, respectively, Israeli Independence Day and Holocaust Remembrance Day.

The historical, evolutionary nature of the Jewish calendar is also demonstrated in the way certain festivals have waned and waxed in their observance. Shmini Atzeret, for example, with its unique prayer for autumn rain, may have made spiritual sense in the context of an agricultural and Temple-oriented society. However, as the Jews became a more urban and Torah-centered people, Simchat Torah, a post-biblical observance, came to overshadow and even preempt the older holiday. For modern Jews, the Holocaust and not the destruction of the Temple has become the focus of communal grief, thus Holocaust Remembrance Day has come to eclipse Tisha B'Av as an observance of public grief and mourning.

Perhaps the most confusing aspect of Jewish holiday observance is the discrepancy regarding celebrations on the second day of Rosh Hashanah, Sukkot, Passover, and Shavuot. For example, some Jews observe two *seders* and eat *matzah* for eight days, while others attend only one *seder* and eat bread again after seven days. The difference in practice dates back to sometime around the fourth century C.E. and is based on doubts as to the exact date of the new moon, which is invisible. Rather than risk celebrating on the wrong date, Jews living outside of the land of Israel began two-day observances of the holidays that required refraining from work and attending worship services. This division continues: Israeli Jews and many Reform Jews outside of Israel celebrate holidays based on the new moon for only a single day; however, many Diaspora Jews continue with two-day observances.[4]

Making yontif. *Yontif* is the Yiddish word for holiday. Literally, it means "good day" and is based in the Hebrew, *yom tov*. Hence the greeting, *"Gut yontif."* (The Hebrew word for holiday is *chag. Chag sameach,* means "happy holiday.")

As with *Shabbat,* the Jewish holidays only have meaning in the doing. The operant verb for holidays is not "celebrating" or "observing," but "making." Thus, making Jewish choices about the holidays is a matter of "making *yontif."*

Jews make *yontif* in many different ways; some are traditional, some brand-new, and the following chapters contain many examples of both. The richness of each holiday makes it impossible to do any of them justice in an introductory book. Books about the holidays are a mainstay of most Jewish home libraries because, in a sense, the holidays are the best curriculum for Jewish education since they encompass nearly every religious, cultural, and historical theme of Judaism.

Each holiday has its own mood, texture, and weight. (Yom Kippur is somber. Purim is hilarious.) While virtually every holiday has some synagogue observance connected with it, some holidays are primarily liturgical and synagogue-centered—Rosh Hashanah is a good example—whereas others like Hannukah are essentially home-based.

Various holidays also have different qualities and different importance in every Jewish household. For example, many people consider Purim primarily a children's holiday and focus on dress-up, plays, and pageants at synagogue or in school. But there are many adults for whom Purim is the occasion for both serious (and silly) study—not to mention the costume party of the year.

Furthermore, individual and family interest in particular holidays may wax and wane, and not only as a result of children's ages. Enthusiasm for a celebration can be sparked by any number of reasons: a good lecture, a book or movie that speaks to the themes of the holiday, an event in the past year. For people who have recently lost a loved one, for example, attending Yom Kippur services can feel like part of the mourning process.

The meaning and joy of the holidays is uncovered year by year in the process of making *yontif*. But perhaps the most important part of that process—the make-it-or-break-it element—is preparation, *hachanah* in Hebrew.

Hachanah includes everything from stocking up on *matzah* for Passover, to making paper chain decorations for Hannukah, from meditating on the unkind words you wish you hadn't said in preparation for Yom Kippur, to reading bedtime stories about Queen Esther during the week before Purim. Preparation is the difference between mechanical holidays and meaningful holidays, between enforced holidays and holidays that are genuinely fun.

Jewish tradition is replete with examples of the importance of preparing for the holidays. The entire forty days before Yom Kippur are considered a period of spiritual preparation. And then, as soon as Yom Kippur is over, even before breaking the fast, preparations for Sukkot begin with the hammering of the first nail in a *sukkah,* the hut in which Jews celebrate the harvest festival. According to the Hasidic view, these preparations are themselves holy; by orienting secular time toward the celebration to come, *hachanah* sanctifies the everyday.

Still, there is a crucial difference between preparing and celebrating, between *hachanah* and *yontif.* The point of getting ready is not merely to have delicious meals or a big party when the day finally arrives. Preparation is what enables us to bask in the present without worrying about what is left unfinished. This sense of celebration—this taste of redemption—is the goal of all Jewish ritual, of *Shabbat,* and of the Jewish holidays.

The menu that follows consists of ideas, strategies, projects, and approaches for making *yontif.* This is not a "to-do" list; there is more here than any one person or any one family can reasonably undertake. This is a "can-do" list—a catalog of the ways that people explore the Jewish holidays.

Getting oriented. One of the easiest ways to focus on the holiday cycle is by purchasing a beautiful Jewish calendar and hanging it prominently. Look for one with room for notes and scribbling, and flip through the months, making note of the week *before* every holiday as a reminder to start getting ready.

One way to focus on holiday celebrations is by picking a primary symbol for each, for instance the *hannukiah* (the eight-candle candelabra of Hannukah) or the Sukkot *etrog* (a citrus fruit imported from Israel). Learn as much as you can about it and feature it in centerpieces on the table, in conversation, in stories and art projects for children.

As markers in time, the Jewish holidays can be a way to organize all kinds of memories. Pictures of ten years' worth of Passover tables make for a moving collage of continuity and change. Or have a family portrait taken every year during the same holiday.

Continuity is good, but so is change. In observing the Jewish holidays, it's a good idea to try to reconcile this seeming contradiction by being flexible. The holidays acquire more and more meaning as they are repeated consistently. The same menus, the same guests, the same ritual objects taken out just once a year, all add to the evocative power of the day. But holidays can also be opportunities for growth. Just as individuals change from one year to the next, so can their holiday observance.

Some holidays may hold more meaning than others for you and your family. Some people "specialize" in certain observances and all their friends know that the So-and-Sos really "do" Hannukah with a big party complete with dancing, a royal feast, and gifts for everyone. As you explore the Jewish calendar from year to year, you'll discover favorites and create ways to make them your own

Family time. There are all kinds of families. And regardless of their size or composition, holidays create time and space for relaxing, sharing, listening, and enjoying one another. For families with children, the holidays are formative Jewish experiences redolent of both continuity and change.

There are many ways to enhance the holidays. Taking time to talk about them at the Friday night *Shabbat* table, for example, is one way to help children prepare and also to let them know that the grown-ups have begun getting ready. Reading stories and drawing pictures about the holiday in anticipation of the celebration is another way to prepare with kids.

In order to associate the holidays with pleasantness, some parents give gifts to their children on the major holidays. A trip to the bookstore or music store for a holiday-related book or CD, followed by an ice cream cone, heightens the anticipation and sweetness of a holiday. And since it is traditional to wear new clothes on holidays (and *Shabbat*), new clothes might be purchased with an eye to a first wearing on *yontif.*

Holidays are like chapter headings in a family history. The light of holiday candles can prompt the telling of "our" stories: of Sarah's first Hannukah, when she tried to eat the candles; of the time everyone went to Grandma's house and all the presents were forgotten at home; of the favorite gifts, and guests, and parties.

It is a good idea to try to strike a balance between activities for children and time for adults. Arts-and-crafts projects may be the perfect way for preschoolers to get acquainted with a holiday, but that's probably not entirely fulfilling for parents. Besides, if children see that their parents are really not involved, they will learn that making *yontif* is essentially kid stuff, that is, something to be outgrown.

Setting the mood. Decorating for the holiday—making tangible preparations—is a good way to enter into a spirit of celebration. This can include everything from buying fresh flowers for the table to making a centerpiece using holiday symbols. Children's artwork about the holiday can be featured on the refrigerator or on the front door.

One nice holiday project is to buy or create special place settings. Commercial place mats are available for Passover and Hannukah, but children can make their own by covering an original drawing or painting with clear Contact paper. Likewise, you can create "dinnerware" for holidays, either by purchasing a new set of plastic tableware, or by going the clear Contact paper route using a paper plate or by getting a "decorate a plate" kit, which is shipped off to the factory so the original design can be permanently baked on.

Another way to set the mood is with music. Recordings of traditional and modern holiday songs abound, as well as music that reflects the diversity of Jewish culture: everything from cantorial singing to Israeli rock and roll, from American Jewish bluegrass to modern classics, such as Leonard Bernstein's "Kaddish" and Steven Reich's "Tehillim." English/Hebrew CDs for children are a popular way to introduce Jewish vocabulary and Hebrew words to youngsters, and their parents.

Eating. The holidays are experienced with all the senses, and special dishes are associated with certain times of the year. It just isn't Rosh Hashanah without apples and honey. Potato pancakes *(latkes) are* Hannukah.

Families create traditions around holiday foods as well. Passover would be weird without Mom's *matzah* stuffing. Shavuot means Aunt Molly's cheesecake. It is easy to start this kind of family table tradition by finding a dish beloved by everyone in the household and more or less reserving it for the holiday. Holidays are also a good excuse for baked treats. Making cookies, cupcakes, and candy can be a great way to involve children in holiday preparations.

Cookbooks are a way to explore the holidays from a sensory perspective. Most Jewish cookbooks contain a special section on holiday food, and there are many titles devoted entirely to holiday recipes. For North American Jews, the vast majority of whom are of Eastern European descent, cookbooks devoted to the Jewish cuisines of Greece and Italy can be a revelation, and not just gastronomically. The fact that holiday traditions include such a breadth of flavors and aromas validates the diversity and variation in modern Jewish life.

Study. One way for adults to enter into the spirit of the holidays is to learn something new about each. Study can take many forms, from going to a lecture about the holiday, enrolling in a course about the holiday cycle, or simply reading a chapter about the upcoming festival. Many holidays also have Torah readings and other traditional texts associated with them.

Tzedakah. It has long been the Jewish custom to share holiday joy by making contributions to the poor. Convening the family to decide where to send money "this season" can be a way to focus on the meaning of the holiday; by sending money to relevant organizations. For example, environmental causes seem an apt choice on Tu B'Shvat, which celebrates trees and the natural world.

Synagogue attendance. The Jewish holidays are marked by special worship services. Many synagogues also offer other activities: from communal candlelighting and meals in the temple *sukkah,* to *Purimshpiels* (Purim plays or pageants), to late-night study sessions on Shavuot. Attending synagogue activities is a good way to participate in communal life and learn about the holidays at the same time.

Spiritual preparation. In the rush to run errands, cook, and get everything finished before a holiday begins, it is easy to forget about making oneself ready for *yontif.* For Jews, spiritual preparation has long been associated with *mikveh,* the ritual bath of purification. A physical manifestation of *kavannah* (intentionality) prior to a holiday, immersion in a *mikveh,* like no othe ritual, permits you to stop and take stock of things, to step outside of time, as it were.[5]

However, there are simple ways to slow down and get centered at home as well. Set aside time to take a solitary walk, to arrange flowers for the table, or to take a long bath; read a poem or prayer to shift mental gears from the everyday into holiday mode.

The *Yontif Seder*

The word *seder*, which means "order," is most closely associated with Passover. The Passover *seder* is made up by the order of the readings, blessings, and rituals that take place before, during, and after the ritual meal on the first and (for many) second nights of the holiday. People have also created seders for Tu B'Shvat, Hannukah, and Purim; ritual menus of songs, readings, blessings, and activities surrounding a meal.

The *yontif seder* is similar to the *Shabbat seder,* which is the order of blessings, customs, and songs surrounding the Friday night meal, described on pages 35–49. Most of the holidays described in the following chapters begin with a festival meal that includes four basic blessings: over candles, wine *(kiddush)*, the season *(shehechiyanu)*, and bread *(motzi)*.

Candles. Festival candles mark the beginning of most holiday celebrations, just as *Shabbat* candles mark the beginning of the Sabbath. If a holiday begins on Friday night, the blessing for the candles concludes with the words *shel Shabbat v'yom tov,* "the lights of *Shabbat* and the holiday."

בָּרוּךְ אַתָּה יְיָ. אֱלֹהֵינוּ מֶלֶךְ הָעוֹלָם. אֲשֶׁר קִדְּשָׁנוּ בְּמִצְוֹתָיו.
וְצִוָּנוּ לְהַדְלִיק נֵר שֶׁל-וֹשַׁבָּת חָן יוֹם טוֹב:

Baruch ata Adonai Eloheynu Melech Ha-olam asher kid'shanu b'mitzvotav vitzivanu l'hadlik ner shel (Shabbat v') yom tov.

You Abound in Blessings, Adonai Our Lord, You make us holy with commandments, and call us to light the lights of (*Shabbat* and of) the holiday.

Wine. The *kiddush,* or sanctification over wine, can be done in a number of ways. The full *kiddush* for holidays usually includes at least a phrase and as much as a paragraph about the specific festival, and is published in most daily prayer books, or *siddurim.* However, many people use the basic *kiddush* for any occasion.

בָּרוּךְ אַתָּה יְיָ. אֱלֹהֵינוּ מֶלֶךְ הָעוֹלָם. בּוֹרֵא פְּרִי הַגָּפֶן:

Baruch ata Adonai Eloheynu Melech Ha-olam boray pree hagafen.

You Abound in Blessings, Adonai Our Lord, You make the fruit of the vine.

The season. *Shehecheyanu* is a blessing recited at many sorts of occasions, ceremonies, and rituals. At the holidays, it acknowledges the advent of a new time in the year, a new time in the life of the people gathered at the table.

בָּרוּךְ אַתָּה יְיָ, אֱלֹהֵינוּ מֶלֶךְ הָעוֹלָם, שֶׁהֶחֱיָנוּ וְקִיְּמָנוּ
וְהִגִּיעָנוּ לַזְּמָן הַזֶּה.

Baruch ata Adonai Eloheynu Melech Ha-olam sheheche-yanu v'kiamanu vihigianu lazman hazeh.

You Abound in Blessings, Adonai Our Lord, You have kept us alive. You have sustained us. You have brought us to this moment.

Bread. Called the *motzi* ("brings"), the blessing over bread represents all the food at the meal. The *motzi* acknowledges that human beings are, ultimately, dependent upon gifts from the earth.

בָּרוּךְ אַתָּה יְיָ. אֱלֹהֵינוּ מֶלֶךְ הָעוֹלָם. הַמּוֹצִיא לֶחֶם מִן־הָאָרֶץ:

Baruch ata Adonai Eloheynu Melech Ha-olam Ha motzi lechem min ha'aretz.

You Abound in Blessings, Adonai Our Lord, You bring forth bread from the earth.

Dinner is served.

ROSH HASHANAH
AND YOM KIPPUR

Picture people running around, sneaking up behind one another with a big ram's horn, giving it a blast, as if to say, "Wake up! It is upon us again." The liturgy of Rosh Hashanah is designed to get you to wake up and pay attention not only to who you are, but to who you have been and who you mean to be.

Yom Kippur is not eating, not drinking, not sleeping very much, not having sex, not dressing in fine clothes and looking in the mirror and seeing what you're going to look like after you've died. And the most joyous noise a Jew can hear is the sound of the shofar announcing the end of Yom Kippur, because it means that you have lived through the day of death and not died.

Rosh Hashanah is about reverence and gratitude for life, the mother lode of all religious insight. Yom Kippur is about telling the worst truth about yourself, and getting new life from that.

RABBI LAWRENCE KUSHNER[6]

Rosh Hashanah (the New Year) and Yom Kippur (the Day of Atonement) are the most liturgical of all the Jewish holidays. The Hebrew word for prayer is *tefila*, which is a reflexive form of the verb "to judge." For Jews, prayer—especially the prayers of these two holidays, known as the Days of Awe—are best understood as a form of reflection and self-judgment.

The two holidays that begin the Jewish year are unlike virtually every other. Neither one is based on an agricultural festival or historical event. And although Rosh Hashanah meals may be elaborate, neither of these holidays is associated with the kinds of symbols, foods, and home celebrations that make other Jewish holidays beloved of children.

The Days of Awe, *Yamim Noraim,* are synagogue-based and exis-tential. They confront every Jew with the fact of his or her own mortal-ity, and thus with an appreciation of life. While these holidays are not inherently "fun" the way that Sukkot, Hannukah, Purim, or Passover can be, they are deeply compelling.

Indeed, Rosh Hashanah and Yom Kippur are the only times when American synagogues are filled to the rafters. Jews who rarely or never attend worship services make a point of going to the longest, most for-mal services of the year. The reasons for this loyalty are complex. Childhood memories and nostalgia draw many people, and some rab-bis have suggested that there is a magical element to High Holiday services that makes attendance seem like the renewal of an ancient Jewish life insurance policy, a hedge against death, or at least a repu-diation of assimilation.

By and large, making *yontif* for the Days of Awe means attending worship services. There are many ways to prepare for these holidays and to mark their observance at home, but because of the importance of community worship, this chapter outlines the liturgy, including some of the religious themes and key Hebrew words found in Rosh Hashanah and Yom Kippur services. However, because individual con-gregations make so many choices about the content and form of ser-vices, this discussion represents only a fraction of the menu from which rabbis, cantors, and ritual committees make their selections.

Preparation

According to tradition, the entire Hebrew month that precedes Rosh Hashanah, Elul, is dedicated to preparing for the Days of Awe. Psalm 27 is added to the daily worship service and the *shofar,* a ram's horn, is sounded every weekday morning. Special penitential prayers called *slichot,* from the Hebrew for "excuse" or "to be sorry," are recited dur-ing Elul, and on the Saturday night preceding Rosh Hashanah, many congregations hold a late-night *Slichot* service. Some synagogues run adult education programs about the approaching Days of Awe during Elul.

The most common personal preparation for these holidays is the sending of New Year's cards. These greetings originated from the custom of signing letters during the month of Elul with the phrase "May you be inscribed [in the Book of Life] for a good year." Commercial cards are available, but some families make their own, featuring artwork by children.

Another way to get into the spirit of the holidays is to buy a *shofar,* the horn of a ram or other animal, available in Judaica stores. A *shofar* is not a sacred object but something both children and adults can play with. A *shofar* can even be used as the family alarm clock in preparation for the holidays to come.

It is also customary to wear new clothes for Rosh Hashanah, and to get a haircut in anticipation of the new year.

Since Rosh Hashanah is associated with both the creation of the first human beings and with the creation of the world, children enjoy decorating the table (or the refrigerator door) with birthday-related projects. They can also decorate the table and the house for the break-the-fast meal that follows the Yom Kippur fast.

Traditionally, the weeks before the Days of Awe are associated with mending relationships, apologizing, and asking for forgiveness for transgressions big and small. People call out-of-town relatives and friends. Some families make a point of resolving conflicts and clearing the air of arguments. It is also customary to visit the graves of family members and loved ones who have died.

Study

Of all the holidays, the Days of Awe seem the most intellectual. Since so much time is spent in services, it can be helpful to browse through the special holiday prayer book or *machzor,* Hebrew for "cycle," you will be using. Getting familiar with the structure and content of the prayers can make the services more accessible and meaningful.

Holiday prayer books contain the holiday Torah and Haftarah portions that are read out loud during services. The Rosh Hashanah Torah readings (Genesis 21 and 22) are among the most powerful and problematic in the Torah. The first includes the story of the birth of Isaac, the casting out of Hagar and Ishmael into the desert, and their subsequent deliverance. Genesis 22 contains the test of Abraham's faith, when he is asked to sacrifice his son Isaac. This story is referred to as "the binding of Isaac," or the *akedah*.

The Haftarah portions (prophetic readings) for both the morning and afternoon Torah services on Yom Kippur also provide complex texts for study and discussion. The morning passage from Isaiah rejects piety divorced from a commitment to social justice; "Behold, on the day of your fast you pursue business as usual, and oppress your workers . . . Such fasting will not make your voice audible on high."[7] The Haftarah for the afternoon of Yom Kippur is the four-chapter Book of Jonah, which is available in illustrated versions for children.

Tzedakah

It is customary to give money to the poor during this season. Since Rosh Hashanah is a celebration of life, some make an annual blood donation before the holiday. Many make a contribution to a hunger-related charity for an amount equivalent to a day's worth of meals at Yom Kippur through Mazon: A Jewish Response to Hunger (www.mazon.org). During the memorial or *yizkor* service of Yom Kippur, one of the prayers pledges *tzedakah* in memory of loved ones who have died, which prompts donations to charities that were important to them.

Another way of performing a *mitzvah,* a holy act, during the Days of Awe is to go to a Jewish nursing home to visit the residents and/or to assist with or attend services with those who cannot get to a synagogue.

Children

Rosh Hashanah and Yom Kippur are days of intense prayer and reflection in the synagogue, clearly not an easy setting for children. Most liberal congregations provide some kind of special programming for little ones, with age-specific activities, including babysitting for toddlers, singing and organized play for preschoolers, and an abbreviated service for school-age children; however, not all temples are able to accommodate all ages. Some parents bring books and puzzles for school-age children, and encourage them to stay in the sanctuary to absorb the melodies and rhythms of the service. Others prefer to leave little ones with babysitters, both for the comfort of the children and fellow congregants, and also for their own prayers. Then again, many parents treasure their memories of spending some (or most) of the High Holidays in the temple foyer or playground, with other parents and children.

Making Rosh Hashanah

At Home

The evening meal that begins the holiday constitutes the high point of home celebration on Rosh Hashanah. Families tend to create their own holiday traditions around this dinner: menus and recipes, special table settings and decorations, guests who return every year. Since Rosh Hashanah is often referred to as the birthday of the world, parents of young children sometimes serve birthday cake or cupcakes, complete with candles, for dessert.

Dinner is preceded by the *yontif seder* that is discussed on pages 149–151, with lighting of candles, *kiddush,* and *motzi.* It is traditional to use a round *challah* on Rosh Hashanah, a symbol of the cycle of the year. *Shehecheyanu* is then recited, the blessing for all "firsts." And to begin the new year sweetly, it is customary to dip apple sections in a bowl of honey and to say:

יְהִי רָצוֹן מִלְּפָנֶיךָ יְיָ אֱלֹהֵינוּ וֵאלֹהֵי
אֲבוֹתֵינוּ שֶׁתְּחַדֵּשׁ עָלֵינוּ שָׁנָה טוֹבָה וּמְתוּקָה:

*Y'hi ratzon milfanecha Adonai Eloheynu vaylohay avotenu,
she'te'chadesh aleynu shana tova u-metukah.*

May it be your will, Adonai, God of our parents, to renew us
for a good and sweet year.

After services, people generally have lunch with family and friends,
go for walks, or search out a body of water for the informal ceremony
called *tashlich,* from the Hebrew for "send off" or "cast away."

Tashlich is a symbolic casting off of sins by emptying pockets into
running water, built around the words of the prophet Micah. "And you
will cast all their sins into the depths of the sea."[8] Short, informal ceremonies have been created for *tashlich,* which include songs about
water and various readings.

Take a bag of stale bread and head for a duck pond—a favorite
with children, especially on a day when they may be asked to sit still a
great deal. Some families use this time to apologize to one another for
the wrongs of the past year and promise to try to be more patient and
kinder in the year ahead.

For those who observe a second day of Rosh Hashanah, it's customary, during the *yontif seder,* to taste a fruit that hasn't been eaten
for several months, providing the occasion to recite *Shehecheyanu,* the
prayer for firsts.

Synagogue Observance

The evening service for Rosh Hashanah is relatively short and, with a
few exceptions, much like other evening services. However, a great
emotional and spiritual transformation is wrought by the distinctive
melodies of the Days of Awe, which are reprised again and again during both Rosh Hashanah and Yom Kippur services. For most Jews, it is
the tunes that evoke the spirit and mood of these powerful holidays.

At the morning service for Rosh Hashanah, the themes of judgment and repentance are repeated. The recurrent image of God as a father-king is given voice in one of the most memorable prayers and melodies of all the Jewish holidays, *"Avinu Malkenu,"* "Our Father, Our King."

One of the overarching metaphors of Rosh Hashanah and Yom Kippur is "the Book of Life." According to legend, on Rosh Hashanah, the first day of the year, the names of the righteous are written in this book, inscribed for another year of life. But those who are not entirely good or righteous, even the wicked, have the next ten days in which to turn away from their wrongs and repent before the book is closed and sealed on Yom Kippur.

Help us to break down the barriers which keep us from You:
falsehood and faithlessness
callousness and selfishness
injustice and hard-heartedness

FROM THE ROSH HASHANAH SERVICE

The Torah scrolls are "dressed" in different coverings for the holidays; usually in white, to denote purity. And their readings are a high point of the service, and often the subject of one of the rabbi's sermons, which are highly crafted and much anticipated. One of the most dramatic parts of the Rosh Hashanah service is the blowing of the *shofar*.

The liturgy for the second day of Rosh Hashanah is largely a repetition of the first, with a different sermon, and often different Torah readers. If the first day of Rosh Hashanah falls on Shabbat, *tashlich* is performed on the second day, as is the sounding of the *shofar*.

The Ten Days

Rosh Hashanah and Yom Kippur begin and end a ten-day period of reflection and repentance, in Hebrew, *teshuvah,* which literally means "turning." The Sabbath between the two holidays is called *Shabbat Shuvah,* the "Sabbath of turning." In some synagogues, these ten days are observed with special services and/or with an ethical will–writing workshop. An ethical will, a form of moral literature that dates back to biblical times, is a personal statement of beliefs, hopes, and advice. A counterpart to a legal will that distributes material goods after a person's death, the ethical will is a way of communicating the values and insights of a lifetime to loved ones. After reading and discussing examples of ethical wills, participants at these workshops sit with pen and paper and write their own. People who have done this say it is a powerfully clarifying exercise, and wonderful preparation for Yom Kippur. Ethical wills are usually stored with legal wills and other important personal documents, and some congregations keep copies on file.

Making Yom Kippur

At Home

Yom Kippur is called *Shabbat Shabbaton,* or the "Sabbath of Sabbaths." The meal prior to the start of the daylong fast is not begun with blessings, although a *motzi* may be said before any meal. However, as with Rosh Hashanah, the meal that precedes Yom Kippur can become a family tradition by virtue of special menus and rituals, such as standing and drinking a glass of water together to end the meal.

After dinner, people who have lost family members light memorial or *yahrzeit* candles (see the chapter on "Death"). Finally, Yom Kippur candles are lit with the following blessing.

בָּרוּךְ אַתָּה יְיָ אֱלֹהֵינוּ מֶלֶךְ הָעוֹלָם אֲשֶׁר קִדְּשָׁנוּ
בְּמִצְוֹתָיו וְצִוָּנוּ לְהַדְלִיק נֵר שֶׁל [שַׁבָּת וְשֶׁל] יוֹם
הַכִּפֻּרִים:

*Baruch ata Adonai Eloheynu Melech Ha-olam asher kid-
shanu b'mitzvotav vitzivanu l'hadlik ner shel (Shabbat v'shel)
Yom HaKippurim.*

You Abound in Blessings, Adonai Our Lord, You make us holy
with commandments and call us to kindle the light of (*Shabbat*
and of) Yom Kippur.

After dinner, some people put a white tablecloth over the table
that will remain empty until the following evening.

This is the last meal eaten before healthy adults undertake a complete fast from food and water, which ends the following sunset. Fasting is only the most obvious form of self-denial on the tenth day of the
seventh month, which the Torah calls "a day for self-affliction."[9] Life's
daily pleasures are avoided in order to focus attention upon the task at
hand, which is repentance.

Children under the age of 13 are not expected to fast during Yom
Kippur, nor is anyone for whom a lack of food or water might cause
physical harm. Pregnant and nursing women are forbidden to fast. People who cannot or do not fast, including children, often choose a modified fast, drinking water only, or eating very little. People who undertake
a complete fast are often advised to cut back on caffeine consumption
several days in advance, since caffeine withdrawal is a common cause of
headaches, grouchiness, and other unpleasant symptoms.

Synagogue Observance

Kol Nidre is the evening service for Yom Kippur, named for its dramatic opening prayer. The *Kol Nidre* prayer is chanted while three
people stand, acting as a ceremonial "court," for the text is legal in nature, declaring all unfulfilled vows and promises null and void. The
full meaning of this prayer has been the subject of debate for genera-

tions, but it clearly addresses the power of words and vows, a recurrent theme in the Yom Kippur liturgy. At least one member of the "court" will hold a white-clad Torah scroll as the haunting melody fills the sanctuary.

The evening service then continues with the stately, somber melodies of the Yom Kippur liturgy and the penitential and confessional language of the Day of Atonement. The communal confession, repeated several times during the holiday, called the *viddui,* is an alphabetical listing of communal sin that begins, "We abuse, we betray, we are cruel. We destroy, we embitter, we falsify."

Kol Nidre is the only evening service at which people wear prayer shawls, and there are other distinctive customs regarding clothing as well. Some people dress in white, a sign of purity and some even don a bathrobelike white garment called a *kittle,* which is sometimes worn at the Passover *seder* or by a groom to his wedding. Some refrain from wearing leather shoes, an ancient symbol of luxury, and others remove their shoes during services and pray barefoot—a universal sign of humility.

In the morning, services continue and last all day long. Not all liberal congregations hold all of the services listed here, nor is the order or content described here universal. Still, this represents the outline of the Yom Kippur liturgy.

Shacharit, the morning service, traditionally includes a Torah reading from Leviticus, which describes the sacrificial rites for Yom Kippur in the Temple. Some congregations choose to substitute another Torah reading, Deuteronomy 29:9–30:20, which ends with the lines "I have put before you this day life and death, blessing and curse. Choose life . . ." The morning Haftarah reading is Isaiah's passionate sermon demanding justice of the Jewish people.

In some synagogues, *musaf,* the additional service, is part of Yom Kippur observance, and includes the recitation of the martyrology, a list of atrocities suffered by the Jewish people, beginning with the murders of Talmudic sages by the Romans and including stories from the Holocaust.

The memorial, or *yizkor,* service is a time for special prayers for the dead. *Yizkor* is scheduled at different times of the day, depending upon the synagogue's custom: at the end of the morning service, or immediately preceding or following afternoon prayers.

Mincha is the afternoon service, which traditionally includes a reading from the Torah that outlines the laws of incest,[10] though this is often replaced with another Torah portion, Leviticus 19, called "the holiness code," which includes the injunction to "love your neighbor as yourself." The Haftarah reading is the Book of Jonah.

Ne'ilah, from the Hebrew "to lock," concludes the day. The name refers to the symbolic closing of heaven's gates and communicates the sense that time is running out. At *ne'ilah,* the liturgy changes in its references to the Book of Life, as "Write us in the Book of Life" becomes "Seal us in the Book of Life." Many people stand throughout this brief service, which ends with a final *shofar* blast. In some congregations, *ne'ilah* is followed by a short evening or *ma'ariv* service.

The final words of the day come from *Havdalah,* the ceremony that ends the Sabbath and holidays and which distinguishes between the holy and the profane. As the braided candle is extinguished in wine, a palpable sense of relief fills the room, which empties quickly as people leave to break the fast with family and friends.

A Few Words about Prayer

Prayer is both a discipline and a spontaneous activity. It requires preparation *(hachanah)* and also a kind of passive receptivity. Sometimes it works. Sometimes it does not. Prayer is not possible for every individual in every synagogue, which is why it is important to find a place where your prayer is a possibility. But even in the most hospitable setting, it can be difficult to sustain prayer for a long period of time. During the long services of Rosh Hashanah and Yom Kippur, there are times when individuals may feel the liturgy is downright hostile to prayer. Repeated references to a King-God, to judgment, and to sin can be offputting. But then, a sentence or a phrase from the prayer book may take your breath away. The challenge is to try to remain open to those flashes of insight, those moments of awe and turning, which are available during the Days of Awe as they are at no other time during the year.

The Hebrew word for prayer, *tefila*, which can be translated as "self-judging," contains the notion that prayer is not about getting God to do something for you, but is a way of affecting change in yourself, a process of meditation, reflection, and stock-taking.

The Hebrew word for sin is *chayt*, a term based in archery that means "missing the mark." A sin is thus a missed opportunity for kindness or righteousness. During Rosh Hashanah and especially Yom Kippur, the liturgy's insistence upon human sinfulness can become a reminder of times during the past year when a generous act was not undertaken, or when a kind word was not spoken. Indeed, the liturgy is replete with references to the ways that people hurt one another with words: through slander and insult, with words that embarrass, and words spoken in anger. During the Days of Awe, prayer can be understood as the process of judging one's own language or conduct with others.

Perhaps the best example of the reflexive nature of prayer and sin is the Jewish approach toward atonement. Prayers to God do not wipe away sins committed against other people. The only way to do that is by asking the person you wronged for forgiveness. It is not necessary for the other person to accept the apology—only that the request for forgiveness be offered sincerely. This is what is meant by "making *teshuva*," which means turning away from your own sin by taking action.

SUKKOT AND SIMCHAT TORAH

Sukkot only makes sense in that it follows a narrow scrape
with death and when it is experienced from inside a sukkah, the
flimsy booth we make our literal home for a week. Sukkot is
about the kind of happiness that comes from looking through a
leafy roof at the sunshine or the starry night and thinking, "I am
glad I am alive."

At the very moment we are about to conclude the reading of
the Torah, a project that we have worked on relentlessly and reli-
giously for the past year, we grab another Torah scroll and lay it
down and, without so much as a pause, start again. Simchat Torah means that learning never stops, and it contains one of the
fundamental insights of the Jews: "How can I be sad, how can I
despair, if there is something more to learn, something more to
know?"

RABBI LAWRENCE KUSHNER[11]

Where Rosh Hashanah and Yom Kippur are intellectual and reflective,
Sukkot (literally, "huts" or "booths") and Simchat Torah ("joy of the
Torah") are sensual and expansive. Five days after the austere Days of
Awe comes a festival cycle that celebrates pleasures and the senses:
the joy of being human.

Sukkot is a seven-day (for some, eight-day) festival described three
separate times in the Torah.[12] It celebrates the end of the growing season and the harvest. The primary symbol of Sukkot is the *sukkah*: a
flimsy, temporary hut, reminiscent of the structures the ancient Israel-

ites constructed near ripened crops during harvest time, and a symbol of life's fragility. In many ways, Sukkot is the autumnal mirror image of Passover. Not only are both week-long festivals that begin at the full moon and involve a great deal of preparation, but the huts of Sukkot are also reminders of the shelters used during the years of wandering in the wilderness after the exodus from Egypt.

As Sukkot ends, another holiday begins. Shmini Atzeret, the Eighth Day of Assembly, is also ordained by the Torah and celebrated with a special synagogue service that features a prayer for rain, reflecting agricultural needs in the land of Israel. In contemporary times, this observance is all but eclipsed by the holiday that falls on the very next day: Simchat Torah. When the Torah reading cycle was established during the 11th century, Simchat Torah became the ninth day of the autumn holiday cycle, celebrating both the completion and beginning of a year's Torah reading. Shmini Atzeret and Simchat Torah are combined and celebrated as one in Israel and by some liberal Jews. The official name for the combined holiday is Atzeret HaTorah, "the Assembly of the Torah," but is usually referred to as Simchat Torah.

Simchat Torah is celebrated with the kind of happiness and enthusiasm associated with Jewish weddings. The last of the autumn holidays—the end of three intense weeks—Simchat Torah closes the circle on a triumphant and joyful note.

Preparation

The biggest part of preparing for Sukkot is building a *sukkah*, the booth or hut in which Jews are supposed to live during the festival. According to tradition, the first nail is driven into the *sukkah* as soon as Yom Kippur ends, even before breaking the fast.

A *sukkah* is a temporary structure and can be made in any number of ways: as a kind of tent, as a lean-to built against the wall of a house, as a freestanding hut. *Sukkot* (the plural of *sukkah*) have been constructed out of all kinds of materials, including bamboo, Plexiglas, aluminum poles, and lumberyard two-by-fours. Walls can be filled in with colorful fabric, old doors, canvas, pieces of plywood paneling, or just about any **other** material. Kits and prefabricated models are widely available on the Internet (keywords: sukkah or sukkah kit).

The most important element of the *sukkah* is the roof, which is supposed to be dense enough to provide shade from the sun, but not solid enough to obscure starlight. The material called for in covering the *sukkah* is called *s'khach,* which is anything that once grew but has been cut, such as evergreen boughs, bamboo, palm branches, and cornstalks.

Inside the *sukkah,* it is customary to decorate with hanging fruits, dried gourds, leaves, and other harvest-type items, which are often hung from the rafters. Posters, paper chains, paper flowers, dolls, toys, and Rosh Hashanah cards may be used to festoon the walls.

If you are not able to construct a real *sukkah,* you can still get into the spirit of the holiday by buying and making special Sukkot decorations for the house and table. A *sukkah*-like canopy can even be raised over the dining room table for a week. Another way to celebrate the harvest is to go pick apples, pumpkins, gourds, and other fall fruits.

There are two other central symbols of Sukkot; the *etrog,* a lemonlike fruit, and the *lulav,* a green bouquet consisting of a palm frond and myrtle and willow branches. These are used in an ancient ritual performed inside the *sukkah* and also during synagogue Sukkot services, described below. Judaica shops stock *etrogim* and *lulavim* in advance of the holiday and many synagogues order them for their congregations. Shopping for the "best" *lulav* and the "perfect" *etrog* is an ancient obsession, and suggests a family outing.

Simchat Torah is much more a synagogue-based holiday than Sukkot, so there tends to be far less home preparation, though some families make flags and banners for the festive processions held in the synagogue. Another art project entails making a child-size Torah, using two dowels and a long sheet of paper, decorated with original renderings of various Bible stories.

To get ready for Simchat Torah, take a close look at a Torah, especially if you have never had the chance to see one. This is relatively easy to arrange by making an appointment with your synagogue's rabbi, cantor, religious school director, or just someone who is comfortable handling the scroll.

Study

In addition to the Torah readings prescribed for the holidays, the traditional text for study at this time of year is the Book of Ecclesiastes, best known for its poetic listing of the seasons of life: "A time to plant and a time to uproot, a time for tearing down and time for building up." As is often the case, the reason why this particular book of the Bible is studied at this season is unclear, which makes a good starting point for discussion. Since the Torah is the focus of Simchat Torah, studying a commentary about the Torah seems most appropriate.

Tzedakah

Sukkot celebrates the harvest of this season in anticipation of the day our harvest will feed everyone on earth; thus it is customary to send money to programs that feed the poor and hungry. Connections between Sukkot and current concerns about ecology, environment, and land use also suggest donations to projects that help foster agriculture in poor countries.

In honor of Simchat Torah, donations to literacy programs and libraries seem especially appropriate.

Making Sukkot

Building and decorating a *sukkah* is a big, engaging project, but the point of building one is to have fun in it. While tradition encourages living inside a *sukkah*, in practice the major activity that takes place inside these little huts is eating. The *sukkah* becomes an al fresco dining room—and more.

Sukkot begins with the *yontif seder*, inside a *sukkah* if possible. In addition to the candles, wine, bread, and the blessing for the new season, there is an additional blessing.

בָּרוּךְ אַתָּה יְיָ. אֱלֹהֵינוּ מֶלֶךְ הָעוֹלָם. אֲשֶׁר קִדְּשָׁנוּ בְּמִצְוֹתָיו. וְצִוָּנוּ
לֵישֵׁב בַּסֻּכָּה:

Baruch ata Adonai Eloheynu Melech Ha-olam asher kid'shanu
b'mitzvotav vitzivanu leyshev ba-sukkah.

You Abound in Blessings, Adonai Our Lord, You make us holy
with commandments and call us to dwell in the *sukkah*.

There is no one dish or menu associated with the Sukkot meal in
Ashkenazi tradition, though harvest foods seem appropriate. It is a good
holiday for beginning a family food tradition, and since it is a meal of
thanksgiving, some people serve their first roast turkey or pumpkin pie of
the autumn, and have their first taste of fresh apple cider in the *sukkah*.

Recall, O Israel, our wanderings,
When life was harsh and insecure.
When cold winds blew,
The stars our only comfort.

May our lives be as upright as the palm,
The coming year as the sweet scent of the etrog.

VETAHER LIBENU, PRAYER BOOK OF CONGREGATION
BETH OF THE SUDBURY RIVER VALLEY, MASS.

A *sukkah* is an opportunity and an excuse for a seven-day picnic. A
week of family breakfasts, solitary lunches, and informal dinners out
of doors is a wonderful way to enjoy the waning light of the autumn—
something to share with family and friends.

Sukkot is a holiday that has always been associated with hospitality. According to a mystical story, the spirits of different biblical ancestors visit each day: Abraham and Sarah, Isaac and Rebecca, Jacob and
Rachel, Joseph and Leah, Moses and Miriam, Aaron and Abigail, Da-

vid and Esther. Sephardic Jews set aside a special chair for these guests. But the *sukkah* is a natural venue for gatherings of flesh-and-blood guests, too. You can host a party to help decorate the *sukkah*, to share the first-night festivities, and to celebrate *Shabbat*. Some families try to have guests for dinner every night, or hold an annual "open *sukkah*" on a weekend afternoon.

A *sukkah* is not only a place for eating, though. It is also a place to sit quietly with a book and a cup of tea, to read aloud and study with friends, to sing, to tell stories and stay up late talking, to set up cots and sleeping bags and look up at the stars. For children lucky enough to do it, sleeping in the *sukkah* becomes a wonderful memory.

Not everyone is able or wants to build a *sukkah* and there are other ways to enjoy its unique pleasures. One is to visit friends' *sukkot*; the other is to make use of your synagogue's *sukkah*. Most congregations build a communal *sukkah* and hold services and potluck meals in it; these may also be available for members who wish to have a family or *havurah* meal there.

If you and your children can't build your own *sukkah* outside, consider making one out of an empty appliance box and creating a miniature version for indoors. A tabletop *sukkah* (made out of a shoe box, for example) can be used as a centerpiece throughout the festival.

Synagogue Observance

Holiday services are held on the first (and in some congregations the second) days of Sukkot. There are a few changes in the liturgy, but most striking are the rituals involving the *lulav* and *etrog*. The bouquet of tree leaves and the citron are ancient symbols of the harvest, possibly associated with some agricultural fertility rite. Over the centuries they have been given many religious interpretations: symbols of the parts of the human body, elements of the Jewish people, the male and female parts of creation.[13] As a blessing is said, everyone who owns a *lulav* and *etrog* holds them close together and then waves them in six directions demonstrating that God is everywhere: to the four points of the compass, skyward and earthward. Then, people—especially children—parade around the sanctuary, holding *lulavim* and *etrogim* aloft as they walk.

Making Simchat Torah

Simchat Torah begins at home with a *yontif seder:* candles, wine, bread, and a blessing for the season. During the Simchat Torah evening service, all the Torah scrolls are removed from the ark and paraded around the sanctuary in circles called *hakafot.* It is considered an honor to carry the Torah, and in some congregations virtually everyone gets the opportunity.

The Hasidic model of celebration for Simchat Torah has inspired spontaneous and joyful observances in many American congregations. Live music, champagne, dancing, and singing may be part of these celebrations, which sometimes even spill out into the street. In some temples, a Torah scroll is completely unfurled in a huge circle, enacting the full cycle of the year, from the final reading from Deuteronomy to the beginning of Genesis.

The mood of Simchat Torah resembles the joyful feeling at a wedding. Indeed, it is customary to call the person honored with reading the last portion of Deuteronomy "the bridegroom (or bride) of the Torah." The person who reads from Genesis is "the bride (or bridegroom) of the Beginning."

At morning services on Simchat Torah, some synagogues call the children up to the Torah, and sometimes a large prayer shawl is draped over their heads for a special blessing. Simchat Torah has also become the occasion for ceremonially welcoming children to religious school with a gift of a mini–prayer shawl, toy Torah, or prayer book.

Here where the end embraces the beginning,
Like the eternal bride and bridegroom joined as one,
Rejoice!

VETAHER LIBENU

HANNUKAH

We watch the days grow shorter and shorter. We become
frightened because it occurs to us that if this keeps up we will all
freeze to death in the dark. We light candles in a transparently
symbolic attempt to get somebody up there to notice and turn on
the lights. We are literally whistling in the dark.

RABBI LAWRENCE KUSHNER[14]

Hannukah falls on the darkest phase of the moon in the darkest season of the year, the 25th day of Kislev. An intimate holiday, it is defined by the circle of light cast by little, colored candles arranged in
rows that recalls two very different stories, one of which rests on a
military victory, one which involves a miracle. But at its emotional
core, Hannukah—like the other holidays of the season—celebrates
the return of the light in the heart of winter darkness.

The historical basis for Hanukkah (from the Hebrew word for
"dedication") is found in the Books of Maccabees, part of the Apocrypha, a collection of ancient writings not included in the Hebrew Bible.
During the second century B.C.E., Antiochus Epiphanes of Syria and
ruler of the land of Israel began a process of Hellenization that included persecutions of anyone who continued to practice Judaism.
Antiochus ordered the desecration of the Temple in Jerusalem and
the killing of those who opposed him. The Jewish guerrilla rebellion
against this oppression was led by Mattathias Maccabee and his five
sons, who defeated the Syrian forces and rededicated the Temple in
164 B.C.E. with an eight-day celebration.[15]

Although the rabbis who codified Jewish law and practice in the Talmud were disturbed by the prospect of a holiday that celebrated a military victory, it was clear that the people were not about to give up their midwinter celebration of lights and merrymaking. Thus, the story of the miracle of the oil became the preferred justification for the lighting of candles, a custom that was probably borrowed from pagan solstice celebrations.

According to this story, the Maccabees found a single jar of consecrated oil, which was used to keep the Eternal Flame alight in the Temple. There was only enough oil to last for one day, but lo and behold, the oil lasted for eight days. With the addition of this miracle, God became a central part of Hannukah's message of redemption.

Preparing

Hannukah celebration can be elaborate or simple, depending on your tastes and family constellation. It can entail little more than buying a box of candles and polishing your Hannukah *menorah,* or *hannukiah.* For many, Hannukah is a wonderful pretext for a midwinter celebration complete with home decorations, special meals and parties, and gift-giving. The eight-branched *hannukiah* is the primary symbol of the holiday. Judaica vendors carry a dizzying array of these, ranging from fine art to happy kitsch. Making *hannukiot* (the plural of *hannukiah*) is a favorite school and home art project for children.

Some people decorate for Hannukah by hanging banners, *draydls,* gold coins, and lights. A shopping trip for a box of Hannukah candles and some new *draydls* (Hannukah tops) is a great way to kick off the holiday.

Study

In addition to the Books of Maccabees, traditional study texts for this holiday include two more stories found in the Apocrypha, both rather bloody tales of heroic women: Judith, a widow who killed a general leading a siege against the land of Judah; and Hannah, the mother of seven sons who died with them rather than bow to a pagan idol. And every year, Hannukah inspires new Jewish children's books and songs. Jewish popular culture has also embraced the holiday with new music, humor, and parties at clubs as well as JCCs.

Tzedakah

At Hannukah, which celebrates a Jewish victory over religious persecution, some people make contributions to organizations that work for religious and political freedom for Jews and for all oppressed people.

Making Hannukah

Hannukah is one of the most home-based of the Jewish holidays. Anytime after sunset when family members and guests are assembled to light the *hannukiah,* you begin by lighting the *shamash* or helper candle, which is usually taller or set apart from the other lights; the *shamash* is then used to light the others. A *hannukiah* is filled from right to left, but lit left to right, so the newest candle is always kindled first.

Any number of *hannukiot* can be lit. In some households, everyone has his or her own *hannukiah,* and on nights when guests are invited they can be asked to bring menorahs and candles, too, so dozens of flames can be kindled. According to custom, the Hannukah lights are set in a prominent window, publicly announcing this is a house where Hannukah is celebrated, and making the night that much brighter.

On *Shabbat,* Hannukah candles are lit before the Sabbath lights.

Every night of the festival, two blessings are recited.

בָּרוּךְ אַתָּה יְיָ. אֱלֹהֵינוּ מֶלֶךְ הָעוֹלָם. אֲשֶׁר קִדְּשָׁנוּ בְּמִצְוֹתָיו.
וְצִוָּנוּ לְהַדְלִיק נֵר שֶׁל־חֲנֻכָּה:

Baruch ata Adonai Eloheynu Melech Ha-olam asher kid'shanu be'mitzvotav vitzivanu l'hadlik ner shel Hannukah.

You Abound in Blessings, Adonai Our Lord, You make us holy with commandments and call us to light the Hannukah lights.

בָּרוּךְ אַתָּה יְיָ. אֱלֹהֵינוּ מֶלֶךְ הָעוֹלָם. שֶׁעָשָׂה נִסִּים לַאֲבוֹתֵינוּ בַּיָּמִים הָהֵם. בַּזְּמַן הַזֶּה:

Baruch ata Adonai Eloheynu Melech Ha-olam sh'asa nissim laa'voteynu bayamim hahem bazman hazeh.

You Abound in Blessings, Adonai Our Lord, You performed miracles for our ancestors in days of old, at this season.

On the first night only, a third blessing, the *shehecheyanu,* is added.

בָּרוּךְ אַתָּה יְיָ, אֱלֹהֵינוּ מֶלֶךְ הָעוֹלָם, שֶׁהֶחֱיָנוּ וְקִיְּמָנוּ וְהִגִּיעָנוּ לַזְּמָן הַזֶּה.

Baruch ata Adonai Eloheynu Melech Ha-olam shehecheyanu v'kiamanu v'higianu lazman hazeh.

You Abound in Blessings, Adonai Our Lord, You have kept us alive, You have sustained us, You have brought us to this moment.

It is customary to sing *"Maoz Tzur,"* "Rock of Ages," immediately after the blessings, and to add other Hannukah songs.

The custom of giving Hannukah *gelt* (Yiddish for money)—gold coins or chocolate coins wrapped in gold foil—dates back to 17th century Poland. As Jews came into closer contact with Christians and

Christmas, since the 19th century, Hannukah has also meant gift-giving.

The extreme commercialization of Christmas and Hannukah drives many people of both faiths crazy. Because it is the business of America to raise every consumer's gift expectations to dizzying heights, many parents devise strategies to keep Hannukah from becoming an eight-day festival of greed, such as designating "book night," or "music night." Some households create a sort of rotating "designated gift-giver" routine, which can be modified to suit any number of people. For example: On night number one, Mom gives the gifts. On night number two, sister distributes presents. Night number three is for Dad. Four is for brother. Five is for gifts from maternal grandparents. Six for paternal grandparents. Seven is for throwing or attending a party, so no gifts are exchanged. And the last night is devoted to *tzedakah,* when everyone in the household puts aside some money and decides on an appropriate organization, agency, or cause with which to share the season's bounty.

Traditional Hannukah foods tend to recall the story of the miracle of the oil with an unswerving devotion to fried foods. For Ashkenazi Jews, Hannukah means potato pancakes, *latkes,* served with applesauce and sour cream. In Israel, jelly doughnuts, called *sufganiot,* are the official holiday treat.

Hannukah is celebrated with parties, which can be held on any and all of the eight nights. After candle lighting, there is singing, eating, and even gambling either with cards or with *draydls* (*sivivon* in Hebrew), four-sided tops. Although Jewish law is extremely hostile to gambling—the rabbis reasoned that a transfer of money in the absence of honest work was a form of theft—at Hanukkah, the ban is lifted and people are encouraged to enjoy themselves.

I have a little draydl
I make it out of clay
And when it's dry and ready
Then draydl I shall play.

HANNUKAH SONG

To play *draydl,* a game of dumb luck, each player antes up with nuts or chocolate coins, buttons or pennies. Each of the *draydl*'s sides bears a Hebrew letter. If the *draydl* falls on נ *(Nun)*, you get nothing; on ה *(Hay),* take half the pot, on ש *(Shin),* add something to the kitty, and on ג *(Gimel),* the winner takes all. The letters are an acrostic for the words נס גדול היה שם—*Nes Gadol Haya Sham,* "A great miracle happened there." (In Israel, the letters spell out נס גדול היה פה—*Nes Gadol Haya Po,* "A great miracle happened here.") The truth is, playing *draydl* is only slightly less tedious than frying potato pancakes. But little kids just love it. To play the "human *draydl*" game, children spin till they drop and the last one standing wins a prize.

While Hannukah is by and large a home-centered holiday, it is also celebrated in synagogues with dinners, concerts, family parties, and the like.

About Christmas

The proximity of Hannukah and Christmas can raise questions and issues for Jewish and intermarried families, partly because Christmas makes many Jews extremely defensive. For one thing, it is the time of year when Jews most acutely feel their differentness in a Christian culture. It is also the season when children confront that sense of being different for the first time, and at successive developmental stages every year. Christmas is when children ask their parents to explain why they are not allowed to take part in the dazzling festival that apparently everyone else gets to enjoy.

Interfaith families may find themselves fighting a symbolic battle over the Christmas tree. To the non-Jewish partner of an intermarriage, the tree may be nothing but a secular symbol of the winter solstice. However, to the Jew, it is a symbol of Christianity, with nearly as much religious meaning as the cross itself. Synagogues run workshops at this season to help couples sort out their differences and learn from each other's choices.

Families deal with the Christmas–Hannukah conundrum in very different ways. For many, Christmas is simply a holiday celebrated in other people's homes—a holiday to enjoy with non-Jewish friends or at Grandma's house, but not in our Jewish home. At the other end of the spectrum, there are households where there is a tree "for Dad."

Some Jews feel the need to compensate for a lack of Christmas by making Hannukah its equal in expectations and gift-giving ("They have only one day of giving; we have eight!"). Others resent that tactic, and, citing the relative unimportance of Hannukah in the Jewish calendar of holidays, try to make as little fuss over it as possible. There is a middle ground.

Hannukah can be celebrated with candles, stories, *tzedakah,* gatherings of family and friends, crafts, and gifts, without collapsing under the strain of Christmas expectations. The Jewish calendar has often accommodated itself to historical change, and making Hannukah into a bigger party than it was in past centuries does not nullify its Jewishness.

However, for Hannukah to retain its integrity, it cannot stand alone. If Hannukah is the only Jewish celebration of a family's year, then it does become that strange creature, the "Jewish Christmas." The truth is, no matter how many candles are lit or expensive gifts are given, Hannukah will never be as big, flashy, and seductive as Christmas; however, if it is just one of many joyful Jewish celebrations, it has no need to compete. Perhaps the best explanation of the differences between the two winter holidays comes from the mouth of a three-year-old, who said, "Christine and Zack have Christmas. We have Hannukah and *Shabbat.*"

TU B'SHVAT

Two men who were fighting over a piece of land brought their dispute to a rabbi. After listening to each man's case, the rabbi put his ear to the ground. After a moment he stood up and said, "The land says that it belongs to neither of you. You both belong to the land."

TALMUD

Once a minor observance, Tu B'Shvat is in the process of becoming a more important Jewish celebration complete with its own *seder,* the most positive celebration word in the Jewish lexicon.

Tu B'Shvat, which means the 15th of Shvat, is not mentioned in the Torah (nor are Hanukkah, Purim, Tisha B'Av, or Simchat Torah). And while the Talmud describes it as "the New Year of the Trees," it mandates no rituals, no blessings, no synagogue observance. Tu B'Shvat may have been noted simply as a way of dating trees, so it would be possible to know when a fruit tree was old enough to be tithed—or when 10 percent of the fruit crop was due to the Temple priesthood. Historically, Tu B'Shvat was a way of maintaining a connection with the land of Israel, where, in the month of Shvat, the winter rains end and the first signs of spring begin. In that hot, arid climate, trees mean food, shade, water—indeed, life itself.

Among Ashkenazi Jews, Tu B'Shvat was observed by eating fruit, especially fruits grown in the land of Israel. Because it traveled well, carob (also known as bosker or St. John's bread) became the traditional food of the holiday. While it was never a major holiday for Sephardic Jews either, they celebrate Tu B'Shvat with more festivity, including readings from a book called *The Fruit of the Goodly Tree,* and with special fruit platter meals, songs, and games for children.[16] After the founding of the state of Israel, Tu B'Shvat became a sort of international Jewish Arbor Day, a day for planting seeds in paper cups at religious school, and for raising money for the Jewish National Fund, which supports the reforestation of Israel.

The modern focus for Tu B'Shvat broadened to include the relationship between people and the natural world—the ecology of the planet upon which we depend for our lives. In Jewish tradition, the primary symbol of this relationship is the tree. The Torah itself is called a tree of life, and the rollers around which the scroll is wrapped are also called trees of life—*atzay hayyim.* The planting of trees was seen as a holy activity. According to Jochanan ben Zakkai, "If you have a seedling in your hand, and someone says to you, 'Look, here comes the Messiah!' go and plant the seedling first, and then come out to meet the Messiah."[17] The Torah forbids the cutting down of an enemy's fruit trees in times of war, even if trees are needed for the siege of a city.[18] The confluence of the traditional concern for trees and contemporary worries about the health of the earth's forests, fields, air, and seas created renewed interest in this midwinter holiday and the Tu B'Shvat *seder.* A once-arcane custom, celebrated by a group of mystics living in the town of Safed during the 16th century, it was modeled after the Passover talking-feast and its four cups of wine, but added the eating of four categories of fruit, which corresponded with the four "emanations" of God.[19]

Preparing

Hosting or participating in a Tu B'Shvat *seder* means shopping for fruit and wine and decorating with greens and flowers. There are all sorts of delightful arts-and-crafts projects for children, such as making a *tzedakah* box in the shape of a watering can, or creating a forest of trees out of recycled cardboard paper towel tubes, or decorating cups for planting parsley seeds to be harvested for use in the Passover *seder.*

To get into the spirit of the growing season, people peruse seed catalogs and select flowers for the coming spring. Other family activities might include visiting a botanical garden or even making a tour of your yard to see whether any of the trees need attention. Since Tu B'Shvat is called the New Year of the Trees, one rabbi even suggests blowing a *shofar* for your own trees.[20]

Study might include reading more about the holiday's history, and reading through a Tu B'Shvat *seder* or two. The ecological aspect of the holiday suggests study of environmental problems and solutions.

Tzedakah

The most common *tzedakah* custom for the holiday is to donate money to the Jewish National Fund, which not only plants trees in Israel, but also works to protect the environment there (www.jnf.org). There is also an old tradition of giving money for fruit, *ma'ot perot,* to the poor, so they could afford a taste of fruit from Israel on Tu B'Shvat. In that spirit, making a contribution to a food program seems appropriate. Some people make donations at this season to national and international organizations dedicated to protecting the environment. For more information about Jewish environmental activism in the United States, check out the Coalition on the Environment and Jewish Life (www.coejl.org).

Making Tu B'Shvat

Tu B'Shvat is a holiday in the making, so there are no formal or standard home or synagogue rituals associated with the holiday. The Tu B'Shvat *seder* takes many forms depending upon who is in charge. Synagogues, *havurot,* and individuals host them, and there are several *haggadot* (plural of *haggadah,* which means "the telling") for the holiday, including many photocopied collections of readings that are rewritten and updated annually. A few have been published by the denominations; check their Web sites.

Feel free to experiment with the Tu B'Shvat *seder;* there is no doing it "wrong." When it is built around a meal, the food is vegetarian with readings, poems, and songs built around two ritual acts: the drinking of four cups of wine and the eating of four kinds of fruits.

The four cups of wine can change in color, starting with white, proceeding to mixtures of white and red, and concluding with red wine. The same blessing is recited before each cup.

בָּרוּךְ אַתָּה יְיָ. אֱלֹהֵינוּ מֶלֶךְ הָעוֹלָם. בּוֹרֵא פְּרִי הַגָּפֶן:

Baruch ata Adonai Eloheynu Melech Ha-olam boray pree hagafen.

You Abound in Blessings, Adonai Our Lord, You create the fruit of the vine.

For the fruit, set out festive platters with as many varieties as possible. One custom is to get 15 kinds of fruit to correspond with the 15th of Shvat; these are then divided into four categories, according to a metaphorical association with the elements, or seasons, or human characteristics. One level consists of fruits with a hard outside and soft inside—nuts, pineapple, pomegranate, and coconut—which may be associated with winter, with the earth, with the physical. The second level includes fruits with a soft outside and hard inner core: cherry, peach, and avocado, which may be associated with spring, with water, with the emotions. The third category comprises fruits that are totally edible: strawberry, fig, grape, raisin, which may be associated with summer, with the air, and with the cerebral. The fourth category is the most abstract and spiritual and is sometimes symbolized by inedible fruits, such as pinecones and acorns, or else it is given no physical representation at all.

The same blessing is recited before eating from each category of fruit.

בָּרוּךְ אַתָּה יְיָ, אֱלֹהֵינוּ מֶלֶךְ הָעוֹלָם, בּוֹרֵא פְּרִי הָעֵץ.

Baruch ata Adonai Eloheynu Melech Ha-olam boray pree ha-aytz.

You Abound in Blessings, Adonai Our Lord, You create the fruit of the tree.

PURIM

Purim elevates laughter to a religious category. It is the one day when taking oneself seriously is a sin. At Purim, we make fun of everything, especially what we consider to be most sacred and reverent. Because religion without humor is blasphemy.

RABBI LAWRENCE KUSHNER[21]

Purim is the Jewish equivalent of Mardi Gras, a giddy outburst of energy and excess. This holiday of the early spring (on the 14th of Adar, which falls near the vernal equinox), celebrates a narrow escape from a disaster that probably never happened and takes its name from the Hebrew word *pur,* which means "lot," as in lottery. In the Purim story, the villains cast lots to determine a date for the slaughter of the Jews. The biblical Book of Esther is bawdy and improbable, but its ironic and dark subtext has struck a chord for hundreds of generations among a people that has suffered and survived terrible persecutions and losses.

According to the Purim tale, a large and prosperous Jewish community once lived in the land of Persia. The Jews were so well integrated into the society that one of them, Mordechai, was a member of the court of the king, Ahasuerus. One day, this feckless king banishes his wife, Vashti, for refusing to obey a command to appear naked before his guests. To replace her, he holds a beauty contest, which is won by Esther, a Jewish woman who only just happens to be Mordechai's relative.

As this Cinderella tale unfolds, a new Grand Vizier is appointed, a dreadful anti-Semite by the name of Haman. Indeed, Haman is considered a prototype of evil, descended as he is, from the wicked Amalek, the archetypal enemy of the Jews described in the Torah.[22] When Mordechai refuses to bow down before this wretched man, Haman decides to punish him by massacring all the Jews in the kingdom.

Mordechai and Esther conspire to foil this plot by having Esther invite King Ahasuerus to her chambers, where she wines and dines him, and then reveals that Haman, despite all his fawning, is actually plotting against his royal highness. She also reveals herself to be a Jew, and asks that he rescind Haman's decree against her and her people. The king has Haman hanged on the scaffold that had been built for Mordechai, who is named Grand Vizier in his place. And as the sun sets, Esther and the Jews of Persia live happily ever after.

The name of God does not appear anywhere in this melodrama, which is probably based on a Persian legend given the fact that the names of its heroes—Esther and Mordechai—are forms of two well-known local deities, fertile Ishtar and warlike Marduk. Furthermore, Purim celebrations—typified by masks, revelry, and drunkenness—recall ancient Persian customs for a springtime new year.

Why is it pointless to put Jews in jail?

They eat lox!

Purim observance has changed over time, and customs vary from nation to city to synagogue. Nevertheless, it is the universal Jewish holiday of release, springtime, laughter, and excess. On Purim, it is a religious obligation to poke fun at Jewish tradition, and piety takes the form of jokes, puns, drinking, cross-dressing, and outrageous behavior in general. According to the Talmud, Purim is the only holiday that will still be celebrated after the Messiah comes to redeem the world and restore peace and harmony. Evidently, even in paradise it will still be necessary to make fun of ourselves.

Preparing

Purim is celebrated in synagogues and schools, but since one of the customs of the holiday involves dress-up, adults as well as children spend time on costumes, which can be either beautiful, silly, or outrageous and may include masks, wigs, and makeup. If you're attending a *megillah* reading or *Purimspeil* (Purim play), you'll need a *gragger*, too—a noisemaker used to drown out the name of Haman. These are available for purchase in Judaica stores and online.

The tradition of giving gifts to friends and to the poor is mandated in the Book of Esther, which says, "the Jews . . . made the 14th day of the month of Adar a day of gladness and feasting, a holiday, and of sending portions to one another (*mishloach manot*)." Thus, some Jews deliver gifts of food to friends, a paper plate or bag filled with *Hamantaschen* (a three-cornered cookie), along with fruit, and candy made in Israel. Baking cookies and assembling and decorating plates or bags is a Purim custom in some congregations and families.

Tzedakah

Giving to the poor on Purim is a *mitzvah* called *mattanot le-evyonim*, and reflects the notion everyone should be able to celebrate. In some congregations, money is collected for *tzedakah* in the synagogue before the Purim story is read. Responding to the command in the Book of Esther that two portions be sent to the poor, some people make contributions to two charities.

Making Purim

The only home ritual associated with Purim is the Purim *seudah*, or Purim feast. Unlike all other holiday meals, which are eaten in the evening, this feast is generally a lunch that features merrymaking, nonsense, and silliness. Putting on a *Purimspiel* is often part of this celebration, the more foolish the better. However, since there is no obligation to refrain from work on Purim, this feast usually only happens on weekends.

Among Jews of Eastern European descent, the traditional food for Purim is a three-cornered pastry called *Hamentaschen*, "Haman's pockets," a delicacy that has been part of Purim celebration since at least the 12th century. Sephardic cooks make Purim ravioli and a deep-fried confection called Haman's ears.

Synagogue Observance

The only religious obligation is that everyone—adults and children— hear a reading of the Book of Esther, which is called the *megillah*, or "scroll." While there are four other scrolls or *megillot* in the Bible (Song of Songs, Lamentations, Ruth, and Ecclesiastes), the Book of Esther is known as *the megillah*.

After the evening service, the ten chapters of the *megillah* are chanted aloud, often in an abbreviated, hilarious performance. Sometimes the story is acted out by costumed players and audience participation is required; whenever the villain's name is mentioned, boos, hisses, catcalls, and the rude sound of noisemakers (whistles, drums and bells, as well as the traditional *graggers*) erupt as the audience does its duty and "stamps out" Haman's name.

"Purim Torah" is the name given to the sacred duty to make fun of all things sacred on this holiday. Rabbis dress up like furry blue monsters and deliver absurd Purim sermons, synagogue newsletters are full of ridiculous articles and advertisements, and even the evening service that precedes the reading of the *megillah* is fair game, as traditional prayers are sung to the melody of "Home on the Range," or "I Want to Hold Your Hand."

Synagogues celebrate Purim with costume parties, parades, dances, theatrical offerings *(Purimspiels)*, carnivals, beauty contests, and fairs. Gambling, forbidden every other day except Hannukah, is permitted on Purim. Drinking is not only permitted, but encouraged to the extent that the Talmud says that Purim obliges every Jew to get so drunk that he or she cannot tell the difference between blessing Mordechai and cursing Haman.[23] Which is mighty drunk. In Israel, Purim is marked by a raucous parade called the *adloyada*, a word based on the Hebrew for "not being able to tell the difference."

PASSOVER

The liturgy of the seder meal is a way of responding to the question, "Why?" The answer to all of the questions asked at the Passover seder begin with the words, avadim hayinu, "because we were slaves." Through song, word, and symbol we not only remember that we were slaves but also reexperience ourselves as slaves. And we learn that our freedom, if it does not translate into making others free, is a sham.

Rabbi Lawrence Kushner[24]

No holiday in the Jewish calendar is more complex or evocative than Passover. The spring holiday that celebrates the return of the sunlight and the first spring fruits on the table, also reflects upon the profound religious themes of the autumn festivals: awakening, life and death, rebirth, gratitude. Passover recalls the crucial event in the history of the Jewish people in which a group of slaves became a nation possessed of the dream called Torah.

No other holiday inspires the same kind of loyalty as Passover. No Jewish ritual word has more positive associations than *seder*, the Passover talking-feast. It is—according to some demographers—the most practiced of all Jewish observances, even more common than the lighting of Hannukah candles. Passover memories—the holiday table, the crunch of *matzah*, songs, phrases, aromas—have inspired a kind of collective unconscious that recognizes the *seder* as *the* Jewish celebration.

Passover can also be the most demanding of the Jewish holidays because it requires a drastic change of diet during its weeklong observance. The Bible forbids not only eating but even owning leavened foods, as a reminder of the time when the Jews were a hunted people who did not have even enough time to wait for dough to rise before baking it. The Talmud elaborated the biblical injunction against leavened food into an entire system for breaking from the normal eating routines of the year. Homes and habits are turned upside down in order to help reenact the essential religious insights of Judaism: that once we were slaves and now we are free; that political liberation and personal change are both necessary for the redemption of the world, a world in which all forms of slavery are forever abolished.[25]

Called the Festival of Spring, the Season of Our Liberation, the Holiday of Matzah, the name *Pesach*, or Passover, comes from the most dramatic story in Jewish history. On the night of the last plague that God unleashed upon the Egyptians to force Pharaoh to free the enslaved Israelites, the Jews were told to sacrifice a lamb and mark their homes by smearing their doorposts with its blood. According to the story, the angel of death stopped in all the unmarked houses, taking the firstborn of every family. But wherever Death saw the blood of the animal that the pagan Egyptians worshipped as a god, Death passed over—in Hebrew, *pasach*.

For this fragment to make sense, the rest of the story must be told, too: the history of how the Jews came to Egypt, the story of Moses, of the resistance of the midwives, and much more. This is both the method and the message of Passover: to tell the story so vividly that it becomes part of memory and consciousness from one generation to the next.[26]

Preparing

No other holiday requires more preparation than Passover, or more choices. Thus, no two households prepare for Passover in the same fashion, and no two *seders* are quite the same. The menu of Passover customs is endless and always changing, but regardless of specifics, preparations may be divided into two general areas: getting ready for the *seder*, and preparing for a week of doing without bread and other leavened foods.

Seder, literally "order," is the meal held on the first and (for some people) second night of Passover. Patterned on the Greek and Roman symposium, where an evening was spent discussing a particular topic over dinner, the Passover *seder* has been celebrated since the days of the Second Temple, though the *seder* that is celebrated by Jews today was essentially set by the 11th century C.E.

Planning for a *seder* begins sometime after Purim, when people draw up guest lists, look over cookbooks, and choose a *haggadah. Haggadah,* literally "a telling," is the name of the book that contains the rituals and readings of the Passover *seder.* Because the *haggadah* is the script that determines the content of the evening, selecting one that suits your needs is one of the most important aspects of the *seder.*

Scores of *haggadot* (the plural) are in use today, in English and Hebrew, with translations and transliterations. Some express contemporary political concerns; some are vividly illustrated; many are annotated, with long footnotes explaining every aspect of the *seder.* The denominations produce *haggadot,* as do many Jewish and secular publishers. There are *haggadot* that feature museum-quality illustrations, and coloring-book *haggadot* for children. Some people use a number of different *haggadot* at the *seder,* comparing and contrasting the variations among them, but most try to purchase or borrow enough copies of the same edition so everyone can follow along together.

A good place to start exploring the options is a synagogue library or other collection of Jewish books. Jewish bookstores usually offer a wide selection. Rabbis, other Jewish professionals, and friends can make helpful suggestions, and synagogues sometimes run a workshop about choosing and using *haggadot.* Of course, you can also put the word "*haggadah*" into your favorite search engine and see what you find.

When shopping for a *haggadah,* it is also important to remember that virtually everyone customizes or edits the *seder.* Few people read every word in the book, so planning requires deciding which readings to include, which to skip, what songs to sing, and how to encourage participation at the table. In families with children, the *seder* changes from year to year, reflecting the changing attention span of the little ones. Some people put together their own seders, cutting and pasting, collecting readings, poems, artwork, and songs from various sources to create their own *haggadah*.

Passover is, first and foremost, a teaching holiday, but it would be a mistake to think of it as a class. The best *seders* are informal and interactive; according to tradition, if no one asks a question at the *seder* table, the meal cannot be concluded. The goal is to provide experiential learning so that everyone, but especially children, will actually *feel* as though they had been liberated themselves. Parents tend to gear at least part of the *seder* to engage their children's participation, and it's not hard to make Passover an annual high point for the young. (See "Elaborations" below.)

Many *haggadot* provide basic information about the holiday and how to celebrate it. Some include explanations and brief histories of various readings and ritual items, as well as descriptions and instructions for setting the Passover table and for preparing a *seder* plate.

The holiday table is never more elaborate than at Passover. While the table is often made festive with spring flowers, the real centerpiece is the *seder* plate, which contains six ritual items: a shank bone (sometimes a roasted chicken or turkey bone) and a roasted egg, both symbolizing the ritual sacrifices of the Temple; bitter herbs (usually horseradish) and salt water to represent the bitterness of slavery; a green vegetable (parsley, celery, or lettuce) is symbolic of the new season; and *haroset* (a sweet paste of fruit, wine, and nuts) symbolizing mortar, a reminder of the heavy labor the Israelites were forced to do. In recent years, an orange has been added to the *seder* plate, as a symbol of the inclusion of once-invisible Jews—gays, lesbians, and women.[27]

Setting the table and making *haroset* are tasks children look forward to all year. Other *seder* plate projects might include harvesting parsley planted at Tu B'Shvat, roasting eggs, and grating fresh horseradish. Arts-and-crafts projects for the table might include making place cards, place mats, napkin rings, or a *matzah* cover, designing a comic-book *haggadah,* or creating a *seder* plate out of a decorated paper covered with clear Contact paper. If the *seder* includes a dramatization of part of the Exodus story, children can collect and create costumes, masks, or puppets.

Some people bake their own *matzah*—or at least a symbolic portion for the *seder*. According to Jewish law, in order to prevent fermentation the *matzah* must be baked precisely 18 minutes after water is added to flour. Since this is quite an elaborate production, some synagogues run a *matzah*-baking workshop, which can become a memorable game of "beat the clock."

In planning the *seder* meal, many cooks stick to family favorites. Roast chicken, turkey, and brisket are among the more popular traditional main courses for Ashkenazi Jews; Sephardic meals often feature roast lamb. Spring foods, such as asparagus and strawberries, recall the seasonal aspect of the holiday. There are many Passover cookbooks on the market, and most Jewish cookbooks have Passover recipes and menus as well. Vegetarian cookbooks are a good resource for planning meatless Passover meals—and there are even vegetarian *haggadot*.

Preparing for the fast from leavened food is the second major task of getting ready for Passover (the first being the removal of *hametz*, a term that designates foods that are not "kosher for Passover"). *Hametz* includes not only leavened foods, but also foods that can easily ferment, such as wheat, malt, and barley. Ashkenazi Jews also refrain from eating beans, peas, lentils, rice, corn, and legumes.

For some families, the days before Passover are taken up with a thorough housecleaning, putting away dishes and cookware, and unpacking china and pots that are used only during the holiday. Children tend to find this process exciting, and it is the source of many powerful memories for adults who grew up with the tradition. In other households, however, dishes and cookware stay the same, and Passover observance is limited to avoiding bread and other leavened foods. Likewise, although some people only buy packaged or processed foods that are specifically designated as "Kosher for Passover," which means they were prepared and packaged under rabbinical supervision, others simply read labels and avoid foods prepared with yeast and other leavening agents. (See also "What Jews Eat.")

Some people try to consume all their leavened foods during the month before Passover. Others put leftovers—including cereals, pasta, beer and other liquors, and prepared foods such as ketchup, many vinegars, and even confectionery sugar (it can contain cornstarch)—in a box or cupboard that is marked and taped or tied shut for the week. Because the Torah says that one should not even own any *hametz* during Passover, it is customary to ritually "sell" it to a non-Jew for the duration of the holiday. Some synagogues fulfill this mandate, complete with a signed contract, in a transaction that ultimately ends with a donation to charity.

The ritual conclusion of preparing a house for Passover is called *Bidikat Hametz,* the search for *hametz.* Pieces of bread may be hidden for a family hide-and-seek, which is traditionally conducted with a candle (it is more fun to do this in the dark) and a feather (for brushing the pieces onto a paper plate). The next morning, it is customary to burn what was found. The Hebrew blessings that precede and follow the search are printed in many *haggadot.*

On the day of the *seder,* it is customary to refrain from eating either bread or *matzah* between breakfast and the evening meal; the purpose of waiting is to sharpen the pleasure of the first taste of *matzah.*

Study

The primary study text for Passover is the *haggadah,* but perhaps the best way of putting the Passover story into context is to read the Book of Exodus, which tells the whole story of the departure from Egypt, the wandering in the desert, and the giving of the Torah. Many people also go back to the chapters in Genesis that tell the story of Joseph and explain how the Jews came to be in Egypt in the first place. It is also traditional to read Song of Songs, the biblical cycle of love poems, filled with images of nature and sexuality, and which addresses the agricultural elements of the holiday.

Books about the Jewish holidays can explicate the theological and historical background of the holiday, and in the weeks before Passover synagogues offer seminars or workshops on making a *seder.* All of which can be a great source of inspiration as well as of basic information.

Tzedakah

Feeding the hungry is a basic theme of the *seder*, which includes the clarion call "Let all who are hungry come and eat." Traditionally, Jewish communities saw to it that their poor could afford *matzah* and wine for the holiday. The American Jewish community continues to honor this tradition by giving special attention to the needs of the poor, the elderly, and recent immigrants. Individuals can participate directly in this *mitzvah* by making room at their *seders* for people who would otherwise have nowhere to celebrate the holiday, such as Jewish travelers, college students, and people in the military service stationed locally. Furthermore, synagogues often match members in need of an invitation with others who have plenty of room at their tables. It is also customary to give money to programs and agencies that feed the hungry at Passover. Many synagogues and other Jewish organizations collect canned goods and other packaged foods that contain *hametz*, which are then donated to local food pantries before Passover.

Making Passover

Three core elements of making Passover are: retelling the story, remembering that "we were slaves in Egypt," and not eating *hametz*. The table rituals, the housecleaning, the special foods, and the family gathering all enhance and celebrate these three elements.

Passover begins at the *seder* table. While synagogues often hold community *seders*, and some people attend them at hotels, resorts, or on cruise ships (and thus avoid the lengthy preparations), the Passover *seder* is one of the most home-identified of all Jewish observances. Family traditions include everything from buying new toothbrushes, to filling the house with daffodils, to closely guarded recipes for Passover cakes, cookies, and candies. The descriptions that follow only suggest the possibilities: they are by no means definitive.

The *Seder* Table

The Passover table is an altar, a classroom, and a theater as well as a place for eating. The tradition of placing cushions or special pillows on the chairs comes from ancient days; tokens of leisure, they demonstrated that the people at the table were free men and women.

In addition to the *seder* plate described above, there are a few other ritual objects on the table as well: a plate containing three *matzot* (plural of *matzah*) covered by a napkin or special *matzah* cover; Elijah's cup, a goblet filled with wine, a symbol of hope that the prophet Elijah, the harbinger of the Messiah, will come to announce the redemption of the world this very night; Miriam's cup, filled with water, a relatively new addition to the table, which honors Moses' sister, also a prophet, who leads the women in song after the people have crossed the sea on their way to freedom.

The Order

A classic Jewish contradiction in terms, variation is the rule when it comes to the order of the *seder*. Some people move things around; others delete some rituals and readings and add others. Some prepare questions to spark discussion; others add singing, dancing, and theatrics. The ceremony can last for twenty minutes, forty minutes, or several hours. Then after the meal, some people spend hours at the table for more readings and songs while others dispense with most or all of the postdinner readings and ritual.

Making a *seder* means making choices. The outline of the Passover *seder* that follows is not exhaustive; there are stories and songs not mentioned here that many people consider essential while others may omit elements. It is your table.

The *yontif seder* described on pages 149–151 is embedded in the Passover *seder*, but changed in many ways. Some scholars believe that some parts of the Passover ritual exist for the sole purpose of getting children to ask "Why?"

Outline

Part I: Introduction

Lighting candles.

Kiddush is recited over the first cup of wine.

Shehecheyanu: the prayer for having reached this moment.

Ceremonial hand-washing, but without the traditional blessing.

Karpas: A blessing is recited over the green vegetable, which is then dipped into salt water and tasted by everyone.

Afikomen: This is the name given to the middle of the three *matzot* on the covered plate. The piece is broken, and the larger part of it is hidden and then ransomed by the children after the meal. *Afikomen* derives from the Greek word for dessert and the *seder* cannot end until everyone eats a piece of it.

Part II: Telling the Story

The *Maggid:* The story. The Passover story begins with the line "This is the bread of slavery which our ancestors ate in Egypt when they were slaves. Let all who are hungry come and eat."

The Four Questions: Customarily asked by the youngest child capable of memorizing the words, the four questions are: Why do we eat *matzah*? Why do we eat bitter herbs? Why do we dip our vegetables? Why do we recline? (In other words, What are we doing here?)

The Four Sons/Children: A parable about the proper way to answer the Four Questions when asked by different kinds of children: wise, stubborn, simple, and those who do not know to enough ask.

The Ten Plagues: As each of the calamities that befell the Egyptians is recounted, a drop of wine is spilled from every glass. The most common explanation for this practice is that when any human life is lost or diminished, all people suffer, which means our cups of joy are diminished as well.

Dayenu: A song that lists the miracles God performed to free
the Jewish people from slavery.

Kiddush: The blessing for the second cup of wine is recited
and drunk.

PART III: PRELUDE TO THE MEAL

Ceremonial hand-washing, with the traditional blessing.

Motzi and the blessing over *matzah*.

Blessing over the bitter herbs.

Hillel sandwich. A mixture of bitter herbs and sweet *haroset* is
prepared on *matzah* and everyone eats of the bittersweet-
ness.

The meal is served.

PART IV: AFTER DINNER

The *afikomen* is "bought" back from children, and a piece is
eaten by everyone.

Blessings after the meal, *birkat hamazon*, are sung.

Kiddush: Blessing for the third cup of wine.

The door is opened for the prophet Elijah.

Singing: Traditionally, psalms of praise called *hallel*.

Kiddush: for the fourth and final cup of wine.

Conclusion: The traditional phrase that ends the *seder* is
L'shana haba-a b'Yerushalayim, "Next year in Jerusalem," a
statement expressing the hope that next year all people will
be free and none will be enslaved.

Elaborations

The Passover *seder* has always inspired creativity and innovation.
Laughter, enchantment, silliness, and argument are all appropriate to
a celebration of the freedom to be fully human. The *haggadah* says,
"To elaborate on the story is praiseworthy." The following examples
demonstrate how people elaborate on the story, the *haggadah*, and the
seder. They are offered as inspiration to your own creativity.

The entire *seder* can be a "potluck" affair. Not only can food courses be assigned to participants, so can sections of the ritual, thus turning the proceedings into a series of surprises, which keeps everyone engaged and eager to find out what will happen next.

A nice way to begin—either before or immediately after candle-lighting—is to invite everyone to share a personal Passover memory, or to talk about what the holiday means to them, or discuss the meaning of "freedom."

To keep people from getting too hungry to enjoy the proceedings, serve a first course of raw and/or cooked vegetables right after the blessing for *karpas* (green vegetables).

There are many customs around the *afikomen*. Parents usually hide it, which leads to a children's treasure hunt later in the evening. In order to get the *afikomen* back, parents pay the winner in coins or treats or prizes. Alternately, older children can hide the *afikomen*, and make their parents search for it. In some households, pieces of *matzah* are hidden all over the house, one for each child who will be attending. When all the previously hidden bits of *afikomen* are found, all the children are given toys.

Giving gifts at Passover is another custom, either as a reward for finding the *afikomen,* or when the door is opened for Elijah. At that point, a bag of treats might be "discovered" on the doorstep. In some families, an adult dresses up like the prophet and brings in a sack of goodies when the door is flung open.

Elijah's cup is on the table as symbol of hope for redemption and a healed world. Some people put an empty cup in the center of the table and, at some point in the *seder,* pass it around so that each person can pour a little wine from their own glass into it, symbolizing how each person needs to help "bring Messiah," how everyone must work to bring about a world of peace. Elijah's cup can also be the subject of fun; some people rig the glass to mysteriously drain during the course of the evening, "proving" that he has been present.

The *maggid,* the telling of the story, offers limitless possibilities. The following suggestions are ways to encourage the sense of personally experiencing the redemption from Egypt:

- Prepare a skit, puppet show, pantomime, musical, or video to recount the story of the exodus from Egypt or some part of it. The story can be scripted and parts can be drawn from a hat (Miriam, Moses, frogs, God, Pharaoh, narrator, etc.). A costume box, masks, and hats heighten the drama.

- Some people have adopted the Sephardic custom of getting up and walking around the table at the point in the story when the Israelites leave Egypt. Similarly, one can play music and dance around the table when the story reaches the moment when the people rejoice at having reached the other side of the Sea of Reeds.

- The plagues have inspired a minor industry, with sacks filled with plastic frogs and bugs. You can make your own plagues with red food coloring (for blood), dolls (death of the firstborn), a burned-out lightbulb (darkness), etc.

- Some people sit in darkness to enact that plague for a few moments, during which everyone names a modern plague: nuclear weapons, AIDS, homelessness, poverty, cancer, racism, anti-Semitism, war.

- Song sheets can encourage everyone to sing. In addition to the traditional Hebrew songs that are printed in many *haggadot,* consider including folks songs and spirituals such as "If I Had a Hammer" and "Go Down, Moses," or any familiar popular songs relevant to the themes of the holiday.

- It's a good idea to aim for a balance between tradition and innovation. *Seders* should change as children grow more able to participate in grown-up conversation, but there's nothing like consistency to plant precious Passover memories; a beloved poem, a silly joke told at the same juncture in the meal, a favorite recipe served only once a year.

- If adults wish to have a longer, more intellectual *seder* than their children can sit still for, they can be excused during discussions and some readings from the *haggadah.* However, at every important "event" of the *seder* (another cup of wine, the Four Questions, the Hillel sandwich) someone can blow a whistle or bang a drum to summon the kids back.

- Where there are no young children or they have all fallen asleep, the *seder* can become an opportunity for intellectual and even esoteric discussion of the story and the other elements of the *seder*. These kinds of meals can go on until past midnight, until everyone is satisfied that they finally understand what it all "really" means—at least for this year.
- Not everyone has such stamina, and by the end of the meal and after four (or more) cups of wine, some people end their seders on a lighter note. One family tradition consists of a tipsy contest for the person with the fastest or funniest performance of the traditional song "Who Knows One?" ("Echad Mi Yodeah," included in most haggadot).

Many people attend two *seders,* on the first and second nights of Passover. To keep the experience fresh, it's a good idea to differentiate between them: for example, a big group one night, a more intimate gathering the next; emphasis on teaching and entertaining children one night, more grown-up conversation the next, which might mean hiring a sitter for the kids.

The Intermediate Days

The only home observance after the *seder* and before the final day of Passover is the eating of *matzah* and the avoidance of *hametz.* As with the practice of *kashrut,* the range of observance is broad. Some people simply do not eat bread or other leavened foods, but otherwise make no change in their kitchens and simply tailor their orders at restaurants. Others clean their homes of *hametz* for the week, with or without a changeover in dishes.

The challenge of cooking without leavening can get tedious as the week goes on, so some people try to plan potluck dinners with family and friends to share recipes and ease the potential monotony of Passover cooking.

Although it is traditional to say the *havdalah* prayer over wine at the end of Passover, for most people, the holiday tends to just peter out with a stop at a pizzeria or Chinese restaurant. However, Sephardic custom ends the holidays with a feast called Maimuna. Named to honor Maimon ben Joseph, father of the great 12th century rabbi Maimonides, Maimuna is still celebrated with festive, elaborate traditions in communities of Moroccan Jews and in the state of Israel. People wear their finest clothes and eat at tables decorated with flowers and wheat stalks. Traditional Maimuna feasts are meatless, featuring buttermilk, sweets, and special pancakes called *muflita*. Some individuals and synagogues have adopted the custom as a way to provide a sense of joyful closure to Passover.

Synagogue Observance

Home observance tends to overshadow all other aspects of Passover; however, holiday services are held on the first (and second) days, which the Torah denotes as days of rest; the same goes for the last day (or two). On the last day of Passover, a memorial service is held and the *yizkor* prayer is recited in memory of loved ones who have died. Some congregations hold a community *seder* on the first or second night. Extra community *seders* are often planned on the intermediate days, when members of the larger community are invited for interfaith and/or interracial teaching-and-sharing ceremonies.

LAG B'OMER

Fifty days after Passover, the holiday of Shavuot marks the giving of the Torah to the Israelites. These observances of liberation and revelation are linked by the counting of those days, which is called the counting of the omer.

An omer was the measure of grain set apart for offerings to the Temple. On the second day of Passover, the first of 50 measures of barley was given, as an offering or gift to God; thereafter, one measure a day was given for the next 49 days. These 50 days eventually came to be associated with terrible persecutions of the Jews, so that certain mourning practices were observed. Some people still do not cut their hair and some rabbis will not officiate at weddings during the counting of the Omer, except on the 33rd day of the Omer, in Hebrew, Lag B'Omer.

Lag B'Omer is considered a semiholiday, and has long been associated with weddings and picnics. However, it was never widely celebrated and its origins and proper observance have been the subject of rabbinic debate. Since it falls in the spring, Lag B'Omer is mostly known today as the occasion for outdoor congregational and community events: family field days, picnics, softball games, and races. In Israel, the air is thick with the smell of outdoor grilling and picnics.

HOLOCAUST REMEMBRANCE DAY AND ISRAEL INDEPENDENCE DAY

Nothing is so whole as a broken heart.

RABBI NACHMAN OF BRATSLAV

In one of its earliest sessions, the Israeli Knesset (parliament) declared that Israel Independence Day would be celebrated on the fifth of Iyar—the Hebrew date corresponding to May 15, 1948, when Israel became a sovereign nation. Three years later, the Knesset proclaimed Holocaust Remembrance Day on the 27th of Nisan, 14 days after the start of Passover and eight days before the celebration of Israel's birth.

The addition of these holidays to the Hebrew calendar reflect the profound impact of two historical events on the Jewish psyche. The world could never be the same after the Shoah, the Holocaust that killed one-third of the world's pre–World War II Jewish population. Nor could the future be the same after the realization of the dream of returning to the land of Israel. The relationship between the two holidays is undeniable, but not simple. The establishment of the state of Israel in no way compensates for the slaughter of European Jewry, but it is, undeniably, a response to that horror and an affirmation of life and Jewish continuity against the overwhelming evidence of death and destruction.[28]

Outside of Israel, Yom HaShoah and Yom HaAtzma'ut are celebrated in communal observances. It is difficult to create ritual responses to the raw emotion and the historical ramifications of the Holocaust and Israel are still unfolding.

Holocaust Remembrance Day

It seems almost blasphemous to attempt to make sense out of the senseless slaughter of six million Jewish men, women, and children. The photographs, film footage, diaries, and memoirs of survivors are excruciating. And yet, the responsibility to remember is absolute and, in some sense, sacred.

It is terrible to remember. It is worse to forget. These are the twin realities of Yom HaShoah and the tension between them is the source of their observance.

In America, commemorations of the Holocaust include a wide range of events including civic ceremonies attended by public officials and clergy of all faiths. There are classroom presentations about the Nazi horror tailored to the age and ability of students to understand what is incomprehensible. Some synagogues and Jewish community centers mark Yom HaShoah with displays of art, photographs, or books, and with seminars, lectures, and film series. Fasting has been suggested as an appropriate way to mark Yom HaShoah and some people abstain from eating sweet foods.

While liturgies have been published and used, many congregations create original services for Yom HaShoah from year to year. Readings from Lamentations and Psalms are often used, but the most common source for commemorations held in hushed and darkened sanctuaries is literature from the Holocaust—the testimony of victims, survivors, and witnesses. Six yellow tulips may be displayed on the *bimah*.

Thus far, the ritual gesture that seems to have taken root is the lighting of six memorial candles, one for each of the six million Jews who were killed. This is done both in synagogues and at home, and some light a seventh candle in memory of non-Jews who were killed in the Holocaust, or to honor the righteous non-Jews who risked their lives to help Jews. Candles and flowers recall the dead and affirm life and hope, even in the heart of the blackest night.

In Israel, on what is called "Holocaust and Resistance Remembrance Day," all public entertainments are closed. A three-minute siren blast is heard throughout the country, and everyone stands at attention.

Yom HaShoah is not associated with any home observances. The Holocaust is still too close, too awful, to bring to the table. However, since it is a time when schoolchildren may be introduced to or reminded of the events of the Holocaust at school, families sometimes use the opportunity to discuss the thoughts and feelings these lessons provoke. There are many good books and films about the Holocaust for all ages.

Donations to virtually any Jewish organization seem appropriate *tzedakah* at Yom HaShoah since the vitality of the Jewish community repudiates its attempted annihilation. Some earmark money at this time for projects devoted to keeping the memory of the Holocaust alive, or for the support of Righteous Gentiles—those who saved and aided Jews during the Shoah.

Israel Independence Day

After nearly two thousand years in exile, the formation of a Jewish state in the land of Israel transformed the self-image of Jews everywhere. Even Jews who have no relatives there or have not visited tend to feel a connection to, commitment to, and responsibility for her existence. While Israel Independence Day is, by and large, a secular event, it is impossible to forget its context in Jewish tradition. From the Torah, where God promises Abraham, "I give all the land that you see to you and your offspring forever,"[29] to the annual Passover wish, "Next year in Jerusalem," the land of Israel has been a focal point of the Jewish hope for redemption. Thus, there is a sense that the modern state of Israel has a profound connection with God's purpose for the Jews. The challenge of living up to the prophetic call for justice while facing virtually constant mortal threats from her neighbors continues to test the spirit and will of Israelis and all Jews everywhere. The test is met with hope, *tikvah,* as in the national anthem of Israel, *"HaTikvah,"* "The Hope."

In North America, Israel Independence Day is the occasion for public gatherings of all sorts, the Israel Day Parade in New York City being the largest. Local community centers and synagogues hold dances, concerts, film series, seminars, and lectures that feature Israeli culture and concerns. Religious schools and day schools usually schedule programs, parties, and pageants in conjunction with the holiday. In Israel, Yom HaAtzma'ut is celebrated with flags, bands, fireworks, picnics, parties, and dancing in the streets. Many American Jews try to schedule trips to Israel to coincide with this gala celebration.

Tzedakah for Israel Independence Day has come to mean supporting the state of Israel by purchasing Israel bonds, by making a contribution to any Israeli charity, and by buying Israeli goods and products.

Yom HaZikaron (Remembrance Day) is an Israeli holiday observed the day before Yom HaAtzma'ut, and honors the memory of those who died fighting for Israel's independence and continuing existence. Another Israeli observance, Yom Yerushalayim (Jerusalem Day), is celebrated three weeks after Israel Independence Day and commemorates the capture of Jerusalem during the Six Day War of 1967.

SHAVUOT

Shavuot celebrates the moment when the Jewish people stood before God at Mount Sinai and received a scroll containing all the secrets of the universe as a memento of their encounter. The scroll was the Torah. She is called a tree of life.

RABBI LAWRENCE KUSHNER [30]

Seven weeks after Passover—seven weeks after leaving Egypt—comes Shavuot, Hebrew for "weeks," and the holiday that celebrates the encounter between the Jewish people and God through the giving of the Torah at Mount Sinai. The Torah is sometimes called a *ketubah,* a marriage contract that describes the covenantal relationship between the people of Israel and God; Shavuot can be thought of as the celebration of this wedding anniversary.

The Bible, however, makes no connection between Shavuot and the Torah; references to Shavuot in Exodus, Leviticus, and Deuteronomy describe an agricultural pilgrimage holiday—a day when people came from all over the land of Israel to the Temple, bearing gifts from the first fruits of the wheat and fruit harvest as an offering to God.[31] The agricultural and seasonal aspects of Shavuot are still reflected in its many names: the Day of the First Fruits, the Day of the Harvest, the Feast of the Flowers (in ancient Persia), and the Feast of the Roses (in Italy).

But after the destruction of the Second Temple in 70 C.E., the holiday was changed to celebrate the Torah, the new center of Judaism. The agricultural roots of the holiday are echoed in seasonal decorations and especially in Israeli celebrations that include public processions featuring singing and dancing. But for the most part, Shavuot is perhaps the most mystical of all the Jewish holidays—the day that celebrates revelation.

Much as Passover encourages every member of every generation to feel as though he or she had experienced slavery and liberation, Shavuot insists that revelation—receiving the Torah—is experienced by every Jew. Shavuot is celebrated with greens and flowers, with dairy meals, sweets, and reading the Book of Ruth, about a woman who was Jewish not by birth but by choice.

Preparing

In recognition of the late spring–early summer season of the holiday, it is customary to decorate with green plants and flowers. An old European craft associated with Shavuot is the paper cut. Called *shavuoslech, raizelech,* or *shoshanta* (the latter two words refer to roses), these were hung on windows so that light would filter through the floral designs.[32] Baking bread for the *yontif seder* is another Shavuot custom. And some people go to the *mikveh* for a ritual of purification to get ready to receive the Torah.

Study

Study is the primary way of preparing for Shavuot. It is traditional to read *Pirke Avot,* "The Ethics of the Fathers," a very accessible section of the Talmud, during the weeks between Passover and Shavuot. In line with the custom of the *tikkun* (described below), some people try to read a little bit of each book of the Bible, with special attention to the Torah and Bible readings for Shavuot: Exodus 19–20 (the Ten Commandments), the Book of Ruth, and Ezekiel 3:12, the strange vision of "the wheel."

In terms of giving *tzedakah,* the themes of learning and agriculture suggest donations to organizations devoted to education, feeding the poor, and restoring the earth.

Making Shavuot

Shavuot begins with a festival meal, including all the blessings of the *yontif seder*: candles, a festival *kiddush, shehecheyanu,* and *motzi*. Since the Torah mentions the offering of two loaves of bread made from newly harvested wheat, it is customary to have two loaves on the table. Some people bake two loaves of *challah* side by side and connected, so that they resemble the popular image of the two tablets of the Ten Commandments.

Shavuot meals feature dairy foods, especially cheese. For Ashkenazi Jews, blintzes (sweet cheese wrapped in a thin pancake) are traditional. Eating outdoors is a nice way to welcome the summer season.

The custom of late-night Shavuot synagogue study sessions can be translated to the home. For children, it can be a special night for staying up late and reading stories about the Bible, or watching Bible movies on DVD.

Synagogue Observance

Synagogue observance of Shavuot begins in the evening with a holiday service that often starts later than usual. Afterward, many congregations run some kind of *tikkun,* or study session. This custom dates back to the 16th century mystics of Safed who stayed up all night long to read and study from the Bible and from the *Zohar,* a mystical book. Modern Shavuot study sessions take many forms: a series of seminars led by members of the congregation or invited scholars; discussion of modern as well as ancient Jewish texts; writing of modern *midrashim*— imaginative commentaries on a biblical passage. Some synagogues run study sessions until midnight or even till dawn, when the morning service is held and breakfast is served.

The Torah portion for the morning service includes the reading of the Ten Commandments. The Haftarah portion comes from Ezekiel, and includes the hallucinatory vision of the *merkavah*—God's chariot or throne, which is attended by marvelous strange creatures: angels, divine beings. The prophet's description of wheels within wheels has been given many interpretations, and remains always a stunning expression of religious imagination.

The Book of Ruth is a popular Shavuot text. Ruth, the archetypal Jew-by-choice, demonstrates that it is not birth or family identity but acceptance of the Torah that distinguishes Jews from the other peoples. Ruth's place as an ancestor of King David celebrates the importance of converts to the continuity of the Jewish people. Some congregations honor Jews-by-choice on Shavuot with panel discussions about people's Jewish journeys.

Many congregations hold confirmation or graduation ceremonies on Shavuot, which has long been associated with Jewish study.

TISHA B'AV

Tisha B'Av, the ninth day in the month of Av, is a day of mourning for the destruction of the Temple in Jerusalem first in the year 586 B.C.E. by Nebuchadnezzar, King of Babylonia, and again seven centuries later in 70 C.E. by General Titus of the Roman Empire.

The destruction of the Temple was, quite literally, the end of the world to the Jews of those times. The end of the Temple meant the end of a way of life, of a religion of sacrifices and priesthoods, and of national identity for the Jewish people, who were dispersed and exiled in the aftermath of military defeat. The destruction of the Temple was also interpreted as a sign that God had withdrawn from the world and from intervening on behalf of the Jewish people. Over time, other sad events were associated with and commemorated on Tisha B'Av, among them: the end of Bar Kochba's revolt against the Romans (135 C.E.), the expulsion of Jews from England (1290 C.E.), from Spain (1492), and from Vienna (1670).

Tisha B'Av is a day of fasting observed with mourning customs, such as not shaving and sitting low to the ground. It also culminates a three-week period of semimourning when weddings and other celebrations are avoided. Those who observe Tisha B'Av light memorial candles and attend services, where there is no singing or chanting. The Torah may be draped with dark or black covers. The text for Tisha B'Av is the Book of Lamentations, a long poem that keens over the destruction of Jerusalem and the First Temple.

In America, Tisha B'Av is the least known of traditional Jewish holidays. In some part this is due to the fact that it falls during the middle of the summer, when many congregations are on summer schedule and many people are on vacation. Also, the destruction of the

Temple does not evoke the emotions of grief and mourning called for by Tisha B'Av and in a sense, Holocaust Remembrance Day has taken its place as a communal day of grief and mourning. Because Tisha B'Av is a holiday mourning the exile of the Jews, the founding of the state of Israel seems to lighten the grief and suggest an element of hope, since there is a legend that the Messiah will be born on Tisha B'Av.

Because it is the only event on the Jewish calendar during the summer months, Jewish camps have made Tisha B'Av a focus for teaching and creative programming. Campers participate in dramatic reenactments and services in candle-lit recreation halls, original poetry-writing workshops, and discussion groups.

THE LIFE CYCLE

Jewish ritual is the art of turning time into celebration. The ceremonies and customs that surround the great transitions of human life—birth, coming of age, marriage, death—provide wise pathways through the soul's uncharted territories; they give us perfect words when the heart is too full to speak. The Jewish life cycle is a venerable guide, but as in all things Jewish, it is also full of choices about how to celebrate, and what to observe, say, and sing. And indeed, the life cycle itself is changing, and adding new choices.

Adding a chapter about conversion and adoption to the list of Jewish life-cycle events acknowledges these changes and also stands as an expression of creative liberal Jewish piety. Although it is difficult to find reliable statistics about conversion and adoption, it is safe to say that there has been no other period in Jewish life to match the present in terms of the numbers entering Judaism through these ancient portals. But it is not merely a matter of numbers: the urge to sanctify life-changing transitions with rituals, prayers, songs, and celebration is part of the DNA of Judaism. Taking the time to honor a profound change of status is simply a Jewish thing to do.

The more that liberal Jews learn of their tradition, the greater their desire to give Jewish dimensions to passages that went unnoted in the past; this means reclaiming customs and *mitzvot* that earlier generations rejected, and inventing new ones. Thus, Jewish women have identified moments in their physical lives that call out for spiritual mindfulness and ritual, including menarche, menstruation, pregnancy, miscarriage, weaning, and menopause. Men and women, boys and girls, have identified other transformational events and passages: graduation from a course of study, becoming an adult *bar/bat mitzvah,* recovery from serious illness, becoming a grandparent. In some cases, the tradition already provides a meaningful response; the recitation of the *gomel*[1] prayer after an illness or escaping injury, is making a return to synagogue liturgy, giving public voice to personal gratitude. Immersion in the ritual bath, the *mikveh,* has returned to the menu of choices for liberal Jews, both for traditional uses (i.e., sanctifying sexuality) and for an array of new purposes, such as those listed above. See www.mayyimhayyim.org.

Some contemporary situations seem to require entirely new prayers and gestures, or new combinations of the old and the new, as in the case of getting a driver's license or of coming out to one's family (www.ritualwell.org).

The repertoire of life-cycle rituals, which once seemed settled for eternity, has become flexible and fluid. This is not a rejection of the past but an embrace of its teaching that the Torah is a "tree of life." The nature of living things is to change and grow.

BIRTH

The first mitzvah—the first "commandment"—in the Bible is "Be fruitful and multiply," from Genesis 1:28. For Jews, having children is both a religious obligation and the crown of human life, the source of the greatest happiness. The birth of Jewish babies is thus greeted with rituals that are both solemn and joyful.

All parents know that *their* baby is the center of the universe, a "fact" that is acknowledged by the Jewish view of time. Every Jewish baby is considered a link in the chain that extends back to the birth of Isaac, the first Jewish baby, and extends forward to the day when the world will be peaceful and whole. After all, any baby might grow up to be the Messiah, the person who will lead the world to redemption. The Jewish traditions and rituals described in this chapter give voice to the powerful feelings that surround the birth of every baby: gratitude, awe, fear, humility, continuity, and hope.

With each child, the world begins anew.

THE MIDRASH

Names

The choice of a name is the first Jewish decision parents are called upon to make, and for Jews, a name is a complicated gift because it bestows not only personal identity but also familial and religious connection. A baby named Daniel or Rebecca is often a living testa-ment to a grandparent who has died, and a link to every Jewish Daniel and Rebecca back to the Bible.

Jewish tradition is very attentive to names and naming. *HaShem,* "The Name," is one way of referring to God, and the Torah contains several dramatic and important name changes. Once Abram and Sarai accepted the covenant with God, they became different people with dif-ferent names: Abraham and Sarah, the parents of the Jewish people. Even more striking is the transformation of Jacob, "supplanter," into Is-rael, "wrestler with God." There is a story that the Jews enslaved in Egypt were saved from complete assimilation by keeping two identifying signs that set them apart: the custom of circumcision and their Hebrew names.

Biblical names have long been a source for parents, but of the 2,800 personal names in the Bible, fewer than 5 percent are used today. And throughout history, Jews have given their children names from many sources, reflecting the fashions and cultures of their times as well as tradition. For example, Esther, a quintessentially Jewish name, is Persian in origin and shares its root with Astarte, also known as Ishtar, the great fertility goddess of the ancient Mid-dle East. The Eastern European custom of naming children after deceased relatives dates back to the Egyptian Jews of the sixth cen-tury B.C.E., who probably borrowed the idea from their non-Jewish neighbors.

The practice of giving a secular name for everyday use and a reli-gious name for prayer and on Jewish legal documents developed dur-ing the Middle Ages in Eastern Europe.[2] This custom is still very much alive in America, where the connection between the secular and Hebrew name is sometimes as tenuous as an initial sound; thus a baby girl named for her grandmother Shayna becomes Susan, and Max is named in memory of Uncle Moshe.

Since the founding of the state of Israel, the lexicon of Jewish names has expanded with the introduction of biblical names that had not been heard for generations, such as Amnon, Yoram, Avital, and Tamar. Israelis also translate names from Yiddish to Hebrew, so, for example, Gittel ("good one") becomes Tovah. Inspired by the land of

Israel, children are named Kinereth (a sea), Arnon (a wadi), Barak (lightning), and Ora (light).

Today, Jewish American parents have embraced biblical names with a passion, and preschools are full of Samuels and Rachels, Benjamins and Sarahs. Modern Israeli names are also growing in popularity: Ariella, Levi, Noam, Shoshana. Increasingly, parents are choosing identifiably Jewish names (from Abigail to Zachariah) because they work well in three settings where American Jews are likely to find themselves: in secular life, in synagogues, and in Israel.

Covenant—*Brit*

A covenant is a contract—an agreement that acknowledges the participation and assent of various parties. Covenant is the term for the relationship of the people of Israel with God. With the birth of every Jewish child, that covenant is renewed again with ritual and celebration.

The ancient ceremony for bringing sons into the covenant of Israel is *brit milah,* a religious ceremony that includes circumcision as a physical sign of the bond between the Jewish people and God. For daughters, American Jews have created a ceremony, *brit bat,* "covenant for a daughter," to invoke the joys and responsibilities of entering the covenant of the people of Israel.

In many ways, the covenant of circumcision and the covenant for a daughter are as different as two ceremonies can be. *Brit milah* is the oldest continuous Jewish rite, celebrated with remarkable consistency throughout the world. *Brit bat,* which goes by many names, is a recent development in Jewish history, and no two are quite the same. What these two celebrations have in common, however, is the element of covenant, expressed with joy, gratitude, and wonder. *Brit* ceremonies give parents a way to express the complex feelings occasioned by the birth of a baby, a way to express new feelings of connection with a Jewish past and faith in the future.

The Covenant of Circumcision
Brit Milah

In this ritual, the foreskin is removed within a religious ceremony, as a physical token signifying the unique relationship between each Jewish male and God. *Brit milah* is called the covenant of Abraham, because the biblical patriarch was the first to practice circumcision as a Jewish ritual. According to the biblical story, Abraham responded to God's command and circumcised himself (at the age of 99) and all the men of his household, including his 13-year-old son, Ishmael. Isaac, the firstborn of a circumcised Hebrew, underwent *brit milah* on the eighth day, which set the precedent for the ritual's timing ever since.

The importance of circumcision as a mark of peoplehood is a recurring theme in the Bible, and the covenant has been renewed in every generation. During periods of persecution, it singled Jewish men out for execution, and circumcision became an act of defiance and courage. In the 20th century, stories from the Holocaust and from the Soviet Union testify to the steadfastness of Jewish practice of *brit milah*—regardless of the consequences.

Such shall be the covenant between Me and you and your offspring to follow which you shall keep: every male among you shall be circumcised. You shall circumcise the flesh of your foreskin, and that shall be the sign of the covenant between Me and you.

GENESIS 17:10–11

The liturgy of *brit milah* was established before the first century C.E., and the laws that regulate and explain it are contained in the

Talmud. *Brit milah* takes place on the eighth day of life,* even if that falls on *Shabbat* or holidays, including Yom Kippur.

However, illness or weakness of any kind requires that the rite be postponed until it is completely safe for the baby. A *bris* (as it is pronounced in Yiddish) may occur anytime before sundown, but it is customarily scheduled early in the day, responding to the tradition that says that one should be eager to perform a *mitzvah*. A *bris* may be held anywhere, but most take place at home.

A father is responsible for his son's *brit milah,* and technically he performs the circumcision; the *mohel* (the Yiddish pronunciation is *moyl,* the Hebrew, *mo-hail*), or ritual circumciser, acts as his representative. The only people who absolutely must be present at a *bris* are the baby, the *mohel,* and one honored assistant called the *sandek;* often a grandfather, who holds the baby. However, since a *bris* is considered a joyful event, it is customary to invite friends and family members.

Choosing *Brit Milah*

Nearly all Jewish parents fulfill this *mitzvah,* arguably the most difficult of all the commandments. It is a choice made even by Jews with little or no connection to community or congregation, by Jews with little or no understanding of the ritual or its meaning. Even so, *brit milah* does pose questions that deserve to be considered and answered: Is it safe? Will my baby suffer? What is the best way to have it done? Why should we continue this tradition at all?

As recently as the 1960s, approximately 98 percent of all boys born in the United States were circumcised for reasons of health and hygiene.[3] For years, this custom excused many Jewish parents from the need to make a decision. But after an official announcement by pediatricians in 1985 that routine circumcision was not medically warranted, that figure quickly dropped to 59 percent.[4] In the late 1980s, the medical debate again shifted somewhat back in favor of universal

*According to the Jewish calendar, a day begins with the preceding nightfall, so if a boy is born on Monday night, his *bris* would be on the following Tuesday.

circumcision. But the fact is, Jews have always performed *brit milah* as a religious obligation, never as a health measure.

Jewish tradition, which is so concerned with the sanctity of life and health, would not require an act that might jeopardize either. Circumcision is a medically safe procedure—complications are extremely rare—and clearly, Jewish sons have survived the procedure for 3,500 years.[5]

Although *brit milah* was performed for centuries with no more anesthesia than a few drops of wine, today most physicians and *mohelim* (plural of *mohel*) numb the area with topical or injectible anesthetic and anyone who has attended more than one *bris* knows that babies are easily comforted after the procedure.

Some Jewish parents, feeling more confidence in medicine than ritual practice, decide to have their sons circumcised by a physician in the hospital before they take the baby home. (This is actually a false dichotomy in many communities; see the section below about the *mohel*.) Apart from the fact that a medical circumcision is not the same as a *brit milah*, which is a religious ritual performed on the eighth day with the deliberate intent of bringing a son into the covenant, there are other important differences between a hospital "circ" and a *bris* performed by a *mohel*.

In many hospitals, residents of varying experience perform the procedure. In order to immobilize the baby, his limbs are strapped onto a board where he may be held for as long as ten or fifteen minutes. After the procedure is over, there may be no one around to immediately comfort the baby. At a *brit milah*, the baby is held by loving hands throughout the procedure, which is performed by an expert at the operation. The baby is given some wine, which is thought to lessen the pain and may help him fall asleep afterward. When the ceremony is over, he is returned to his mother, who can nurse and comfort him.

As to the "why" of *brit milah*, the most compelling reasons are not always the easiest to explain. For many parents the answer to the question is: If we stop doing *brit milah*, we stop being Jews. *Brit milah* is a physical connection to the ancient Jewish past and to all subsequent generations to this day, and it is one of the few ritual practices upon which virtually all Jews still agree. Choosing not to circumcise a son

may, in effect, cut him off from full membership in the Jewish community, or present him with the choice of undergoing a painful operation as an adult. The implications of the decision not to circumcise a
Jewish baby are best discussed with a rabbi.

The mohel. Traditional *mohelim* learn their skills by apprenticeship to and supervision by an accomplished, established practitioner.
The Reform and Conservative movements now train board-certified
physicians as *mohelim* with a course on the theology, Jewish law, folklore, and liturgy of *brit milah*. Indeed, more and more *mohelim* of all
denominations are doctors.

On the day of a *brit milah*, the *mohel* examines the baby, and if there
is the slightest question about the child's health, Jewish law requires that
the circumcision be postponed. The *mohel* will usually act as the "master
of ceremonies" for the *brit*, leading prayers and explaining the ritual as well
as performing the circumcision. Sometimes, a rabbi, cantor, the parents,
or others will share the liturgical honors. After the ceremony, the *mohel*
again examines the baby, gives instructions for caring for the circumcised
penis, and then remains "on call" for questions about healing.

Word-of-mouth recommendation is the best way to find a *mohel*,
and since rabbis and cantors go to many circumcisions, they are probably the best people to consult. Local denominational offices may also
be able to provide a list of names, and some *mohelim* place advertisements in local Jewish newspapers.

The ceremony. The liturgy of *brit milah* is ancient and, as with
most Jewish life-cycle rituals, the ceremony is very brief—no more than
five or ten minutes long. A *bris* consists of three parts. The first is as
normative and universal as any part of Jewish religious life: a blessing is
recited, the circumcision is performed, and another blessing follows.
The second part begins with *kiddush*, the blessing over wine, and includes a longer prayer that gives the baby his name. The third segment,
required by Jewish law, is the *seudat mitzvah*, the ritual meal of celebration.

There are variations and many customs attached to this simple
outline. The father may hand the circumcision knife to the *mohel*,
demonstrating that he bears responsibility for the act; sometimes, the
mother joins in this ritual gesture. Sephardic Jews follow the blessing

over wine with the scent of fragrant spices—Moroccan Jews use dried rose petals—and recite the blessing over spices, familiar from the Sabbath *havdalah* service.

Parents can customize and personalize the ceremony with readings, prayers, or a short *d'rash,* or teaching, but additions to the liturgy tend to be brief, since the comfort of the baby is paramount. Sometimes, when the baby is brought into the room, he is passed from one generation to the next, from great-grandparents to grandparents to parents. If an older sibling is mature enough to participate, he or she might carry the baby into the room, or light a candle, or say a few words.

Most parents take the opportunity to talk about the baby's name. This is a time for remembering Uncle Jake, for whom little Jacob has been named, and to hope he will grow up to be as learned, as quick to laugh, and as devoted a friend and father as his namesake. After the naming or at the meal of celebration, guests can offer personal blessings for the new baby: "May he be blessed with long life," "May he grow up in a world free of want and fear," "May he inherit his mother's good looks and his father's appetite."

There is an old custom of distributing *kibbudim,* "honors," to family members and friends during the ceremony. The most important of these is the role of the *sandek* (the word derives from the Greek *syndikos,* or "patron"); the *sandek* assists the *mohel* by holding the baby during the circumcision. The other traditional ceremonial roles are that of *kvatterin* (godmother), who carries the baby from the mother to the room where the *bris* takes place, and *kvatter* (godfather), who in turn brings the baby to the chair of Elijah. (*Kvatter* and *kvatterin* are entirely ceremonial roles. There is no formal Jewish role analogous to that assumed by Christian godparents, who become responsible for the child in case of his parents' death. The Jewish community as a whole is responsible for the education and support of orphaned children.)

According to the ancient legend, the prophet Elijah, who is associated with the coming of the Messiah, attends every *bris*. The special chair set aside for the prophet is a symbol of hope that this baby will bring peace and redemption to the world.

Covenant for a Daughter—*Brit Bat*

Although not as universally familiar as *brit milah,* ceremonies for baby girls are hardly a new invention. Sephardic tradition is rich in rituals and customs to celebrate a daughter's birth, including a ceremony called *Seder zeved habat,* "celebration for the gift of a daughter." The Jews of Spain held a special party at home after the mother's recovery called *las fadas,* a celebration that welcomed good fairies and was probably adapted from non-Jewish folk beliefs.[6]

American Jews have adopted this tradition with enthusiasm and variety, replacing the simple Ashkenazi custom of announcing a baby girl's name at services with new rituals, liturgies, and customs. Many rabbis officiate at "baby namings" in their synagogues, introducing the little girl and announcing her Hebrew name. Her parent(s) and grandparent(s) are invited up to the *bimah* (the raised platform, usually in front of the ark where the Torah scrolls are kept), usually during *Shabbat* services, with songs and words of welcome.

But many *brit bat* ceremonies take place in the home. Of the many new ceremonies being written and celebrated in America today, it may be that a single, standard liturgy for daughters will eventually become as normative as the words associated with *brit milah.* However, it is possible that this ceremony will continue to be given many interpretations like the Passover *seder,* which retains its identity even as it is interpreted anew every year.

Where and when. There are no rules for *brit bat,* but current practice offers a menu of choices. As noted above, the ceremony can take place at home or in the synagogue; although a sanctuary or social hall encourages a larger community celebration, some people prefer the intimacy of home. When *brit bat* takes place at home, the baby's parents usually lead the ceremony, sometimes with a rabbi's or cantor's assistance. When it is held in a synagogue, the rabbi tends to officiate, sometimes with parental participation. In general, grandparents tend to be given the most important *kibbudim* or honors, sometimes using the honorary roles and titles of *brit milah:* for example, the *sandek* (or if a woman, *sandeket*) holds the baby during part of the ceremony, and the *kvatterin* and *kvatter* may carry her to and from the room.

Generally, parents schedule *brit bat* for a time when the mother is sufficiently recovered to enjoy the event, and when it will be possible for out-of-town family members to attend. Various intervals are used and justified on traditional grounds. For example, holding the ceremony on the eighth day mirrors the ancient customs of *brit milah*. However, since mothers often do not feel ready for a party so soon after giving birth, this is a relatively infrequent choice and thirty days after birth is a popular choice, which has a basis in tradition, since the rabbis of the Talmud believed children were viable only after thirty days.

Elements of the ceremony. There are countless *brit bat* ceremonies in circulation. Some are short and simple, others are long and elaborate. Some incorporate music, some use a lot of Hebrew, and others use very little. It is difficult to generalize about these ceremonies, but despite the variety, there are some nearly universal elements.

1. The introductory section begins with the greeting "Blessed is she who enters," *B'rucha haba'a.* Songs may be sung, and candles are sometimes lit. There are usually prayers or readings by the parents, rabbi, and/or cantor. *Kiddush*, the blessing for wine that is part of all Jewish rituals marking significant events or times, is recited.

2. The second part of the ceremony is about covenant. Using blessings and symbolic actions, a baby daughter is entered into the people of Israel. While daughters are most commonly entered into the covenant simply by saying a blessing, many parents add a symbolic gesture as well as words. Washing the baby, or sometimes just her feet or hands, is an earthy yet gentle physical act that recalls the water imagery of the Torah, much of it associated with women: Rebecca and Rachel make their first appearances at wells, and Miriam the prophetess is associated with a well of living water that sustained the Israelites in the wilderness.

Generally, the covenant is followed by some version of the threefold wish recited at *brit milah:* "As she has entered the covenant, so may she enter a life devoted to Torah, *huppah,* and the accomplishment of good deeds."

3. In the third section, the baby's name is announced and her namesake(s) recalled. Anything said about how a name was chosen can be very moving, especially since most American Jews name children to honor the memory of a family member who has died. The Hebrew or biblical meaning of a name can also suggest ways for parents to talk about their hopes and dreams for a daughter.

Other kinds of readings, prayers, poems, and songs are added here and family and friends may be invited to offer spontaneous prayers and wishes for the new baby: "May she live to be 120," "May she sleep through the night soon." If the group is small and the baby placid enough, she might even be passed from person to person as they speak.

4. The end of the ceremony is signaled by one, some, or all of the following three prayers: *Shehecheyanu,* which is the generic prayer of thanks for anything new, and may be the most common element of all *brit bat* ceremonies; the traditional blessing for a daughter, which is recited on Friday night, part of the *Shabbat seder;* the threefold or priestly benediction, which concludes many Jewish rituals and services, and which some parents include in the *Shabbat* blessing of their children. (Check the index for references to these blessings.)

5. *Brit bat* concludes with the *seudat mitzvah,* a celebratory meal. The Jewish term for this kind of party is *simcha,* a word that means both joy and its celebration.

Celebrating

According to Jewish law, all major life-cycle events are marked, concluded, and celebrated with a *seudat mitzvah,* the "meal of the *mitzvah.*" The celebrations to honor the birth of a new baby boy or girl range from catered dinners to potluck buffet brunches. However plain or fancy, large or small, these meals traditionally begin with the blessing over *challah (motzi).*

The meal can also be an informal continuation of the *brit* ceremony, a time for guests to offer their blessings and wishes for the baby and family. Messages from people who could not be present might be read aloud, or older siblings can be given a chance to shine during a day in which they are eclipsed.

Tzedakah

Traditionally, Jews mark happy occasions like births with contributions of *tzedakah*, righteous giving or charity. Giving *tzedakah* is a way of both sharing the joy of the occasion and of acknowledging that personal happiness is incomplete in a world so badly in need of repair. A donation to honor the birth of a child is a kind of investment in a more just world for all children.

In ancient Israel, it was customary to plant a cedar sapling at the birth of boy, a cypress when a baby girl was born. The cedar symbolized strength and stature, the cypress gentleness and sweetness, and eventually, branches were cut down from each tree to hold up a wedding canopy. Some parents have revived this custom, planting a sapling in the yard when a baby is born. And many people have a tree planted in Israel's Children's Forest in honor of a birth (www.jnf.org).

God commands us to perform countless acts of love.

How can we begin to obey such a difficult commandment? It is not such a mystery really.

Every lullaby, every diaper change, every smile, every sleepless night, every wordless prayer of thanks for this perfect baby—in these and the unending ways we care for and teach and protect our children, we perform countless acts of love.

And the world is made holier. And so are we.

ADAPTED FROM THE MIDRASH

BAR AND BAT MITZVAH

May you live to see your world fulfilled,
May your destiny be for worlds still to come,
And may you trust in generations past and yet to be.

May your heart be filled with intuition
and your words be filled with insight.
May songs of praise ever be upon your tongue
and your vision be on a straight path before you.
May your eyes shine with the light of holy words
and your face reflect the brightness of the heavens.
May your lips ever speak wisdom
and your fulfillment be in righteousness
even as you ever yearn to hear the words
of the Holy Ancient One of Old.

PARENTS' BLESSING [7]

According to the rules of Hebrew grammar, no one is ever *bar mitzvah*-ed. One *becomes* a *bar mitzvah*, "son of the commandment," or *bat mitzvah*, "daughter of the commandment." There is more to this distinction than grammar. The ceremonies called *bar* and *bat mitzvah*—the preparation and study, the public recognition, the celebration—do not confer the status of *bar* or *bat mitzvah*. At the age of 13, Jews automatically become *bar* or *bat mitzvah*, full-fledged members of the community.

Nevertheless, the ceremony associated with this change of status has become one of Judaism's most potent rites of passage. *Bar* and *bat mitzvah* mark and celebrate a fundamental and irrevocable life change: the end of childhood. While no one treats a 12-year-old or 13-year-old as an adult, the beginning of adolescence is a momentous transition, one that many human cultures mark with ritual and ceremony.

Traditionally, *bar/bat mitzvah* is understood as a ceremony that welcomes a young Jew into the formal, adult prayer life of the community. In a religious culture that stresses communal rather than individual action and prayer, it is a unique moment and the only ceremony that features one Jew acting upon his or her own behalf solely. In celebrating the transition from childhood to puberty, *bar/bat mitzvah* ceremonies are also family rituals of transformation, marking the beginning of major changes for everyone, including parents.

Looking in the mirror, parents suddenly see people who are old enough to have a child of *bar/bat mitzvah* age—a child who is maturing sexually, a child who suddenly has strong opinions about everything under the sun. Watching a son or daughter stand, Torah in arms, in front of a crowded sanctuary, can be a revelation. As this poised and somehow mature child begins a new stage of their development, parents need to change, too.

History. *Bar mitzvah* does not appear in the Bible, which gives the age of 20 as the time when adult obligations begin.[8] However, by the first century C.E., adulthood was universally held to begin at 13 for boys and 12 for girls, a view codified in the Talmud, which states, "At age 13, one becomes subject to the commandments."[9] The earliest reference to any ceremony to mark this change dates from the Second Temple period, when a special blessing was recited for 13-year-old boys who had completed their first Yom Kippur fast.[10] But in fact, until the Middle Ages, the religious distinction between a 10-year-old and a 13-year-old was strictly theoretical. Children were regularly counted for the purposes of creating a *minyan,* the quorum of ten needed for certain prayers, so that reaching the age of 13 was not associated with any particular rituals or celebrations.[11]

That approach to ritual maturity changed drastically sometime between the 14th and 16th century in Germany and Poland, where minors were no longer permitted to read from the Torah or to be counted in a *minyan*. From that point in history, *bar mitzvah* became an important life-cycle event throughout the Jewish world. Boys were called to the Torah to symbolize the attainment of adult status in the prayer life of the community.

The central act of the ceremony was receiving the honor of an *aliyah*—of being called to bless and/or read from the Torah. However, other elements were soon added to the ceremony. As early as the 16th century, a *bar mitzvah* boy was expected to deliver a *d'rash,* a discourse on the Torah portion he had read. In the 17th and 18th century, some synagogues permitted accomplished students to lead part of the service as well. As with every joyful occasion, or *simcha, bar mitzvah* carried with it the obligation of a *seudat mitzvah,* a commanded meal of celebration.

Bat mitzvah. Because girls' coming-of-age was not connected with the performance of public religious rites, the notion of a parallel synagogue ceremony for girls was basically unthinkable before the modern era. In some German communities, families would hold a *seudah,* or party, on the occasion of a daughter's 12th birthday, and while a girl might deliver a speech and her father recite a blessing, this was not a religious celebration.

Bat mitzvah was invented in the 20th century. Although the Reform movement officially instituted equality between the sexes in the late 19th century, the first recorded *bat mitzvah* did not occur until 1922, and was celebrated by Judith Kaplan (Eisenstein), the eldest daughter of Mordecai Kaplan, the founder of the Reconstructionist movement. The practice did not become commonplace until the 1950s, first in Reform congregations and then in Conservative synagogues.

For many years, *bar* and *bat mitzvah* were distinctly different. Boys were usually expected to read or chant a Torah and/or Haftarah portion on Saturday morning while girls were limited to a Friday night reading of the Haftarah. The differences between *bar* and *bat mitzvah* have been steadily diminishing to the point that today, in most congregations, they are virtually indistinguishable.

Current practice. The custom of bar/*bat mitzvah* has become a focal point of Jewish identity. For many parents, the prospect of a child's turning 13 is the impetus for the first contact with the organized Jewish community since their wedding. Indeed, *bar* and *bat mitzvah* are the main reason many American Jews send their children to religious school, or even affiliate with a synagogue.

Synagogues prepare students for *bar/bat mitzvah*. In addition to regular religious school classes, there may be smaller and/or individual tutorial sessions with teachers and/or the rabbi or cantor. These sessions focus on the text the student will read or chant: a portion of Torah (the first five books of the Bible) and/or a reading of the Haftarah, selections from the Prophets associated with each week's Torah portion, and some kind of speech or *d'rash*.

To offset the tendency to stress a one time performance over the process of Jewish learning, most congregations have instituted special programs for children studying for *bar/bat mitzvah*. The content of Torah portions might be explored in depth, and guest teachers may be invited to the classroom to talk about more "grown-up issues," everything from sexual ethics to Israeli politics. Rabbis may schedule private meetings with each child. There are often *mitzvah* requirements, such as doing volunteer work, and/or collecting money for a charity. Many congregations have enriched the *bar/bat mitzvah* year curriculum to include weekend retreats, special one-on-one sessions with the clergy, field trips, and parent-child classes.

In theory, *bar/bat mitzvah* can take place at any service where the Torah is read. Although most take place on *Shabbat,* some families opt for a Sunday (if it coincides with Rosh Hodesh) or Monday of a holiday weekend, for a variety of reasons. In Conservative synagogues where there is a ban on music and photography on the Sabbath, those prohibitions do not apply, and for families with *Shabbat*-observant relatives, the complications and expense are fewer on a weekday. Children are commonly assigned a date more than a year in advance. Some people try to schedule the occasion for the first *Shabbat* after the 13th birthday, though in large congregations with many students and a limited number of dates, the results can be rather random and there may even be "double headers."

Bar/bat mitzvah ceremonies vary enormously from one congregation to the next. In some synagogues, the *bat mitzvah* leads part of the service, reading prayers in Hebrew and English, and leading songs and responsive readings. In other congregations, participation is limited to reading a Torah portion and making a speech. In some congregations, the liturgical participation for *bar/bat mitzvah* is always the same, but in others, more accomplished students are given more to do.

Synagogues tend to have a more or less standard format for *bar/bat mitzvah* ceremonies, but some rabbis and congregations are flexible and open to creative changes in the service. Special-needs children who wish to become *bar/bat mitzvah* are almost always accommodated with sensitivity and respect.

It is customary in some synagogues for the parents to "dress" their son/daughter in a *tallit* (perhaps for the very first time) before the ceremony, in private, and then to address their child publicly during the service, talking about their thoughts, feelings, and wishes on this occasion. Another lovely custom is for the Torah scroll to be passed from grandparents to parents to the *bar/bat mitzvah*, in a symbolic passing of the tradition from one generation to the next.

Despite the great variety in how a *bar/bat mitzvah* is conducted, there are three elements that are virtually universal: the *aliyah*, the speech, and the celebration.

The aliyah. Receiving an *aliyah* means being called up to the raised platform in the front of the synagogue, the *bimah*, to recite the blessings for the Torah reading and/or to read from the scroll. A *bar/bat mitzvah* may read or chant as little as three verses or as much the entire weekly Torah portion. In some congregations, s/he will only read a Haftarah, and in others both a Haftarah portion and from the Torah.

On the day of a *bar* or *bat mitzvah*, it is also customary to honor the young person's relatives with *aliyot* (the plural of *aliyah*). Parents, grandparents, siblings, uncles, aunts, and cousins may be called up to recite the Torah blessings, open the ark where the Torah is stored, and lift or "dress" the Torah.

The speech or d'rash. At some point in the service, the *bat* or *bat mitzvah* usually delivers a speech of some kind. While these are very personal and tend to include a "thank you" to parents, siblings, and teachers, the real purpose of this presentation is to demonstrate the young person's understanding of the text s/he has read in Hebrew. The *d'rash*, sometimes written as part of a religious school class or in consultation with the rabbi, cantor, and/or parents, may focus on the content of the portion for the week, or just start from there. Many teachers see the *d'rash* as an opportunity for a young person to make an important statement about who s/he is and what s/he believes in. There is also almost always a second speech delivered by the rabbi. Often called the rabbi's "charge," this tends to be a kind of personal sermon addressed to the *bar/bat mitzvah*.

The celebration. Important rites of passage are always celebrated with a festive meal. While tradition dictates a *seudat mitzvah* to mark the occasion of a *bar/bat mitzvah*, there are no Jewish laws that regulate the nature of that celebration; local and congregational custom and children's peer groups tend to dictate what these events look like.

Many families put enormous amounts of energy and money into the celebration of *bar/bat mitzvah*, largely in response to social pressure. If everyone in the congregation puts on a lavish party, it seems shoddy not to do the same. Likewise, hiring clowns, offering a children's menu, and buying expensive party favors may seem mandatory if your child has been so entertained. Unfortunately, some parents use the *bar/bat mitzvah* reception as a way to repay social and business obligations.

Many people have ridiculed and bemoaned the commercialization of *bar/bat mitzvah*, and unfortunately there are many accounts of bad taste: huge ice sculptures in the shape of the *bar mitzvah boy,* a caped superhero character called "Captain Bar Mitzvah," even monkeys wearing *yarmulkes.*

The problem of conspicuous consumption is not new. During the Middle Ages, rabbis promulgated laws limiting the number of guests who could be invited to *bar mitzvah* celebrations, and even regulated what kinds of finery could be worn. In part, sumptuary laws were an attempt to stave off anti-Semitic sentiments about Jewish wealth and ostentation; however, the rabbis were also concerned about unseemly excess that could overwhelm the religious significance of the day.

In reaction to modern excesses and to help keep the focus on the ritual rather than social aspects of the day, some families plan more intimate parties, less formal receptions. While there is still great pressure to conform, there is a growing desire to personalize the celebration.

From this perspective, "personalize" means more than engraved match-book covers or *yarmulkes* with the *bar/bat mitzvah*'s name inside. Making a celebration that genuinely reflects a family's beliefs and tastes can start with designing an invitation that features the *bar/bat mitzvah*'s own art-work or poetry, or contains a request that guests bring a can of food for distribution at a local shelter.

Increasingly, *tzedakah* is becoming a focus of *bar/bat mitzvah* prep-arations and celebrations. In small, close-knit Jewish communities of the past, beggars were invited to wedding and *bar mitzvah* feasts. To-day, many families symbolically invite the poor to their celebratory meals by setting aside a voluntary tax of 3 percent of the money spent for food to MAZON, A Jewish Response to Hunger, which funds soup kitchens, food pantries, and other feeding programs in the United States and around the world (www.mazon.org). Likewise, leftover food may be donated to local shelters for the homeless.

There are many other ways to make *tzedakah* an important part of the *bar/bat mitzvah experience.* In some families, a percentage of all money spent on the event is donated to charity, or a portion of cash gifts is earmarked for *tzedakah*. If parents know that a particular rela-tive plans to give money as a gift, they may request that donations be made to a charitable endowment instead; the *bar/bat mitzvah* then becomes trustee for this fund and decides which charities should re-ceive interest payments. If there are floral centerpieces at the *simcha,* the *bar/bat mitzvah* and his/her family can deliver them to a local nurs-ing home after the party. Alternately, money that might have been spent on flowers may be donated to some worthy cause, with a note on each table explaining that decision.

It is, however, important to remember that children have social pressures of their own to contend with. Young adolescents want their parties to be just like their friends' parties, and ignoring or dismiss-ing the strong emotions of kids at this age can be counterproductive. It makes sense to listen to their concerns and even compromise on details that seem especially crucial to your 13-year-old. For example, if the local custom "demands" a candle-lighting cake ceremony at the reception (a practice that, as far as anyone can tell, probably origi-nated with Long Island caterers interested in selling big cakes), there's little to be gained by making a stand on that essentially minor matter.

Nevertheless, parents of 13-year-olds should be making most of the decisions that affect their children's lives, and setting limits is as much a part of planning a *bar/bat mitzvah* party as deciding on the menu. Besides, virtually every decision parents make about the *bar/bat mitzvah* celebration becomes a lesson in making Jewish choices. If parents pay more attention to the color scheme than to the Torah portion, the child learns that the religious ceremony is secondary to putting on a pretty show.

Alternatives. While the overwhelming majority of families choose to hold *bar/bat mitzvahs* in a synagogue, they have also been celebrated in living rooms, function halls, and backyards. Do-it-yourself *bar/bat mitzvahs* tend to be small, intimate, and modest, and tend to be made by families who are part of or active in a *havurah* or *minyan,* small, self-directed groups of Jews who meet for study, community, and worship. As Jewish religious services do not absolutely require the presence of a rabbi, the proceedings may be led by a learned family member or friend, or by the *bar/bat mitzvah* him/herself. Some people consult with a teacher or rabbi for advice and assistance, or hire someone to run the service.

The most common alternative to the synagogue *bar/bat mitzvah,* however, is to take the ceremony to Israel. Families can hold the ceremony at the Western Wall in Jerusalem (for boys only, as Orthodox rulings restrict public and communal observances and services for women at the Wall), at the historical ruins of Masada (for both boys and girls), and at other sites, both sacred and secular.

This kind of trip has had a very powerful impact on many families, who consider it a turning point in their Jewish lives. Tour companies that specialize in *bar/bat mitzvah* trips to Israel make all necessary arrangements, and even provide the Torah. Some families celebrate a *bar/bat mitzvah* twice; once at their synagogue and again in Israel.

Afterward. Traditionally, *bar/bat mitzvah* marks the beginning of adult Jewish commitment. In terms of Jewish law, a *bar/bat mitzvah* can be counted in a *minyan,* the quorum needed for prayer, and may act as a witness in a legal proceeding. *Bar/bat mitzvah* also signals the start of more mature learning, and certainly few people are ready to tackle the moral, ethical, and theological questions of Jewish tradition before the age of 13.

In practice, however, many parents permit *bar/bat mitzvah* to be a "graduation" from Jewish learning and, indeed, from Jewish life. If parents permit their children to quit religious school, and if they themselves give up synagogue membership after their last child's "big day," young adults will understand that Jewishness is hardly a priority. On the other hand, parents who remain active in synagogue life, and who insist that religious school confirmation is no more optional than high school graduation, send the message that Jewishness is essential, and an ongoing choice for adults—a powerful lesson.

MARRIAGE

To the Jewish imagination, the wedding is a prototypical act of creation and thus the premier life-cycle event. The Zohar, the great book of Jewish mysticism, states, "God creates new worlds constantly. In what way? By causing marriages to take place."[12] Although the core of the Jewish wedding ritual is simplicity itself, the customs, symbols, and rituals associated with marriage spill over into more than a year's worth of celebration and joy.

Reb Nachman of Bratslav, a 17th century Hasidic master, is credited with a wonderful story about keeping the focus of a wedding on what's really important:

A group of people who have been to a wedding are walking home when one says, "That was a beautiful wedding. The food was out of this world." One of her companions says, "It was a great wedding. The band was terrific." A third friend chimes in, "I never had more fun at a wedding. I got to talk to people I hadn't seen in years."

But Reb Nachman, who overhears this conversation, says, "Those people weren't really at a wedding."

Then a fourth person joins the group and says, "Isn't it wonderful that those two people found each other!" At that Reb Nachman says, "Now that person was at a wedding!"

At their best, Jewish weddings are simultaneously reverent and hilarious, delicious and schmaltzy, intimate and communal, mysterious, romantic, and revealing. And everyone who has been there feels like they witnessed some sort of miracle.

Symbols, Laws, and Customs

The season of preparation and celebration that surrounds Jewish weddings includes parties and rituals, customs and symbols, documents and gifts that take the happy couple and their families from the first announcement of an engagement to the wedding day, and beyond. The following discussion of laws and customs includes only selections from the much longer wedding menu.

The huppah. Jewish marriage ceremonies take place beneath a *huppah*—a canopy supported by four poles. Although there are customs and conventions about the most appropriate location for a wedding, a *huppah* can be raised anywhere, reflecting the Jewish notion that almost any place can be made a holy place by human action and intention.

The *huppah* is a multifaceted symbol: of home, garment, bedcovering, and a reminder of the tents of the ancient Hebrews. During the 16th century, the vogue was for a portable canopy held aloft by four friends, a custom that remains popular to this day.

Some couples* have embraced the old custom of using a prayer shawl, or *tallit,* as a canopy, a symbol that affirms a commitment to creating a Jewish home. People also commission or make beautiful canopies using batik, silk screen, weaving, quilting and embroidery. These become instant heirlooms and are often displayed in the couple's home, on a wall, or even suspended as a canopy over the bed. Some couples raise their *huppah* again, over a child's *brit* ceremony (see "Birth").

Timing. While a *huppah* can be raised almost anywhere, Jewish law is far more prescriptive about the timing of weddings. Marriages do not take place on the Sabbath, nor on the major holidays and festivals, including Rosh Hashanah, Yom Kippur, Passover, Shavuot, and Sukkot, nor, traditionally, during the days between Passover and Shavuot.

---

*Many liberal rabbis and congregations welcome same-sex couples under the *huppah,* both in places where their union will have secular legal sanction, and in those where "gay marriage" is illegal. This introduction to the Jewish wedding, while it occasionally employs the terms "bride" and "groom," applies in all particulars to gay and lesbian couples as well.

Weddings are forbidden on *Shabbat* not only because the work and travel involved could violate the Sabbath spirit of rest, but also because of the injunction against mixing one *simcha*—or joy—with another. The combining of two kinds of happiness risks that one or both of them will not be given their full due, which is why double weddings are discouraged.

From every human being there rises a light that reaches straight to heaven. And when two souls that are destined to be together find each other, their streams of light flow together, and a single brighter light goes forth from their united being.

THE BAAL SHEM TOV

The ketubah. The Jewish marriage contract is one of the oldest elements of Jewish weddings. It is also one of the least romantic. In its traditional form, the *ketubah*—a word derived from the Hebrew for "to write"—does not mention love, trust, the establishment of a Jewish home, or God. The *ketubah* is a legal contract, plain and simple, written in Aramaic, the technical language of Talmudic law, not the poetic biblical Hebrew of Song of Songs.[13]

When it came into use during the first century C.E., the *ketubah* was considered a great advance for its time, in part because it provided women with legal status and rights in marriage. Over the centuries, it has changed very little, and indeed, a contemporary traditional *ketubah* is very much like a marriage contract from over a thousand years ago, complete with phrases such as:

And I here present you with the marriage gift of virgins, two hundred silver zuzim, which belongs to you, according to the law of Moses and Israel; and I will also give you your food, clothing and necessities, and live with you as husband and wife according to the universal custom. And this maiden consented and became his wife. The trousseau that she brought to him from her father's

*house in silver, gold, valuables, clothing, furniture and bedclothes,
all this the bridegroom accepted in the sum of one hundred silver
pieces.*

Clearly, these terms are archaic, at best, in describing relationships between women and men today. In order to sign a marriage contract in good faith (and also to reflect the realities of same-sex couples)
rabbis and calligraphers, brides and grooms, and loving partners have
written many new *ketubah* texts to reflect the realities of contemporary
marriage and partnership. Contemporary documents not only express
mutual and egalitarian obligations and commitments, they can also be
a way for couples to give voice to their feelings for each other and
hopes for their marriage. Some *ketubot* use the traditional text with
additions, but many are wholly original. In general, modern *ketubot* are
written both in English and Hebrew, and are signed by the bride and
groom, as well as witnesses and the rabbi, cantor, or other officiant.

Beautifully calligraphed, illustrated, and illuminated, there are a
wide variety of *ketubot* available for sale. Individuals may also commission unique works by artists. (Search *"ketubah"* on the Internet for a
huge selection.)

Here is an example of a modern *ketubah* text:

*On the first day toward Shabbat, the _____ day of _____, in
the year five thousand _____ since the creation of the world
according to our accustomed reckoning in _____, _____
_____ (bride's name) and _____ (groom's name), in the
presence of beloved family and friends entered into this covenant
with each other.*

*We promise to consecrate ourselves, one to the other as hus-
band and wife, according to the tradition of Moses and Israel; to
love, honor and cherish each other; to work together to create a
home faithful to the teachings of Torah, reverent of the Divine,
and committed to deeds of loving-kindness. We promise to try
always to bring out in ourselves and in each other qualities of
forgiveness, compassion, and integrity. All this we take upon ourselves to uphold to the best of our abilities.*

Rabbis and witnesses. In a Jewish wedding, the bridal couple actually marry each other through their own words and actions. However, it is customary to have an officiant, a person called a *mesader kiddushin,* "one who leads [literally, orders or arranges] the sanctification." Although any knowledgeable Jew can recite the necessary blessings at a wedding, cantors and rabbis almost always perform this honor. Most clergy also meet with the couple in advance of the wedding to discuss marriage and the establishment of a Jewish home, as well as plans for the ceremony.

Two impartial witnesses are required to make a Jewish wedding "kosher," or proper. Neither of the witnesses may be related to either the bride or groom, so they can have no emotional, social, or economic stake in the marriage. Because they are such important participants, it has been suggested that witnesses assume a special kind of responsibility for the marriage, especially in times of trouble.

The wedding. The essence of the Jewish wedding ceremony can be summed up in a few words: the bride accepts an object worth more than a dime from the groom, and the groom recites a ritual formula of consecration. If these two actions are witnessed by at least two other people, a wedding has taken place.

Over the centuries, some of the customs and traditions that surround this simple ceremony have taken on almost equal authority and importance. They are described here, in brief.

The processional. In a standard Hollywood wedding, the father escorts his daughter down the aisle and gives her away. The Jewish custom is very different. Both parents lead their children—sons as well as daughters—to the *huppah* and to marriage. No one is "given away." Indeed, the Jewish processional demonstrates how a marriage is a union of families, not just individuals.

In some communities, it is customary for a handheld *huppah,* carried on long poles, to precede the couple, and for members of the processional to light the way with candles. Perhaps the most common way of welcoming the bride and groom to the *huppah* is with music. In ancient times, the sounds of flutes greeted the bride and groom, and Yemenite brides are sometimes preceded by a group of singing women.

In America, string quartets, organs, choirs, soloists, or the guests themselves perform this customary honor.

Under the **huppah.** Before the 11th century, the Jewish wedding was composed of two distinct rituals separated by as much as a year. The first of these was betrothal or *kiddushin,* from the same root as the word *kadosh,* or holy. After betrothal, the bride and groom were considered legally wed, and a formal bill of divorce was necessary to dissolve the marriage. Even so, the marriage was not consummated until after the next ceremony, the nuptials or *nissuin,* a word derived from the verb *nasa,* which means to carry or lift, and may refer to the days when a bride was carried through the streets to her new home. The nuptials are not accomplished by words, but in a symbolic act of intimacy called *yichud.* Betrothal designates the bride and groom for each other only; nuptials give them to one another.

It has been nearly ten centuries since these two ceremonies were made into one, but Jewish weddings still show the seam where the two rituals were joined. The presence of two cups of wine, one for each ceremony, is a reminder of the time when two separate ceremonies were begun with *kiddush,* the prayer of sanctification recited over wine.

Circling. Just before the ceremony begins, it is customary for the bride to circle the groom, either three times or seven times, according to various customs. Circling is a magical means of protection, so the bride builds a wall against evil spirits by walking around the groom. The bride's circle has also been interpreted as a gesture that binds the groom to her.

A custom once abandoned because of its magical connotations and the implied subservience of the bride, the gesture has been reclaimed by many couples. In some ceremonies, both partners circle each other in turn, or simultaneously, holding hands.

Betrothal (**Kiddushin**). Most Jewish weddings begin with two introductions. The first one is addressed to the people gathered—especially the bride and groom.

B'ruchim haba'im b'Shem Adonai.

Welcome in the name of Adonai.

The second, a prayer asking for God's presence at and blessing of the marriage, is called the *"Mi Adir."*

Splendor is upon everything.
Blessing is upon everything.
May the One Who is full of this abundance
Bless this groom and bride.
                         TRANSLATION BY DEBRA CASH[14]

Next comes the recitation of *kiddush* over wine, which begins virtually all Jewish observances and celebrations. The betrothal blessing, which follows, was once recited a full year before the nuptials and includes a specific warning that betrothed couples are not sexually permitted to one another until after the next ritual takes place. Today, it is often translated loosely. For example:

"Praised are you Adonai, Ruler of the universe, who has made us holy through Your commandments and has commanded us concerning marriages that are forbidden and those that are permitted when carried out under the canopy and with the sacred wedding ceremonies."

The wine is drunk after this blessing is recited. In some communities the first cup of wine is shared with members of the immediate family.

The core of the ceremony follows, with the groom's giving and the bride's acceptance of a ring. As he gives her the ring, the groom recites the words that literally marry them. This part of the ceremony is called the *Haray aht* (from the first two words), and because it is essential that both people understand the meaning of these words, the phrase is recited both in Hebrew and English, or whatever language the couple knows best.

הֲרֵי אַתְּ מְקֻדֶּשֶׁת לִי, בְּטַבַּעַת זוֹ,
כְּדַת מֹשֶׁה וְיִשְׂרָאֵל.

Haray aht m'kudeshet li b'taba'at zo k'dat Moshe v'Yisrael

By this ring you are consecrated to me in accordance with the traditions/laws of Moses and Israel.

The bride is not legally required to say or do anything when she receives the ring. However, in many ceremonies today, the bride replies, either with a line from Songs of Songs ("I am my beloved's and my beloved is mine") or with the same words the groom addressed to her (adapted for gender), which in effect, equalizes the wedding ritual.

הֲרֵי אַתָּה מְקֻדָּשׁ לִי, בְּטַבַּעַת זוֹ,
כְּדַת מֹשֶׁה וְיִשְׂרָאֵל.

Haray ata m'kudash li b'taba'at zo k'dat Moshe v'Yisrael.

By this ring you are consecrated to me in accordance with the traditions/laws of Moses and Israel.

The Jewish wedding liturgy contains no wedding vows or "I do's." However, since an expression of intention is such a powerful image in American culture, and since couples often feel a need to say "yes" during the ceremony, many rabbis and couples add vows either just prior to or immediately following the ring ceremony. Most rabbis and cantors avoid the "To have and to hold, to honor and obey" formulas common to secular and Christian wedding ceremonies. Instead, vows or promises can be personal and specific. Sometimes they are taken from the *ketubah,* or are written by the bride and groom themselves.

The ring ceremony completes betrothal/*kiddushin.* At this juncture it has been customary, almost since the beginning of the combined betrothal-and-nuptials wedding in the 12th century, to make a clear separation, traditionally done by reading the *ketubah* or part of it; generally, this is also the time when the rabbi makes a short speech.

Sometimes, there are personal additions to the ceremony as well: songs, poems, or personal prayers by family members and friends.

Nuptials (nissuin). This ceremony consists of two elements: the seven wedding blessings, *sheva b'rachot,* and the seclusion of the bridal couple, called *yichud*.

While a wedding requires only two witnesses to be valid, a *minyan*—ten adult Jews—must be present for the seven blessings to be recited. Generally, the rabbi or cantor chants the wedding blessings, but there is also a long tradition of honoring special guests by asking them to read or chant one or more of them. In one Sephardic tradition, parents cover the bride and groom with a prayer shawl before the seven wedding blessings are recited.

Although the seven blessings constitute the longest part of the wedding liturgy, only the last two have anything to say about weddings or brides and grooms. Read as a whole, however, they situate the bride and groom within the entire span of Jewish time. The seven blessings mention the beginning of time in Eden when life was perfect, and the end of days when that perfection, or wholeness, will be restored. A fulcrum between the first and the last, every wedding becomes the embodiment of union. And since Judaism has no concept of individual redemption, the *huppah* provides the whole community with a glimpse into an unbroken, healed reality.

The Seven Blessings

You abound in blessings, Adonai our God, who creates the fruit of the vine.

You abound in Blessings, Adonai our God, You created all things for Your glory.

You abound in Blessings, Adonai our God, You created humanity.

You abound in Blessings, Adonai our God, You made humankind in Your image, after Your likeness, and You prepared for us a perpetual relationship. You abound in Blessings, Adonai our God, You created humanity.

May she who was barren rejoice when her children are united in her midst in joy. You abound in Blessings,

Adonai our God, who makes Zion rejoice with her
children.

You make these beloved companions greatly rejoice even
as You rejoice in Your creation in the Garden of Eden
as of old. You abound in Blessings, Adonai our God,
who makes the bridegroom and bride to rejoice.

You abound in Blessings, Adonai our God, who created
joy and gladness, bridegroom and bride, mirth and ex-
ultation, pleasure and delight, love, fellowship, peace
and friendship. Soon may there be heard in the cities
of Judah and in the streets of Jerusalem, the voice of
joy and gladness, the voice of the bridegroom and the
voice of the bride, the jubilant voice of bridegrooms
from their canopies and of youths from their feasts of
song. You abound in Blessings, Adonai, our God, You
make the bridegroom rejoice with the bride.

The seven blessings conclude the marriage service. Some rabbis
give the wedding sermon at this point, and others end with the official
secular pronouncement, "By the power vested in me by the state
of . . ." Most cantors and rabbis conclude with a benediction.

The broken glass. The shattering of a glass to mark the end of the
wedding is a practice that dates back to the writing of the Talmud and
has become one of the most kaleidoscopic of all Jewish wedding symbols. The broken glass is a joyous conclusion that encourages merriment
and rejoicing at the meal to follow. The wedding ritual can become
rather solemn, and the shattering gives permission for levity to break
out. There is an irony in this since, according to one explanation, the
glass-breaking may have originated at one particularly raucous wedding
party, as a way of calming things down.[15]

By the 14th century, the broken glass was generally interpreted as
a reminder of the destruction of the Temple in Jerusalem, and of the
fact that even at moments of personal joy, Jews remember that terrible
loss. This remains the dominant interpretation, although it is generally
broadened to include all of the losses suffered by the Jewish people,
and also the need for the repair and redemption of the whole world.

The breaking is not only a reminder of sorrow, but also an expression of hope for a future free from all violence.

There are other interpretations as well. A broken glass cannot be mended, likewise marriage is irrevocable, a transforming experience that leaves individuals forever changed. The fragility of glass also suggests the frailty of human relationships; even the strongest love is subject to disintegration. In this context, the glass is broken to "protect" the marriage with the wish that, "As this glass shatters, so may our marriage never break."

Loud noises are also an ageless method for frightening and appeasing demons, who, it was widely believed, were attracted to the beautiful and the fortunate—people like brides and grooms. In a more general way, the breaking glass hints at the intensity and release of sexual union (the classic Freudian interpretation of this custom is that it represents the breaking of the hymen), which is not only allowed married couples but required of them.

The sound of breaking glass signals the end of the ceremony. The silence that surrounded the *huppah* ends with an explosion. People exhale, shout *"Mazal tov!"* clap their hands, embrace, talk, and sing the traditional wedding song, *"Siman Tov u Mazal Tov"* ("a good sign and good luck" or "a good omen and a good star") as the couple departs.

Yichud. After they leave the *huppah,* bride and groom traditionally spend ten or fifteen minutes alone together. *Yichud,* or seclusion, is a custom that dates from ancient days when a groom would carry the bride off to his tent to consummate the marriage. Although consummation has not immediately followed the wedding ceremony for many centuries, these moments of private time have remained as a demonstration of the couple's new level of intimacy.

Yichud is a precious pause in a hectic day, an island of privacy and peace before the public celebration begins. It is a time for bride and groom to hold each other, to face each other, to let it all sink in. And since it is customary for a bride and groom to fast on the day of their wedding, *Yichud* also permits the couple to break the fast as husband and wife.

Celebrating. "Reception" is too formal a word for the celebration of a wedding. *Simcha* is more accurate; it means joy as well as the celebration of a joyous event, and the purpose of Jewish wedding parties is to increase the joy of the bride and groom. The Talmud says that anyone who enjoys a wedding feast but does nothing to rejoice the hearts of the bride and groom has transgressed against the "five voices": the voice of joy, the voice of gladness, the voice of the bridegroom, the voice of the bride, and the voice that praises God.

The meal that follows a Jewish wedding is a *seudat mitzvah,* a meal that fulfills a religious commandment to rejoice. At a wedding, everything that increases happiness—words of Torah, blessings, songs, dances, toasts, riddles, jokes, parodies, indeed anything that makes the bride and groom laugh—is considered a religious act, a way of praising God.

In order to ensure the *mitzvah* of entertaining the bride and groom, it is customary to have someone play the role of *badchan,* or "jester." The *badchan's* job is to act as master of ceremonies for the celebration by making toasts, telling jokes, and organizing and eliciting performances from other guests. Sentiment as well as foolishness play a part in this assignment, thus a *badchan* may start by reading a love poem, then lead the guests in a song or cheer, crown the "royal" couples with paper crowns, and lead the dancing.

One of the best known of all Jewish wedding customs is the moment at which the bride and groom are raised up on chairs and whirled around each other holding either end of a handkerchief. The custom may have originated as a way for the bride and groom to catch a glimpse of each other over the physical barrier that separates the rejoicing of the women from the men. But it may also be an echo of the privileges of royalty, who have been carried in chairs and on litters from earliest times.

The first year. Since biblical times, a couple is referred to as "bride and groom" for their entire first year together. That year begins with a week of parties. According to one tradition, a *minyan* of friends gather with the couple each night for a week, for a meal, blessings, and songs; this practice is also called *sheva brachot* for the "seven blessings" recited nightly in their honor.

The yearlong public recognition of the special status of brides and grooms is a way for the couple and the community to savor the joy and gladness of the wedding. The designations "husband" and "wife" only apply after the first anniversary.

Intermarriage. A fact of life for more than 50 percent of couples in North America, intermarriage is perceived by the Jewish community as a threat to the continuation of the Jewish people. It may be difficult to find a rabbi to officiate (or co-officiate) at a wedding where one of the partners is not a Jew, and it is difficult not to feel personally rejected by this rejection.

It is important to remember that a Jewish wedding has legal (*halachic*) standing when two witnesses see the bride accept a ring from the groom and hear him say, "With this ring you are consecrated to me according to the laws of Moses and Israel." A rabbi does not marry a bride and groom; they marry each other with these words and gestures. Thus, if one of the parties is not bound "by the laws of Moses and Israel," the marriage has no standing.

Another reason for rabbis' reluctance to participate in intermarriage ceremonies is that the major function of Jewish weddings is to establish Jewish homes and families. According to Jewish law, children born to non-Jewish mothers are not considered Jews. Demographic evidence seems to show that few children of mixed-faith marriages identify as Jews as adults.

The ongoing debate and hair-pulling over intermarriage tends to overwhelm and ignore the dilemmas facing many intermarrying couples. However, there are individuals in most cities and towns—among them counselors at Jewish agencies, rabbis, cantors, and marriage counselors—who are willing to listen to and discuss the ways intermarrying couples can affirm their connection to Judaism, beginning with the wedding. Many rabbis suggest that couples seek out a judge or justice of the peace to perform a ceremony that includes Jewish references and symbols.

Some rabbis and cantors will officiate at weddings between Jews and non-Jews, not as a matter of course but on a case-by-case basis. Such rabbis agree to officiate when the non-Jew has no religious affiliation and both people express a willingness to create a Jewish home. These interfaith weddings, which may not include all the liturgical elements of a traditional Jewish wedding, are seen as a way of encouraging couples to become members of the Jewish community, and to raise Jewish children. Alternately, Jewish tradition can be incorporated into a wedding ceremony by a justice of the peace.

Divorce. Divorce has always been a fact of Jewish life, which means that there has always been a body of law attached to this transition as well. While Jewish law permits a few instances where a wife can dissolve a marriage, it is by and large a male prerogative. According to traditional practice, a husband commissions a religious divorce decree called a *get,* which is formally delivered to his wife. If she accepts it, the divorce is then certified by a court of three rabbis, a *bet din.*

When a marriage ends, the altar sheds tears.

TALMUD

In fact, only a small fraction of divorced American Jews seek a Jewish divorce, and since between one-third and half of all Jewish marriages end in divorce, it seems clear that most people consider civil divorce sufficient, valid, and final. However, as rabbis have been called upon to do more family and marriage counseling, many people have expressed the need for a formal Jewish conclusion to a relationship that began with Jewish blessings. Thus, some liberal rabbis offer a Jewish divorce ritual to help give the parties a sense of resolution and closure.

Liberal *gittin* (the plural of *get*) and accompanying divorce rituals are egalitarian, reciprocal agreements, which can be initiated by either partner. The *get* may be written either in English or Hebrew, or in both languages. It may include specific clauses relevant to the couple that is divorcing, but the core of the document is a formal statement of dissolution. For example:

I, _____, son/daughter of _____ and
_____, of my own free will grant you this bill of
divorce. I release you from the contract which established our

*marriage. From this day onward you are not my husband/wife
and I am not your wife/husband. You belong to yourself and are
free to marry another.*[16]

Such a document can be executed in a rabbi's study or any place
agreeable to the parties involved, and is usually signed by the couple,
the rabbi, and, in some cases, by witnesses. In order to physically enact
the dissolution of the marriage covenant, a corner of the document
might be cut or ripped.

This form of divorce differs substantially from a traditional Jewish
divorce and may not be recognized as legitimate by Orthodox Jews.
Since divorce is one of the most divisive issues in the community, affecting remarriage and the Jewish status of children, this is an issue to
discuss fully with a rabbi.

---

*For everything there is a season
and a time for every purpose under heaven
a time to be born and a time to die
a time to plant and a time to uproot . . .
a time for tearing down and a time for building up
a time for weeping a time for laughing
a time for embracing and a time to refrain from embracing.*

ECCLESIASTES

CONVERSION AND ADOPTION

The Jewish community is changing. More people are choosing to become Jews than at any point since the beginning of the Common Era, and more Jews are creating and enlarging their families through adoption.

Of course, conversion and adoption are not new to Judaism. Both are honored in the biblical stories of Ruth and Moses, and the Talmud speaks of converts with admiration. "The convert is dearer to God than Israel. When the nation assembled at the foot of Mount Sinai, Israel would not have accepted the Torah without seeing the thunders and the lightning and the quaking mountains and hearing the sound of the *shofar*. Whereas the proselyte, without a single miracle, consecrated himself to the Holy One, praised be God, and puts upon himself the yoke of the kingdom of heaven. Can anyone be deemed more worthy of God's love?"[17]

For centuries, conversion was discouraged because it posed a danger to the Jewish community. Renouncing Christianity for Judaism was a capital offense, which extended to the Jews who welcomed any convert. Jewish attitudes toward converts and conversion was slow to change, and the tradition that required rabbis to rebuff people interested in converting three times is still in effect in some parts of the community.

However, for the most part, the door is wide open to those who choose Judaism. Where conversion for the purpose of marriage was once treated as suspect, today rabbis and Jewish organizations welcome and even solicit interest from non-Jews planning to marry or already married to Jewish spouses.

In large part, this change is a response to the fact that as many as half of all American Jews marry non-Jews, but it also reflects a recognition that, in the marketplace of ideas and in a world of seekers, Judaism is an intrinsically fulfilling way of life that appeals to people for many different reasons.

Whatever the circumstances, choosing Judaism is a profound and momentous decision, and one who takes this path with a full heart is called a *ger tzedek,* "righteous proselyte," from the same root as *tzadik,* which means a righteous or pious person.

For those interested in finding out whether Judaism is right for them, the liberal movements offer a variety of introduction-to-Judaism courses. These programs vary both in content and form, but they generally cover a broad range of subjects, including history, theology, Sabbath and holiday observance, Israel, the Holocaust, an introduction to the Hebrew alphabet, and some basic prayers. Students are also encouraged to practice making some Jewish choices, by attending worship services and trying out home observances.

Although classwork is important in these courses, the primary experience of study is done one-on-one with a rabbi. The content and duration of meetings with the rabbi depend upon his/her requirements and the student's level of interest and diligence. When a rabbi determines that a student is ready, s/he will explain and schedule the ritual elements of conversion.

Not all liberal rabbis require their students to undertake all of these rituals, but according to tradition, conversion requires *mikveh* (ritual immersion) for men and women, and circumcision or ritual circumcision (drawing one drop of blood from an already circumcised foreskin) for men. Converts also meet with a *bet din,* literally, "house of law," a Jewish court that usually consists of three rabbis, who examine the candidate about his/her her knowledge of Judaism, and, perhaps even more important, try to discern the sincerity and motivation for making this extraordinary choice. A public ceremony of acknowledgment is part of the process in some, though not all, congregations.

Mikveh entails immersion in a ritual bath (also called a *mikveh*), and the recitation of two short prayers. Like virtually all religious traditions, Judaism treats water as a symbol of rebirth and renewal; the *mikveh* represents the source of human life, the waters of the womb, and according to one legend, the "living water" of *mikveh* flows from the mystical source of all water and all life, the river whose source is in Eden.[18] Of all the rituals associated with conversion, *mikveh* is often counted the most powerful. For a tradition that is so intellectual, the pure physicality of being completely nude in a body of warm water is a revelatory and radical enactment of changing one's status from not-Jewish to Jewish.

The importance of *brit milah,* the covenant of circumcision, is discussed in the chapter on "Birth" and is best discussed with one's rabbi.

People get very nervous at the prospect of meeting with a *bet din;* however, it is best not to think of this as a pass-fail test for which you need to cram. Although it is not a pro forma meeting, rabbis will not bring unqualified candidates before a panel of their peers. As a rule, *batei din* tend to be far less concerned with dates and Hebrew fluency than they are with learning about a candidate's motivation for conversion and his/her commitment to basic Jewish concepts and practices.

Historically, conversion to Judaism was a strictly private event; indeed, focusing public attention on the process was seen as an abrogation of respect. Since a Jew-by-choice is a Jew, *period,* there was a sense that reminding people of the distinction was somewhat denigrating. Now that conversion is more common and widely seen as a source of strength and pride, the reluctance to go public has faded. Indeed, understanding conversion as a Jewish life-cycle event means that, like birth or marriage, it has an impact beyond the individual; every time a person becomes Jewish, s/he transforms at least one and usually two families. Furthermore, every new Jew changes the entire Jewish community forever.

With this in mind, celebrating conversion seems not only appropriate but necessary. Some people bring close friends or family members to the *mikveh* or to the meeting with the *bet din* for support, and then go to celebrate afterward, with gifts, a meal, or even an excursion to shop for a *tallit,* or a *kiddush* cup, or a *mezuzah.*

In some congregations, new Jews are acknowledged at a worship service, where they might be called up to the Torah for a blessing.

Some Jews-by-choice address a speech or *d'rash* to the congregation and then sponsor a festive meal afterward—a *seudat mitzvah*.

Conversion raises complex issues within the Jewish world about "who is a Jew" and the authenticity of liberal Jewish life. The Orthodox community and the state of Israel recognize only conversions performed under Orthodox auspices, a position that may have ramifications for the children of Jews converted by Reform, Reconstructionist, and Conservative rabbis. Becoming Jewish means taking part in this and many other contentious debates; it is essential to begin this discussion with a rabbi you know and trust.

Adoption

As adoption has become more common, it has become the source for public joy, celebration, and *nachas*—a word that conveys the intense pleasure parents take in their children. All kinds of Jews now complete their families through adoption, including single people who wish to become parents, gay and lesbian couples, and those who have difficulty conceiving. For people who struggled for a biological child, adoption may be a difficult choice, and experts stress the need to grieve for that loss before moving on. However an adoptive child arrives, his/her arrival always brings gratitude and awe at the fulfillment of a cherished dream.

Although there is little about adoption in the Bible or Talmud, Jewish law assumes that foster or adoptive parents bear all the responsibilities of biological parents, and the rabbis tended to favor "nurture" over "nature." "Those who raise a child are called its parents, and not the ones who conceived it."[19]

During the Second Commonwealth (538 B.C.E.–70 C.E.), Jews were known to rescue gentile children who were orphaned or outcast, and reared them as Jews.[20] But that was before Christian and Muslim laws made converting to Judaism a capital crime, and since then, Judaism has concerned itself, for the most part, with the needs of orphans born to Jewish parents. Nevertheless, the adoption of non-Jewish children happened often enough that Jewish law made the conversion of minors provisional until a child reached maturity. Thus, when a child reared as a Jew but born to a non-Jewish mother reached the age of 13, he or she was given the right to affirm or renounce his or her Jewishness.[21] In this way, Judaism always mandated full disclosure of children's adoptive status, an openness supported by psychologists and adoption experts today, when nearly all children adopted by Jews are born to non-Jewish parents.

Although adoption has become far more normative and accepted than ever before, Jewish adoptive parents do face challenges as they begin the process and as they navigate their family's unique path. However, there is no need to go it alone. Virtually every congregation includes some adoptive families who can provide guidance and support, as can staff at the local Jewish Family and Children's Services.

Stars of David, a nonprofit, national support network for Jewish adoptive parents, creates links to other families and professionals through local support groups; its members include Jews of all affiliations and beliefs, and it welcomes intermarried couples, single parents, gay and lesbian families, prospective parents, interracial couples with biological children, and grandparents (www.starsofdavid.org). Another support group is the Jewish Multiracial Network, which connects Jews of color and multiracial Jewish families for mutual education and advocacy (www.isabellafreedman.org/jmn/jmn_intro.shtml).

According to Jewish law, the adoption of a baby born to a non-Jewish mother requires a formal conversion, which entails ritual immersion, *mikveh*, for both girls and boys, and circumcision, *brit milah*, for boys. *Mikveh* is the only ritual requirement for the conversion of girls. Baby girls are named either immediately following immersion or sometime later in a synagogue or at home in a *brit bat* ceremony. An uncircumcised adopted male newborn is given a *brit milah* on the eighth day after birth, or as soon as possible. For a baby adopted at four months or older, circumcisions are generally done under anesthesia in a hospital, with both a physician and a *mohel* (ritual circumciser) in attendance. If a boy was circumcised without religious ceremony, a ritual is performed in which a *mohel* draws a drop of blood from the site of the circumcision and recites the appropriate blessings. (See "Birth" for more about ceremonies for both girls and boys.)

Liberal rabbis interpret Jewish law in different ways. The Reform and Reconstructionist movements recognize the Jewishness of children not born of a Jewish mother who are given a Jewish upbringing both in religious school and at home, who celebrate Jewish holidays, and who publicly identify with the Jewish people. Parents who are in the process of adopting the child of a non-Jewish mother are advised to discuss these issues with a rabbi.

For some parents, the special feelings of joy, gratitude, and awe inspired by adoption call out for an additional ritual, and have created Jewish ceremonies that speak to this need. Since there is no precedent for these rituals, their timing, location, and content are entirely determined by the parents, often with assistance from a member of the clergy.

DEATH AND MOURNING

The primary principle underlying every Jewish law, ritual, and custom having to do with death and mourning is *kavod*, a word that means "honor" and "respect." The Jewish approach to bereavement is also based on respect for the powerful emotions of loss.

Unlike the widespread American practice of encouraging mourners to hide or repress their grief and get back to work within a matter of days, Jewish law and custom create time for grief and provide a methodology for grieving. The specific laws regarding the mechanics of burial—even to selecting a coffin—give mourners guidance during a time when making necessary decisions is so difficult. And after the funeral, mourners are given a structure to encourage feeling their loss, and thus heal.

While this chapter provides an introduction to Jewish burial and mourning practices, when a death occurs it is crucial to seek out assistance and support from members of the Jewish community: rabbis, Jewish funeral home personnel, members of your synagogue or the deceased's congregation. It is relatively easy to find such help, even for people who are unfamiliar with Jewish burial and mourning practices. For those coping with a loss in a strange city, hospital chaplains—of all denominations—can direct you to local Jewish resources.

Burial

From the moment of death until a body is buried, Jewish law and custom are entirely focused upon honoring the deceased. Symbolic gestures of respect include closing the eyes and mouth, lighting a candle, and opening a window for the soul's release.

The traditional prayer said upon witnessing or hearing of a death is a statement of total acceptance.

בָּרוּךְ אַתָּה יְהוָה אֱלֹהֵנוּ מֶלֶךְ הָעוֹלָם
דַיַּן הָאֱמֶת.

Baruch Ata Adonai Eloheynu Melech Ha-olam Dayan Ha-emet.

Holy One of Blessing Your presence fills creation, You are the True Judge.

Jewish tradition stresses that the body should not be left alone from the time of death until burial, which takes place as quickly as possible. The custom is to have someone read Psalms beside the body, a duty that can be performed by family members, friends, or by synagogue members. Upon request, Jewish funeral homes will provide a ritual guardian, or *shomer*, for this purpose.

If a death occurs in a hospital, family members should inform the staff of their wishes regarding respectful treatment for the body. Autopsies are not automatically approved because they are seen as a desecration of the body and thus an abrogation of respect. However, since the rabbinic principle that saving a life takes precedence over nearly every other law, autopsies, organ donation, and donation of the body for medical research may be authorized with this *mitzvah* in mind. These issues are best discussed on a case-by-case basis with a rabbi.

While some people make their own burial and funeral arrangements in advance of their own deaths, family members are often left to make the decisions surrounding burial. Jewish tradition is quite specific in this regard: embalming, viewing the body, and holding a wake are considered disrespectful to the body and to the memory of the deceased.

Mahogany caskets with silver hardware may be purchased from a

Jewish funeral home for the price of a luxury car, but according to Jewish tradition, respect for the dead is expressed not by "burying money," but by contributing to *tzedakah*—especially to charities and causes that were important to the deceased. A plain wooden coffin is seen not as a sign of cheapness or disrespect, but as a way to promote the natural processes of death and decomposition, a way of returning to the earth, to the source of life.

A desire for simplicity can be expressed to representatives of a Jewish funeral home with a request for "the least expensive kosher casket available." In this context, "kosher" means "in conformance with Jewish law," in other words, made of plain wood by Jews for the purpose of burying a Jew.

According to Jewish tradition, the body is prepared for the grave with the utmost simplicity. No attempt is made to preserve or prettify the body, which is washed and cleaned according to specific regulations. All people, male and female, rich and poor, are buried alike, wearing nothing but plain, white shrouds, without pockets. Jews are sometimes buried wearing a *tallit;* however, the fringes on the prayer shawl will be cut, since they are reminders of the *mitzvot* or obligations that are binding only in this world.

These practices are known to Jewish funeral home personnel, however, it may be necessary to ask for them to be performed.

A baby enters the world with closed hands. A person leaves the world with open hands. The first says, "The world is mine." The second says, "I can take nothing with me."

ECCLESIASTES RABBAH

Cremation

Jewish law prohibits cremation, based on a belief that the natural process of the decomposition of the flesh shows respect for the body.

Jewish burial methods stress a return of the body to its source, unadulterated, reuniting one part of creation with the rest. Cremation is seen not only as a repudiation of the natural pace of "dust to dust," but as the desecration of that which was created in God's own image. In modern times, the Holocaust has cast cremation into an especially problematic light. The very word conjures up images of ovens, chimneys, and the charred remains of thousands of Jewish bodies that were never laid to rest.

In the past, someone who chose cremation was treated as one who had cut him or herself off from the Jewish community. In traditional circles, official forms of mourning are not permitted for one who has been cremated and survivors may not be permitted to say *Kaddish* or sit *shiva*; the response is rarely so drastic in liberal circles.

Despite the legal, historical, and emotional arguments against it, some Jews express wishes and even make arrangements for their own cremation, often with the intention of sparing their families the trauma and expense of a funeral. A loved one's wish to be cremated can create an emotional dilemma for family members who would prefer to follow a more traditional Jewish path. The son or daughter of a parent who wishes to be cremated is asked to choose between not obeying Mom or Dad's last wishes, and doing something that violates a belief or need as mourners. For many people, having a grave to visit is an important part of healing after a loss.

While it is difficult to speak about these matters with a healthy parent, sibling, or spouse, this is a conversation worth having. The counsel of a sympathetic rabbi can also be extremely helpful.

The Funeral

Jewish funerals take place as soon as possible following death, although they may be postponed until relatives and friends can arrive, as a way to honor the dead. Burials are not permitted on *Shabbat* and most holidays.

Funeral services usually take place at a funeral chapel or in a syna-

gogue, though they may also be conducted at a home or at the cemetery. While anyone knowledgeable about Jewish burial customs may
conduct a funeral, it is a function performed almost exclusively by rabbis and cantors. The decision about whether or how much family
members want to participate in the funeral service, reading a eulogy or
prayers, for example, is entirely personal and should be made in consultation with the officiating clergy member. Many families leave the
service entirely up to him or her.

Compared with the specific rules and requirements for treatment
of the body and burial, there are few liturgical requirements for a funeral service. Psalm 23, "The Lord is my shepherd," is nearly universal
and certain prayers are traditional, especially the *El Maley Rachamim*,
"God Filled with Compassion":

God who is full of compassion, dwelling on high
Grant perfect peace to the soul of _____.
May s/he rest under the wings of Your Presence
Holy and Pure, Who shines bright as the sky.
And may his/her place of rest be as Eden
We pledge tzedakah *for the sake of her/his memory.*
We pray that You comfort her/his soul in eternal life,
under the protection of your wings.
Adonai, You are our heritage.
May s/he rest in peace.
Amen.

The single most important element of the funeral is the eulogy, or
hesped, which honors the dead by speaking of him/her in personal
terms. Typically, eulogies are delivered by rabbis, who meet with mourners in advance of the funeral to talk about the one who has died and to
solicit stories and suggestions for his or her remarks. Sometimes members of the family write the eulogy or parts of it for the rabbi. In some
cases, a relative or close friend will deliver the *hesped* him/herself.

The tearing of a mourner's garments, called *k'riah*, is an ancient,
physical enactment of the feeling that the world has been torn apart.

K'riah is often done just prior to the funeral service, although it can take place at the graveside or when someone first hears of the death. For men, the tear is usually made on the lapel of a sport coat or jacket. Women will tear a sweater, dress, or blouse. It is also common to substitute a torn black ribbon, which is then worn on the lapel for the next seven days.

At the Cemetery

It is considered both an honor and duty to help bury the dead.[22] Carrying a loved one to his or her grave is seen as a way of paying loving tribute, which explains the custom of having those present participate in the burial by lifting a shovel of earth, a process usually initiated by close family members. Inviting participation in the physical act of burial makes it extremely difficult to deny the reality of death, which in turn makes it possible for grief and healing to begin. Those in attendance generally do not leave the grave until the body is placed into the earth and the coffin is covered with earth, although this, too, is a choice left to family members in consultation with clergy.

Even if there was a chapel or synagogue service, a brief service is also held at the graveside, consisting of Psalms and the recitation of the *Kaddish*. *Kaddish,* from the word *kadosh,* or "holy," is a familiar and much-recited prayer, which has several forms and purposes. Written in Aramaic, the Mourner's *Kaddish* does not mention death at all, but praises God for the gift of life. Sometime during the Middle Ages, this prayer became associated with mourning and today its recitation evokes the pain of loss and the consolation of remembrance for Jews everywhere. There is a legend that angels brought *Kaddish* to earth. The 20th century writer S. Y. Agnon imagined that the prayer was first recited by a human mourner to comfort God, Who is said to grieve over the deaths of men and women.[23]

The recitation of the *Kaddish* at the graveside begins the mourner's obligation to repeat this prayer during the formal period of mourning, and again at appropriate occasions, such as during a synagogue service.

Mourner's **Kaddish**

Exalted and hallowed be God's greatness
In this world of Your creation.
May Your will be fulfilled
And Your sovereignty revealed
In the days of our lifetime
And the life of the whole house of Israel
Speedily and soon.
And say, Amen.

May You be blessed forever,
Even to all eternity.
May You, most Holy One, be blessed,
Praised and honored, extolled and glorified,
Adored and exalted above all else.

Blessed are You,
Beyond all blessings and hymns, praises and consolations
That may be uttered in this world,
And say, Amen.

May peace abundant descend from heaven
With life for us and for all Israel,
And say Amen.

May God, Who makes peace on high,
Bring peace to all and to all Israel,
And say, Amen.[24]

Mourning

The Talmud says, "Do not comfort the bereaved with their dead still before them."[25] In other words, it is considered inappropriate to offer words of condolence to mourners until after the funeral. But from the moment the mourners turn away from the grave, the focus shifts from honoring the deceased to comforting the bereaved.

Jewish tradition designates official mourners very narrowly to include people who have one of seven relationships with the deceased: father, mother, son, daughter, sister, brother, spouse. The laws and customs regarding mourning apply only to this small and intimate circle. This does not mean that cousins, grandchildren, and friends are not bereaved or should not express their grief. However, limiting this circle also limits the time one must spend on the official acts of mourning, which call for some withdrawal from the world and from joyful activities.

Jewish mourning practices are arranged in a series of concentric circles that reflect and respond to the diminishing intensity of grief and concurrently reintroduce mourners to the world of the living.

Aninut, the period between death and burial, is a time filled with shock and even denial. Mourners essentially do nothing but prepare for the burial, funeral, and the mourning period to follow. They make necessary phone calls, meet with the rabbi, and spend time with only their closest friends. This is generally not a time when visitors call. *Aninut* ends with the sound of earth being thrown onto a coffin.

Shiva, from the Hebrew word for seven, refers to the seven days that include and follow the funeral.

This is the most intense period of formal mourning. People often refer to this period as "sitting *shiva,*" because of the custom of sitting on or near the floor, an ancient gesture of being struck low by grief. Funeral homes sometimes provide *shiva* benches or low stools. Some people remove cushions from couches and chairs and simply sit lower to the ground. Only mourners, not guests, sit on or near the ground.

Shiva usually begins as soon as the mourners return from the cemetery. Since *Shabbat* and certain holidays affect the counting of these seven days, a rabbi can help determine when this period begins and ends. There are circumstances where *shiva* is postponed or even canceled, and some people choose to observe *shiva* for fewer than seven days.

When the family returns from the grave, hands may be washed at the door—a symbolic acknowledgment of the sad duty just completed at the grave and an act of symbolical purification after contact with death. A seven-day candle, usually provided by the funeral home, is lit. Then, a meal is served. This *seudat havra'ah,* "meal of consolation," is a graphic reminder of the fact that life must go on, even for those with the taste of death in their mouths. It is considered a great act of kindness, a *mitzvah,* for friends to provide and serve this meal to mourners. Eggs and other round foods, such as lentils, are often served as a symbol of the continuing cycle of life, but this not a festive meal. It is eaten quietly.

During *shiva,* mourners refrain from business and pleasure. They do not go to work, or watch television, or even leave the house. Mirrors are covered to discourage vanity. Mourners often do not shave, wear new clothing, or have sex. Some Jews do not wear leather shoes, which were a sign of luxury in the ancient world.

The purpose of *shiva* is not to make mourners feel better or to cheer them up, but to encourage them to grieve. *Shiva* means taking time to remember and cry, to feel anger, loss, sorrow, panic—whatever feelings are present—fully and without distraction. For seven days, mourners speak of the life that is over; they tell and retell stories, weeping over their loss and also laughing at happy memories. Some families read and discuss books about Jewish mourning customs and books about death and dying during *shiva.*

If mourners are observing the custom of not going out during *shiva,* a daily *minyan* is held in the home so that the bereaved can say *Kaddish.* The task of organizing a *minyan* is often done by a synagogue committee set up for that purpose.

Paying a **shiva** *call.* Visiting a house of mourning is considered a *mitzvah,* a good and holy thing to do. Many rules of etiquette are suspended where people are sitting *shiva.* First of all, one enters without ringing the bell or knocking; mourners are not hosts, nor are guests emissaries of good cheer. People come not to console the mourner so much as to share his or her grief. There is very little that can be said at times like this, but words are not as important as the presence of friends. It is enough that people just come, in the words of the prophet Ezekiel, to "sigh in silence."[26]

Generally, it is inappropriate to send or bring flowers to a Jewish house of mourning. A donation to charity in the name of the deceased is considered a far more meaningful tribute. Gifts of food are traditional, but rather than bringing the sixth plate of brownies, it may be more helpful to call whoever is taking responsibility for food in the house to find out what is most needed: a dinner casserole, a trip to the grocery store, a few hours of babysitting for small children, or someone to take out-of-town relatives to the airport. These sorts of arrangements, among others, may be performed by a group of friends or a synagogue committee.

Shiva ends on the morning of the seventh day. The memorial candle is blown out in silence, and sometimes mourners go for a walk around the block, as a way of taking a first step back into the real world.

People used to bring food to a house of mourning. The wealthy brought it in baskets of silver and gold, the poor in baskets of willow twigs, and the poor felt ashamed. Therefore our sages taught that everyone should use baskets of willow twigs out of deference to the poor and in hopes of fostering unity.

TALMUD: MO'ED KATAN 27A–B

Shloshim refers to the 30 days following burial and includes the seven days of *shiva*. During *shloshim*—but after *shiva*—many of the prohibitions against work and pleasure are lifted. Mourners return to their jobs, sit on real chairs again, go out of their homes, wear perfume, have sex. However, some restrictions still apply, and some people will not attend parties or other social functions, or go to movies or listen to music. Some Jews go to services every day to say *Kaddish*; others attend services every *Shabbat* with the same intention. On the 30th day, all outward signs of mourning are suspended, except for those who have lost a parent, who may continue to abstain from attending joyful events and continue to say *Kaddish* regularly.

Avelut, literally "mourning," is the 12-month period observed only by people who have lost a parent. It is counted from the day of death and ends after 12 Hebrew months. Jewish law requires that mourners recite *Kaddish* daily for 11 months, which means attending a prayer service where a *minyan* will be present. Some liberal Jews observe *avelut* by saying *Kaddish* at *Shabbat* services every week for a year.

The year of mourning also mandates refraining from "joyous" activities, so some people do not go to movies or parties. This practice is a way of reminding oneself, "I am not finished mourning. I am not entirely ready to be soothed." As with many practices, the transformative power of accepting such restrictions becomes clear only in retrospect. If one, for example, chooses not to listen to music as a way of mourning a parent, the first notes one hears after such a year are extraordinarily powerful.

Another way to observe the year of remembering a loved one is with gifts to charities that were especially important to the deceased. Similarly, some people volunteer and work for a social service or religious organization, in memory of a parent.

Unveiling. The dedication of a gravestone takes place anytime between the end of *shloshim* and the anniversary of the death. A cloth or veil is removed from the grave marker in the presence of the immediate family and perhaps a few close friends. An unveiling is not a second funeral, and while rabbis sometimes officiate, it is common for family members to gather on their own to read Psalms or prayers, or just reminisce. There is no set ceremony for an unveiling.

Simplicity tends to be the rule regarding Jewish gravestones. As the Talmud puts it, "We need not make monuments for the righteous— their words serve as their memorial."[27] Generally, the marker includes the full Hebrew and secular name of the deceased, the Hebrew date of death, the secular calendar dates of birth and death. There are usually a few Hebrew letters on the stone, which stand for, "Here is buried," or "May his/her soul be bound up in the bonds of life." Jewish symbols, such as the six-pointed star of David, are commonly inscribed, as are quotes from scripture, or personal notes.

The custom of leaving pebbles on a gravestone may date back to biblical days when people were buried under piles of stones. Today, pebbles are usually left as tokens that people have been there to visit and remember.

Yarzeit *and* **yizkor.** *Yarzeit,* from the Yiddish for "a year's time," is the anniversary of a death. A special, 24-hour memorial candle is lit on the eve of the day of the death, and also on the eve of Yom Kippur. It is also traditional to light these candles at the end of the festivals of Sukkot, Passover, and Shavuot. No special prayer is associated with this act of remembrance. Sometimes, silence is the most eloquent tribute.

Yizkor, which means "remember," is the name of a prayer and also the name of the short memorial service that takes place four times every year: on Yom Kippur and at the end of Sukkot, Passover, and Shavuot. The prayer consists of a series of paragraphs that all begin with the words *"Yizkor Elohim,"* "May God remember." It is recited by anyone who has ever lost a parent, a child, a sibling, or a spouse. The Memorial Service also includes paragraphs for those mourning other relatives and friends.

As in all aspects of Jewish life, the traditions surrounding death present mourners with choices. One of the most common alterations in mourning practices among liberal Jews is the choice to attend a weekly rather than a daily *minyan* during the month of *shloshim* and the year of *avelut*. Liberal Jews also reinterpret *shiva* restrictions in ways that respect the spirit, if not the letter, of the law; for example, while the tradition is not to leave the house during *shiva* or listen to music, some people make long, meditative walks a regular part of those seven days, or spend time listening to music that was especially beloved by the deceased.

Traditional Jewish burial and mourning customs respond to two fundamental needs, practical and psychological. During the emotional crisis that follows a death, it is comforting to have a set of clear directions to follow. Equally compelling is the way that Jewish burial and mourning customs reflect modern insights into the healing processes of grief. The image of Jewish tradition as a mirror, a tool of reflection, seems particularly apt for mourners. During the week of *shiva*, the mirrors in a mourner's house are draped to encourage people to look within and also to seek answers from those gathered around them in sympathy. Recovering from the death of a loved one is never easy or speedy, and there is much evidence that people who do not fully explore the depth of their feelings immediately following a death, tend to suffer more depression and disorientation years later. The "schedule" of Jewish mourning customs insists both that people take time to fully grieve, and that they reenter the world of the living, step-by-step.

The memory of the righteous is a blessing.

PROVERBS 10:7

GLOSSARY

Afikomen From the Greek for "dessert." In the PASSOVER SEDER, the *afikomen* is the middle of three pieces of *matzah,* which is usually hidden and ransomed.

Akeda "Binding." The name given to the story of the binding of Isaac in Genesis 22.

Aleph-Bet Name of the Hebrew alphabet; also, its first two letters.

Aliyah "To go up." Receiving an *aliyah* means being called to the TORAH, usually to recite a blessing or to read. "Making *aliyah*" refers to moving to the land of Israel.

Aninut The name of the period between death and burial.

Apochrypha Fourteen writings, including the Books of Maccabees, not included in the final redaction of the Bible, but which are, nevertheless, important Jewish texts.

Aramaic An ancient Semitic language closely related to Hebrew. Aramaic was the lingua franca of the Middle East, and is the language spoken by Jesus. The GEMARA, the later part of the TALMUD, was written in Aramaic.

Ashkenazi Jews and Jewish culture of Eastern and Central Europe.

Aufruf The honor given to a couple called up to the TORAH on the SHABBAT before their wedding.

Avelut "Mourning"; an *avel* is a mourner. *Avelut* refers to the yearlong (or 11-month) observances for the death of a parent.

B.C.E. Before the Common Era. Jews avoid the Christian designation B.C., referring to Christ.

***Baal* Shem Tov** "Master of the Good Name." Israel ben Eliezer, the founder of HASIDISM, the 18th-century mystical revival movement.

***Baruch* ata Adonai** Words that begin Hebrew blessings, most commonly rendered in English as "Blessed art Thou, Lord our God, King of the Universe." This book contains many alternatives to that translation.

Bat Daughter, or "daughter of," as in *bat mitzvah*, which means "daughter of the commandment."

Bench, also **Benching** Yiddish for "to bless"/blessing.

Bible The Hebrew Bible, in Hebrew called TANACH, which includes the TORAH, Prophets, and Writings.

Bimah Raised platform in the synagogue from which the worship service is led.

Brit Covenant; also covenant ceremony. (*Bris* is the Yiddish form.)

***Brit* Bat** Covenant of the daughter—a term applied to ceremonies that welcome baby girls into the covenant of the Jewish people.

***Brit* Milah** The covenant of circumcision.

Cantor A Jewish professional trained in liturgical music who leads services or co-officiates with a rabbi.

Challah Braided loaf of egg bread, traditional for SHABBAT and holidays.

Cholent A hearty meat stew served for lunch on SHABBAT by Eastern European Jews.

Conservative A modern religious movement, developed in the United States during the 20th century as a more traditional response to modernity than offered by the Reform movement.

***Day* School** Jewish parochial school.

D'rash Religious insight, often based on a text from the TORAH.

***D'var* Torah** "Words of Torah"; an explication of a portion of the TO-RAH. (Plural: *divrei Torah*).

Daven (Yiddish) Pray.

Diaspora Exile. The dwelling of Jews outside the land of Israel.

Draydl (Yiddish) A spinning top used for playing a game of chance during the festival of HANNUKAH; in Hebrew, *sivivon*.

Erev Eve. "The evening of," especially a holiday. *"Erev Shabbat"* is Friday evening.

Etrog Citron. A lemonlike fruit, used in observance of the holiday of SUKKOT.

Flayshig (Yiddish) Meat food, which according to *kashrut,* may not be mixed with dairy products.

Gemara An expansive commentary on the MISHNA, completed around the fifth century C.E. The Gemara and the Mishna together are called the TALMUD.

***Gemilut* Hassadim** Acts of loving-kindness.

Get A Jewish divorce document.

Haggadah The book containing the liturgy of the PASSOVER SEDER.

Haimish (Yiddish) Homelike; giving one a sense of belonging.

Halachah Probably from the Hebrew for "to go"; the umbrella term for Jewish law.

Hametz Food prepared with leavening, which is not eaten during PASSOVER.

Hannukah The eight-day winter festival of lights.

Hannukiah A candelabra with nine branches used during the festival of Hannukah.

Haroset A mixture of apple, nuts, and wine used as a part of the PASS-OVER SEDER.

Hasidism Eighteenth-century mystical revival movement that infused the traditional ritual and liturgy with song, dance, and joy.

Havdalah Hebrew for separation. The Saturday evening ceremony that separates SHABBAT from the rest of the week.

Havurah "Fellowship." Small, participatory groups that meet for prayer, study, and celebration.

Hazzan Hebrew term for CANTOR.

Hazzanit Hebrew term for female CANTOR.

Hechsher A symbol on food packaging that means its contents are KOSHER and prepared under rabbinical supervision.

Hesped Eulogy.

Hiddur Mitzvah The beautification of a MITZVAH and the rabbinic precept of adorning or decorating something used for religious purposes.

Holocaust Remembrance Day Established in 1951 as a memorial to those who died in the Holocaust. Held on the 27th of the Hebrew month of Nissan—a week after PASSOVER.

Huppah Wedding canopy.

Israel Independence Day Spring celebration that corresponds to the fifth of Iyar in the Hebrew calendar marking the creation of the state of Israel in 1948.

K'riah The mourning custom of tearing a garment as a sign of grief.

Kaballah From the Hebrew for "receive" or "tradition." The tradition of Jewish mysticism.

Kaddish A prayer recognizing the supreme nature of God, which appears in many forms, written in Aramaic. Often appears in liturgy to separate parts of the service; the best-known form is associated with mourning.

Kallah Bride. Also, a name for SHABBAT.

Karpas A green vegetable used as a part of the PASSOVER SEDER.

Kashrut System of laws that govern what and how Jews eat.

Ketubah A Jewish marriage contract.

Kibbudim Ceremonial honors.

Kibbutz Israeli collective farm.

Kiddush Sanctification; the blessing over wine recited on SHABBAT, festivals, and other occasions.

Kohane/Kohen One who traces his/her line to the ancient priesthood.

Kosher Fit and proper; foods deemed fit for consumption according to the laws of KASHRUT.

Kvatter, Kvatterin Godfather, godmother.

Lulav A bouquet consisting of palm, willow, and myrtle branches, used during the holiday of SUKKOT.

Ma'asim Tovim Good deeds, righteous actions.

Magid From the Hebrew for "telling"; the telling of the story of PASSOVER at the SEDER.

Maimonides Rabbi Moshe ben Maimon, also known as the Rambam, lived from 1135 to 1204 in Spain and North Africa. One of the great scholars and philosophers in Jewish history, he is best known for two books: the *Mishneh Torah* and *The Guide for the Perplexed*.

Martin Buber An Austrian-Jewish philosopher, educator, and theologian (1878–1965), who wrote about religious consciousness, interpersonal relations, and community.

Maven (Yiddish) An expert.

Mazel Tov "Good luck." In daily use, it means "Congratulations."

Menorah A candelabra. The term is often used to refer to the HANNUKAH *menorah*, the HANNUKIAH.

Mensch Person; an honorable, decent person. *Menschen* is the plural. *Menschlichkeit* means "person-ness," the quality of being a *mensch*.

Mesader Kiddushin One who "orders" or leads a wedding ceremony.

Mezuzah A small, decorative container, affixed to the doorways of and inside Jewish homes, which holds a handwritten parchment scroll of the first two paragraphs of the SHEMA.

Midrash A body of literature consisting of imaginative exposition of and stories based on the BIBLE.

Mikdash Ma'at A little sanctuary; a Jewish home.

Mikveh Ritual bath.

Milah Circumcision; *brit milah* is the covenant of circumcision.

Milchig (Yiddish) Dairy foods, which, according to the laws of KASHRUT, may not be mixed with meat products.

Minhag Custom (plural: *minhagim*).

Minyan A prayer quorum of ten adult Jews needed for certain worship services and rituals.

Mishna The first part of the TALMUD, composed of six "orders" of debate and law regarding everything from agriculture to marriage.

Mitzvah A commanded deed. A fundamental Jewish concept about the obligation of the individual to perform commandments put forth in the TORAH and elaborated by Jewish law. (Plural: *mitzvot*).

Mohel One who is trained in the rituals and procedures of BRIT MILAH, circumcision.

Motzi Blessing over bread recited before meals.

Nachas (Yiddish) Special joy derived from the achievements of one's children.

Niggun A wordless prayerlike melody.

Oneg Shabbat "Joy of the Sabbath." The informal gathering for conversation and community after Friday night Sabbath services.

Orthodox The modern Orthodox movement developed in the 19th century in response to the Enlightenment and Reform Judaism.

Parasha The weekly TORAH portion or reading.

Pareve Neutral foods, including all fruits and vegetables, which can be eaten with either dairy or meat meals.

Passover The spring holiday recalling the exodus from Egypt. In Hebrew, PESACH.

Pesach PASSOVER.

Pharisees Jews who lived during the period of the Second Temple (536 B.C.E.–70 C.E.), and the progenitors of what is known as rabbinic or traditional Judaism.

Purim A late winter holiday based on the Book of Esther.

Pushke A coin box used to collect money for TZEDAKAH or charity.

Rabbi Teacher. Today, "rabbi" refers to an ordained member of the clergy. "The rabbis" refers to the men who codified the TALMUD.

Reconstructionist Religious movement, begun in the United States in the 20th century by Mordecai Kaplan. It views Judaism as an evolving religious civilization, which is constantly being "reconstructed."

Reform A movement, begun in 19th century Germany, that sought to reconcile Jewish tradition with modernity.

Responsa An ongoing body of rabbinic legal literature containing decisions and opinion about contemporary questions.

Rosh Hodesh First day of every lunar month; the New Month, a semiholiday.

Rosh Hashanah The New Year—the head of the Jewish year when the SHOFAR is sounded.

Safed A town in northern Israel (pronounced S'fat in Hebrew) associated with Jewish mysticism.

Sandek Godfather; the one who holds the baby during the circumcision. *Sandeket,* godmother, is the feminine form.

Seder Hebrew for "order"; usually refers to the talking-feast of PASSOVER.

Seudat Mitzvah A commanded meal; the festive celebration of a milestone.

Shalom Peace; also a term of greeting.

Shalom Bayit Peace of the home.

Sh'chitah Laws governing the KOSHER slaughter of animals.

Shabbat Sabbath. In Yiddish, *Shabbos* or *Shabbes.*

Shamash Usually refers to the "helper" candle used to light the other eight candles on the HANNUKIAH.

Shavuot A holiday that takes place seven weeks after PASSOVER and celebrates the harvest of first fruits and the giving of the TORAH on Mount Sinai.

Shechinah God's feminine attributes, sometimes referred to metaphorically as a separate entity.

Shehecheyanu A common prayer of thanksgiving for new blessings.

Shloshim The month following the burial of a loved one—a period during which mourners attend services and refrain from joyful activities.

Shema The most-often-recited Jewish prayer that declares God's unity.

Sheva B'rachot Seven marriage blessings.

Shiva From the Hebrew word for "seven", the seven-day mourning period that begins on the day of a funeral.

Shmooz (Yiddish) To chat.

Shochet A person who is familiar with the laws of SH'CHITAH and performs ritual KOSHER slaughter.

Shofar A ram's horn, an instrument blown at ROSH HASHANAH.

Shtetl Small town, especially one inhabited by ASHKENAZI Jews before the Holocaust.

Shul Synagogue.

Siddur Daily and SHABBAT prayer book.

Simcha Joy; a celebration of joy or party.

Simchat **Torah** The joyful holiday at the end of SUKKOT, marking the end and beginning of the annual TORAH reading cycle.

Siman **Tov u'Mazal Tov** "A good sign and good luck"; a song of good wishes sung at celebrations.

Sukkah A temporary hut or booth erected for the holiday of SUKKOT.

Sukkot The fall harvest festival.

Tallis/Tallit Prayer shawl.

Talmud Collection of rabbinic thought and laws, codified between 200 B.C.E. and 500 C.E.

The **Temple** The first building associated with Jewish worship is referred to as "the Temple." Built in Jerusalem by King Solomon beginning in 868 B.C.E., the rituals of animal sacrifice described in the book of Leviticus took place there. In ancient times, Israelites traveled from all over the land for festivals and holidays celebrated there.

Tikkun **Olam** Repairing the world; taking responsibility for correcting the damage done by people to one another and to the planet.

Tisha **B'Av** The ninth day of the Hebrew month of Av, a day of mourning and fasting recalling the destruction of the Temples in Jerusalem and other tragedies that have befallen the Jewish people.

Torah First five books of the Hebrew BIBLE, portions of which are read every SHABBAT. Also, Jewish learning in general.

Trafe The opposite of KOSHER. Literally, "torn."

Tu B'Shvat The 15th of the Hebrew month of Shvat, the new year for trees.

Tzedakah Righteous giving, charity.

Ulpan An intensive course in conversational Hebrew.

Yahrzeit Yiddish for "a year's time." The anniversary of a death.

Yeshiva An academy of Jewish learning.

Yichus (Yiddish) Family status; also pride in family members' achievements.

Yiddish Language spoken by ASHKENAZI Jews, a combination of early German and Hebrew.

Yizkor A memorial service recited on YOM KIPPUR, SUKKOT, PESACH, and SHAVUOT.

YMHA/YWCA Young Men's Hebrew Association/Young Women's Hebrew Association; the Jewish versions of the YM/YWCA.

Yom Kippur Day of Atonement, the holiest of the High Holidays.

Zohar A mystical commentary on the TORAH and several other biblical books.

TIMELINE

These dates are provided to give historical context to places, events, and names that appear in *Living a Jewish Life*.

Secular Calendar		Hebrew Calendar
	Before Common Era	
3761	Creation of Adam, the sixth day of Creation	1
2704	Birth of Noah	56
2104	The Flood	1656
1812	Birth of Abraham	1948
1764	Tower of Babel	1996
1742	Covenant between God and Abraham	2018
1712	Birth of Isaac	2048
1675	Binding of Isaac	2085
1652	Births of Jacob and Esau	2108
1589	Isaac blesses Jacob	2171
1568	Jacob marries Rachel and Leah	2192
1544	Joseph sold by his brothers	2216
1522	Jacob and his family move to Egypt	2238
1505	Death of Jacob	2255
1451	Death of Joseph	2309
1428	Beginning of slavery in Egypt	2332
1392	Birth of Moses	2368
1312	Exodus from Egypt, giving of the Torah	2448
1272	Death of Moses	2488
1106	The story of Deborah	2654
1000	First Temple completed	2648
950	The story of Samson	2810
879	Samuel anoints Saul as king of Israel	2881

Secular Calendar		Hebrew Calendar
877	Samuel anoints David as king of Israel	2883
836	King Solomon begins his rule	2924
796	Split of the kingdom of Israel	2964
586	First Temple destroyed, Babylonian exile begins	3174
356	The story of Purim	3404
352	Construction of the Second Temple	3408
312	Alexander the Great conquers Persia, beginning of Greek rule	3448
139	Miracle of Hannukah, kingdom of the Hasmoneans begins	3622
36	Hasmonean dynasty ends, Herod begins his rule	3724
32	Leadership of Rabbi Hillel begins	3728
18	Herod begins Temple reconstruction	3748
Common Era		
68	Second Temple destroyed by the Romans	3828
73	Fall of Masada	3833
80	Leadership of Rabbi Akiva begins	3840
93	Josephus completes *Jewish Antiquities*	3853
120	Rebellion of Bar Kochba	3880
219	Mishna compiled	3979
306	Constantine makes Christianity the state religion of the Roman Empire	4066
325	Council of Nicea, Christians begin to celebrate Sabbath on Sunday	4075
358	The permanent Jewish calendar is instituted	4118
368	Jerusalem Talmud compiled	4128
476	Fall of Rome, beginning of Byzantine rule over Israel	4236
500	Babylonian Talmud completed	4260
622	Hegira—Muhammad flees from Mecca to Medina	4382
638	Islamic conquest of Jerusalem	4398

Secular Calendar		Hebrew Calendar
814	Death of Charlemagne	4574
1040	Birth of Rashi, biblical and Talmudic commentator	4800
1096	First Crusade	4856
1131	Birth of Maimonides, Rambam	4891
1144	First Blood Libel against the Jews in England	4904
1215	Magna Carta	4975
1290	Expulsion of the Jews from England	5050
1305	Death of Rav Moshe DeLeon, author of the Zohar	5065
1337	Beginning of the Hundred Years War	5097
1348	The Black Death	5108
1394	Expulsion of the Jews from France	5155
1480	Inquisition established in Spain	5240
1492	Expulsion of the Jews from Spain; Columbus discovers America	5252
1516	Ottoman Turks conquer Palestine	5276
1544	Martin Luther, Protestant Reformation	5304
1569	Rav Isaac Luria comes to Safed to teach Jewish Mysticism (Kaballah)	5329
1582	Gregorian Calendar established	5342
1620	*Mayflower* arrives at Plymouth Rock	5380
1648	Chmelnitzki massacres in Poland; end of Thirty Years War	5408
1654	First Jewish settlement in North America (New Amsterdam)	5414
1760	Death of Baal Shem Tov, the founder of Hasidism	5520
1776	American Revolution	5536
1789	Beginning of the French Revolution	5549
1791	French National Assembly grants full civil rights to Jews Pale of Settlement established in Russia	5551

Secular Calendar		Hebrew Calendar
1804	Napoléon crowned Emperor	5564
1806	End of Holy Roman Empire	5566
1815	German Jewish immigration to America begins; Waterloo	5575
1844	First meeting of German Reform leaders	5604
1861	American Civil War	5612
1881	Czar Alexander II is assassinated; Pogroms against the Jews	5641
1882	Mass immigration of Russian Jews to America begins	5642
1885	Pittsburgh Platform (Statement by American Reform Movement)	5645
1894	Dreyfus trial (France)	5654
1897	First Zionist Congress (Basel)	5657
1902	Conservative Movement emerges in U.S.	5662
1914	World War I begins	5674
1917	British defeat Turks, capture Jerusalem; Balfour Declaration	5677
1920	England receives Mandate over Palestine	5680
1933	Hitler comes to power	5693
1938	Kristallnacht riot against Jews in Germany	5698
1939	World War II begins	5699
1947	Dead Sea Scrolls first discovered	5707
1948	State of Israel is declared	5708
1967	Six Day War. Reunification of Jerusalem	5727
1972	First woman rabbi ordained by Reform Movement	5732
1976	Entebbe Rescue	5736
1978	Camp David Peace Accord	5738
1979	Israeli-Egyptian Peace Treaty	5739
1984	Operation Moses, rescue of Ethiopian Jews	5744
1987	Intifada, Arab uprising in Israel begins	5748
1988	Elie Wiesel receives Nobel Peace Prize	5749
1989	Berlin Wall comes down	5750

Secular Calendar		Hebrew Calendar
1991	Operation Solomon: Rescue of remainder of Ethiopian Jews in massive 24-hour airlift	5751
1993	Israel and PLO sign Oslo Accords	5753
1994	Israel and Jordan sign peace treaty; Arafat, Rabin, and Peres share Nobel Peace Prize	5754
1995	Israeli Prime Minister Rabin assassinated	5755
2000	Israel withdraws from Lebanon; second Intifada begins	5760
2001	Terrorist attacks on the United States	5761
2005	Israel withdraws military personnel and settlers from Gaza Strip	5765

Sources: *Encyclopedia Judaica*; *Seder Hadorot* by Rabbi Yechiel Heilpern; *Toldot Am Olam* by Rabbi Shlomo Rottenberg, as compiled by Tzvi Black.

FURTHER READING

SHABBAT

Heschel, Rabbi Abraham Joshua. *The Sabbath: Its Meaning for Modern Man*. Shambhala, 2003.

For children

Schwartz, Amy. *Mrs. Moskowitz and the Sabbath Candlesticks*. Jewish Publication Society, 1991.

Hirch, Marilyn. *Joseph Who Loved the Sabbath*. VikingPenguin Puffin Books, 1988.

Schwartz, Howard. *The Sabbath Lion: A Jewish Folktale from Algeria*. HarperTrophy, 1996.

TZEDAKAH

Heschel, Rabbi A. J. *The Prophets*. Harper Perennial Classics, 2001.

Siegel, Danny. Books for adults and children including, *Gym Shoes and Irises: Personalized Tzedakah*. 1987. *Munbaz II and Other Mitzvah Heroes*. 1988. http://www.ziv.org/danny_sbooks.html.

For children

Zellman, Sella, and Brigitte Evans. *The Man with Many Telephones*. United Synagogue Book Service, 1987.

KASHRUT

Dresner, Samuel H. *The Jewish Dietary Laws*. United Synagogue Book Service, 1980.

Greenberg, Blu. *How to Run a Traditional Jewish Household*. Jason Aronson, 1997.

Schwarts, Richard H. *Judaism and Vegetarianism*. Lantern Books, 2001.

COMMUNITY

Borowitz, Eugene, and Naomi Patz. *Explaining Reform Judaism*. Behrman House, 1985.

Kaplan, Dana Evan. *American Reform Judaism*. Rutgers University Press, 2003.

Dorff, Elliot. *Conservative Judaism: Our Ancestors to Our Descenders*. United Synagogue of America, 1977.

Alpert, Rebecca, and Jacob Staub. *Exploring Judaism: A Reconstructionist Approach*. Reconstructionist Press, 2000.

ISRAEL AND TRAVEL

Hoffman, Rabbi Lawrence A. *Israel: A Spiritual Travel Guide: A Companion for the Modern Jewish Pilgrim*. Jewish Lights Publishing, 2005.

Tigay, Alan M., ed. *The Jewish Traveler*. Jason Aronson, 1994.

The Jewish Travel Guide 2006: International Edition. Vallentine Mitchell, 2006.

For children

Burstein, Chaya. *A Kid's Catalog of Israel*. Jewish Publication Society, 1998. School-age.

Carmi, Giora. *And Shira Imagined*. Jewish Publication Society, 1988. Preschool–2.

Sofer, Barbara. *Kids Love Israel, Israel Loves Kids*. Kar-Ben, 1995. For families.

THE HOLIDAY CYCLE

Greenberg, Irving. *The Jewish Way: Living The Jewish Holidays*. Jason Aronson, 1998.

Nathan, Joan. *The Jewish Holiday Kitchen: 250 Recipes from Around the World to Make Your Celebrations Special*. Schocken Books, 1998.

Strassfeld, Michael. *Jewish Holidays*. Collins, 1993.

Waskow, Arthur. *Seasons of Our Joy*. Beacon Press, 1991.

For children

Sofer, Barbara. *The Holiday Adventures of Achbar*. Kar-Ben Copies, Inc., 1983. For young readers.

Cashman, Greer Fay. *Jewish Days and Holidays*. Adama Books, 1988. Grade 4 and up.

ROSH HASHANAH AND YOM KIPPUR

Agnon, S. Y. *Days of Awe*. Schocken Books, 1995.

Reimer, Gail Twersky, and Judith Kates. *Beginning Anew: A Woman's Companion to the High Holy Days*. Touchstone, 1997.

Speigel, Shalom. *The Last Trial: On the Legends and Lore of the Command to Abraham to Offer Isaac as a Sacrifice: The Akedah 1899–1984*. Jewish Lights Publishing, 1993.

For children

Singer, Marilyn. *Minnie's Yom Kippur Birthday*. HarperCollins Children's Books, 1989.

Weilerstein, Sadie Rose. *K'Tonton's Yom Kippur Kitten*. Jewish Publication Society, 1995.

HANNUKAH

Singer, Isaac Bashevis. *The Power of Light*. Farrar, Straus and Giroux/ Sunburst Edition, 1990.

For children

Chaiken, Miriam. *Alexandra's Scroll: The Story of the First Hanukkah*. Henry Holt and Co., 2002.

Erlich, Amy. *The Story of Hannukah*. Dial, 1989.

Hirsh, Marilyn. *Potato Pancakes All Around*. Jewish Publication Society, 1982.

Koons, Jon. *A Confused Hanukkah: An Original Story of Chelm*. Dutton Juvenile, 2004.

Rouss, Sylvia. *Sammy Spider's First Hanukkah*. Kar-Ben Publishing, 1993.

TU B'SHVAT

Appelman, Harlene Winnick. *A Seder for Tu B'Shevat*. Kar-Ben Copies, 1984. For families with children.

Fisher, Adam. *Seder Tu BiShevat; The Festival of the Trees*. Central Conference of American Rabbis, 1989.

Waskow, Arthur. *Trees, Earth, and Torah: A Tu B'Shvat Anthology*. Jewish Publication Society, 1999.

PURIM

Novak, William, and Moshe Waldoks. *The Big Book of Jewish Humor*. Harper & Row, 1981.

For children

Feder, Harriet K. *It Happened in ShuShan*. Kar-Ben Copies, 1988.

Rouss, Sylvia. *Sammy Spider's First Purim*. Kar-Ben Publishing, 2000.

Simpson, Lesley. *The Purim Surprise*. Kar-Ben Publishing, 2004.

PASSOVER

Haggadot

Passover Haggadah; The Feast of Freedom. United Synagogue Book Service, 1982. Conservative movement publication.

Levitt, Joy, and Michael Strassfeld. *A Night of Questions: A Passover Haggadah*. Reconstructionist Press, 2000.

A Passover Haggadah. Central Conference of American Rabbis, 1994. Reform movement publication.

Stern, Chaim. *Gates of Freedom, A Passover Haggadah*. Behrman House Publishing, 1998.

The Shalom Seders: Three Haggadahs. Compiled by New Jewish Agenda. Adama Books, 1984.

Kalechofsky, Roberta. *Haggadah for the Liberated Lamb*. Micah Press, 1988. Vegetarian Passover handbook.

A Sephardic Passover Haggadah. Prepared by Rabbi Marc D. Angel. Ktav Publishing, 1988.

Silberman, Shoshana. *A Family Haggadah II*. Kar-Ben Publishing, 1997.

Books

Arnow, David. *Creating Lively Passover Seders: An Interactive Sourcebook of Tales, Texts and Activities.* Jewish Lights Publishing, 2004.

Sarna, Nahum. *Exploring Exodus: The Origins of Biblical Israel.* Schocken Books, 1996.

Walzer, Michael. *Exodus and Revolution.* Basic Books, 1986.

For children

Cohen, Barbara. *The Carp in the Bathtub.* Kar-Ben, 1987.

Miller, Deborah Uchill. *Only Nine Chairs: A Tall Tale for Passover.* Kar-Ben, 1982.

Rouss, Sylvia. *Sammy Spider's First Passover.* Kar-Ben, 1995.

Schwartz, Lynn Sharon. *The Four Questions.* Puffin, 1994.

BIRTH

Cohen, Debra Nussbaum. *Celebrating Your New Jewish Daughter: Creating Jewish Ways to Welcome Baby Girls into the Covenant.* Jewish Lights Publishing, 2001.

Diamant, Anita. *The New Jewish Baby Book.* Jewish Lights Publishing, 2005.

Kolatch, Alfred, J. *The Comprehensive Dictionary of English and Hebrew First Names.* Jonathan David Publishers, 2004.

Kunin, Samuel A., M.D. *Circumcision: Its Place in Judaism, Past and Present.* Isaac Nathan Publishing, 1998.

BAR/BAT MITZVAH

Davis, Judith. *Whose Bar/Bat Mitzvah Is This, Anyway?: A Guide for Parents through a Family Rite of Passage.* St. Martin's Press, 1998.

Salkin, Rabbi Jeffrey K. *Putting God on the Guest List: How to Reclaim the Spiritual Meaning of Your Child's Bar/Bat Mitzvah.* Jewish Lights Publishing, 2005.

Siegel, Danny. *The Bar and Bat Mitzvah Book: A Practical Guide for Changing the World through Your Simcha.* http://www.ziv.org/danny_sbooks.html.

MARRIAGE

Diamant, Anita. *The New Jewish Wedding.* Simon & Schuster, 2001.

CONVERSION/ADOPTION/NEW TRADITIONS

Diamant, Anita. *Choosing a Jewish Life: A Handbook for People Converting to Judaism and for Their Families and Friends.* Schocken Books, 1997.

Orenstein, Rabbi Deborah. *Lifecycles: Jewish Women on Life Passages and Personal Milestones.* Jewish Lights Publishing, 1998.

DEATH AND MOURNING

Diamant, Anita. *Saying Kaddish: How to Care for the Dying, Bury the Dead, and Mourn as a Jew.* Schocken Books, 1998.

Grollman, Earl A. *Talking about Death: A Dialogue between Parent and Child.* Beacon Press, 1991.

Reimer, Rabbi Jack, and Nathaniel Stampfer. *So That Your Values Live On: Ethical Wills and How to Prepare Them.* Jewish Lights Publishing, 1994.

JEWISH PARENTING

Abramowitz, Yosef, and Susan Silverman. *Jewish Family and Life: Traditions, Holidays, and Values for Today's Parents and Children.* St. Martin's Press, 1997.

Diamant, Anita, with Karen Kushner. *How to Be a Jewish Parent: A Practical Handbook for Family Life.* Schocken Books, 2000.

Fuchs-Kreimer, Rabbi Nancy. *Parenting as a Spiritual Journey: Deepening Ordinary and Extraordinary Events into Sacred Occasions.* Jewish Lights Publishing, 1998.

Friedland, Ronnie, and Edmund Case. *The Guide to Jewish Interfaith Family Life: An Interfaithfamily.com Handbook.* Jewish Lights Publishing, 2001.

Mogul, Wendy. *The Blessing of a Skinned Knee: Using Jewish Teachings to Raise Self-Reliant Children.* Penguin Compass, 2001.

ACKNOWLEDGMENTS

This book is a collaboration between a writer and a teacher; it began in an adult education class taught at Congregation Beth El of the Sudbury River Valley, in Sudbury, Massachusetts. Howard Cooper, then director of education, was teaching a course titled "Making a Jewish Home Now That You Have a Family of Your Own," which offered people the opportunity to peruse the menu of Jewish practice: "prior knowledge or experience not necessary." Howard, who holds an undergraduate degree in Judaic Studies and a master's degree in education, is the kind of teacher who inspires students with his obvious love of his subject. A silly sense of humor doesn't hurt either. His approach to Jewish tradition, which I share, suggested this collaboration and this book.

The process of creating *Living a Jewish Life* began with and regularly returned to long conversations between us, many of them held at an ice cream shop halfway between our respective homes. Over endless cups of watery coffee and a few sundaes, we hammered out the contents of each chapter, discussed philosophy and vocabulary, and worried about what to leave out.

Howard collected source material from a variety of Jewish texts, as well as anecdotes and bibliographies, which became the backbone of my own research. He also drew heavily upon his own personal experience. Some of the original material in this book came from a questionnaire we sent to people around the country, asking about their holiday and *Shabbat* observance. More information and ideas came from conversations with colleagues, teachers, friends, and acquaintances. We polled many rabbis, but also listened carefully to the voices of laypeople—the people we imagined as readers, people with varied levels of Jewish knowledge, who are interested in making more meaningful Jewish choices.

Three people, extraordinarily generous with their time, read every chapter: Rabbi Neil Cooper (Howard's brother) was our "on call" rabbi. Leslie Tuttle, a student of Judaism who was raising two Jewish children, pointed out places that needed better definition or further amplification. Rabbi Barbara Penzner's contributions were practical, creative, spiritual, learned, loving, and always on target.

Many others read, criticized, and suggested changes in one or more chapters, including: Fran Addison and Rob Gogan, Marsha Feder, Rabbi Lawrence Kushner, Joan Kaye, Billy Mencow, Rabbi Nehemia Polen, Jenique Radin, Brian Rosman, Danny Siegel, Larry Sternberg, Rabbi Gerald Teller, Moshe Waldoks, and Jonathan Woocher.

The following people answered our questionnaire, made comments on specific chapters, engaged in helpful conversations, or provided other kinds of support during the research and writing of this book, for which we are most grateful: Velda Adams, Rabbi Herman Blumberg, Rabbi Lester Bronstein, Debra Cash, Betsy Cohen, Rabbi Richard Israel (whose memory is a blessing), Sherry Israel, Jay Fialkov, Lev Friedman, Rabbi Janice Garfunkel, Ora Gladstone, Mitchell Silver, Rabbi Devorah Jacobson, Rabbi Stuart Weinberg Gershon, Karen Kushner, Maddy and Peter Langmann, Jeff Liberman and Joni Levy Liberman, Cantor Riki Lippitz, Rabbi Norman Mendel, Joel Rosenberg, Marion Ross, Arthur Samuelson, Rabbi John Schechter, Ella Taylor, Craig Taubman, Scott Tepper, Betsy Platkin-Teutsch, William Whalen, Susan and Marty Wieskoff, and the office staff at Temple Emmanuel in Worcester, Massachusetts.

Howard Cooper also wishes to thank Rabbi Gerald Teller, a lifelong teacher and mentor. He also acknowledges the support of his family: siblings par excellence, Marsha and Bob Feder, and Neil and Lori Cooper; wonderful stepchildren, Hanan and Gavriella; daughter, Hannah Evy, in whose eyes I see the bright light of the future, and the warm glow of the past; and his wife, best friend, and lover, Ellen, who made me whole, keeps me laughing, and helped me become a *mensch.*

I would also like to thank my family and friends for their support and patience during the writing of this project, especially my husband, the one and only Jim Ball.

Finally, Rabbi Lawrence Kushner has had the most profound influence on both Howard and me—as Jews and as people. His imagination and his erudition continue to inspire us to learn and to teach. He is the godfather of this book. And we thank him with love.

Anita Diamant

NOTES

INTRODUCTIONS AND DEFINITIONS

1. The phrase came from the 1866 poem "Awake My People," by Judah Leib-Gordon, a Russian-Hebrew poet of the *Haskalah*, the Jewish enlightenment. The exact line is, "Be a man abroad and a Jew in your tent." The early-nineteenth-century Jewish Enlightenment poet Judah Leib Gordon coined the slogan (in Hebrew) for Jews: "Be a Jew in your tent and a human being when you go out of it."

2. However, the opportunity to perform some of them, for example, the commandments related to the rituals of the Temple in Jerusalem, is not available.

3. William Novak and Moshe Waldoks, *The Big Book of Jewish Humor* (New York: Harper & Row, 1981), p. 288.

4. "The Divine Authority of the Mitzvah," in Herman E. Schaalman, *Gates of Mitzvah*, ed. Simeon J. Maslin (New York: Central Conference of American Rabbis), p. 103.

5. Schaalman, p. 103.

6. Hasidism was a mystical revival of the 18th century. This idea is attributed to Rabbi Yehudah Aryeh-Leib of Ger, in *S'fas Emes*, a five-volume classic of Hasidic spiritual insights, and was suggested to the authors by Rabbi Nehemia Polen.

7. Exodus 24:7

HOME

1. Deuteronomy 6:4–9, 11:13–21. Translation from *Vetaher Libeynu, Purify Our Hearts*, the prayer book (*siddur*) of Congregation Beth El of the Sudbury River Valley, Sudbury, Massachusetts, p. 35.

2. This translation/adaptation, taken from the verse written on the *mezuzah* parchment is by Rabbi Rami Shapiro.

3. *Baruch ata Adonai Eloheynu Melech Ha-olam* are the words that introduce many blessings. The most familiar English translation for the Hebrew is "Blessed art Thou, Lord our God, King of the Universe." Alternatives to this translation are found throughout this book, none of which refer to God as a male monarch.

4. Genesis 2.

5. Abraham Joshua Heschel, *The Sabbath* (New York: Farrar, Straus and Giroux, 2005) p. 110.

6. Deuteronomy 5:15.

7. Ezekiel 20:12.

8. Talmud: Shabbat 118b.

9. Exodus 16.

10. Isaiah 58:13.

11. Hayyim Schauss, *The Jewish Festivals* (New York: Schocken Books, 1962), pp. 11–12.

12. Samuel H. Dresner, *The Sabbath* (New York: The Burning Bush Press, 1970), p. 66.

13. *Hasidic Tales of the Holocaust,* by Yaffa Eliach (New York: Avon Books, 1982).

14. The kinds of work that are forbidden on Shabbat are based on a list of 39 specific jobs listed in the Mishna, which is part of the Talmud. The rabbis theorized that these tasks, which are largely agricultural in nature, were derived from the work of constructing the portable Tabernacle in the wilderness. Rabbis have based other restrictions—including the modern prohibition against using electricity—both on the Mishna and on subsequent codes of Jewish law.

15. Schauss, p. 33.

16. Bella Chagall, *Chagall: Burning Lights* (New York: Schocken Books, 1969; reprint of 1946 edition, reissued in March 1988), p. 48–49. This volume is described as a "double portrait of the warm world of Russian Jewry." The text is by Bella Chagall, and the book is illustrated by 36 line drawings by her husband, the artist Marc Chagall.

17. This translation and others in this chapter come from *Vetaher Libeynu,* op. cit.

18. Exodus 20, Deuteronomy 5.

19. Herbert C. Dobrinski, *A Treasury of Sephardic Laws and Customs* (Hoboken, N.J.: Ktav, 1986), p. 231.

20. Actually, since *Shabbat* begins at the very moment the candle is lit, actively extinguishing a flame is forbidden by Jewish law.

21. Used by permission. © Marcia Falk, *The Book of Blessings* (HarperSanFrancisco, 1996), pp. 124–25. www.marciafalk.com.

22. Genesis 1:31; 2:1–3.

23. Numbers 15:17–21.

24. *Pirke Avot* 3:17.

25. Ibid., 3:4.

26. Translation from *Vetaher Libeynu*.

27. *"Y'did Nefesh"* was written by Rabbi Eleazar Azikri, who lived in Palestine during the 16th century. Translation from *Vetaher Libeynu*.

28. *Pirke Avot* 2:21.

29. Deuteronomy 16:20.

30. Talmud: Baba Bathra 9a.

31. Danny Siegel, *Gymshoes and Irises* (Spring Valley, N.Y.: Town Mill Press, 1982), pp. 120–24.

32. Sota 14a, quoted in ibid., p. 126.

33. Isaac Luria's book, *Sefer Yetzirah*, is one the basic books of Jewish mysticism, called Kabbalah.

34. Isaiah 57:14–58:14.

35. See Barry Holtz, *Back to the Sources* (New York: Summit Books, 1984), p. 13.

36. *Pirke Avot* 1:14.

37. Talmud: Shabbat 25b.

38. Rabbi Lawrence Kushner, *River of Light* (Woodstock, NY: Jewish Lights Publishing, 2000), p. xii.

39. *Genesis Rabbah*, VIII, 5

40. Quoted in Samuel H. Dresner, *The Jewish Dietary Laws* (New York: The Burning Bush Press, 1970), pp. 15–16.

41. Rabbi Hayim Halevy Donin, *To Be a Jew* (New York: Basic Books, 1972), pp. 98–99.

42. Leviticus 11.

43. The rule is repeated three times in the Torah: Exodus 23:19 and 34:26; Deuteronomy 14:21.

44. Rabbi Seymour E. Freedman, *The Book of Kashruth* (New York: Bloch Publishing Company, 1970), p. 3.

45. Genesis 1:29–30.

46. Isaiah 11:7

47. Sheila Weinberg, "Kashrut: How Do We Eat?" in *The Jewish Family Book,* ed. Sharon Strassfeld and Kathy Green (New York: Bantam Books, 1981), p. 85.

48. Edda Servi Machlin, *Classic Cuisine of the Italian Jews* (New York: Dodd, Mead & Co., 1981), p. 11.

49. Josephine Levy Bacon, *Jewish Cooking from Around the World* (Woodbury, N.Y.: Barron's, 1986), p. 2.

50. Blu Greenberg, *How to Run a Traditional Jewish Household* (New York: Simon & Schuster, 1983), p. 109.

COMMUNITY

1. *Pirke Avot* 2:5.

2. Ta'anit 22b.

3. Midrash Sefer Eliahu Rabba 7.

4. Midrash Rabba 4:11, Song of Songs.

5. Jewish confirmation ceremonies were begun in the 19th century by the Reform movement as a substitute for *bar mitzvah* in response to the consensus that 13-year-olds were too young to be admitted as adult members of the community. Today, however, confirmation is a collective ceremony that occurs somes year later than and in addition to bar/bat mitzvah.

6. Hillel: The Foundation for Jewish Life on Campus is named for one of Judaism's most beloved teachers. Hillel the Elder, who lived toward the end of the first century B.C.E., engaged in a lifelong debate with another great teacher, the brilliant but impatient Shammai. Hillel was known for his benevolence, gentleness, and humility and is credited with many famous aphorisms. Perhaps the most famous story about him involves the impatient student who asks him to explain all of Judaism while standing on one foot. Hillel answered, "Love your neighbor as yourself. The rest is commentary. Go and study" (Shabbat 31a).

7. Talmud: Eruvin 54a.

8. According to the Policy Planning Institute of the Jewish Agency in Israel, Only about 35 percent of American Jews have actually visited Israel (2005).

9. Rabbi Lawrence A. Hoffman, *The Journey Home: Discovering the Deep Spiritual Wisdom of Jewish Tradition* (Boston: Beacon Press, 2002), p. 110.

10. Ibid., p. 111.

THE CYCLE OF THE YEAR

1. Heschel, p. 8.

2. The Gregorian calendar was brought into use by Pope Gregory XIII during the 16th century.

3. There are also agricultural and pagan sources.

4. For an excellent treatment of this subject, see Arthur Waskow, "The Second Day of Festivals," in *Seasons of Our Joy* (New York: Bantam Books, 1982), pp. 226–27.

5 For more information about this use of *mikveh,* see www .mayyimhayyim.org.

6. From an interview with the author.

7. Isaiah 57:14–58:14.

8. Micah 7:20.

9. Leviticus 23:26–32:3.

10. Leviticus 18.

11. From an interview with the author.

12. Exodus 23:16–16, Leviticus 23:33–44, Deuteronomy 16:13–17.

13. For further discussion of these interpretations, see Michael Strassfeld, *The Jewish Holidays* (New York: Harper & Row, 1985), and Philip Goodman, *The Sukkot/Simchat Torah Anthology* (Philadelphia: Jewish Publication Society, 1973).

14. From an interview with the author.

15. According to the revisionist version of the "official" Hannukah story, the war was, in fact, a civil conflict between the devout masses in the countryside and the assimilated city-folk who had adopted Greek ways. Years after the Maccabee victory, they, too, became Hellenized.

16. Dobrinski, pp. 376–80.

17. Avot de Rabbi Natan 31b.

18. Deuteronomy 20:19

19. For a good description of the Tu B'Shvat *seder* of the mystics of Safed, see Waskow, pp. 108–9.

20. Rabbi Zalman Schachter-Shalomi, in Strassfeld, *The Jewish Holidays,* p. 183.

21. From an interview with the author.

22. Deuteronomy 25:17.

23. Talmud: Megilot 7B.

24. From an interview with the author.

25. This description of Passover as the essential Jewish holiday owes a great deal to Rabbi Irving Greenberg's views, expressed in *The Jewish Way: Living the Holidays* (New York: Summit Books, 1988).

26. Actually, most of the story is not told at the *seder* table. Passover sets in motion a season of study.

27. See Anita Diamant, "The Orange on the Seder Plate," in *Pitching My Tent: On Marriage, Motherhood, Friendship and Other Leaps of Faith* (New York: Scribner, 2003), p. 148.

28. Greenberg, p. 339.

29. Genesis 17.

30. From an interview with the author.

31. Exodus 23:16, Leviticus 23:17, Deuteronomy 16:10–12.

32. Waskow, p. 202.

THE LIFE CYCLE

1. The *gomel* blessing may be recited by one who has recovered from illness, escaped danger, returned from a perilous journey, or been released from prison or captivity. It is typically said in conjunction with an *aliyah* to the Torah. From the Reconstructionist prayer book: "Blessed are You, Abundant One, our God, the sovereign of all worlds, Who bestows good things on one in debt to you, and who has granted me all good." *Kol Haneshamah* (Wyncote, Penn.: The Reconstructionist Press, 1996), p. 400.

2. Alfred Kolatch, *The Name Dictionary* (Middle Village, N.Y.: Jonathan David Publishers, 1967), p. xi.

3. Lawrence K. Altman, M.D., "Pediatricians Find Medical Benefit in Circumcision," *New York Times*, March 6, 1989.

4. Betsy A. Lehman, "The Age-old Question of Circumcision," *Boston Globe*, June 22, 1987.

5. Rabbi Lawrence Kushner, "Save This Article," Bulletin of the Congregation Beth El of the Sudbury River Valley, Sudbury, Mass., Vol. VIII, No. 6., Sivan/Tammuz 5742, p. 3.

6. Toby Fishbein Reifman with Ezrat Nashim, *Blessing the Birth of a Daughter: Jewish Naming Ceremonies for Girls* (Englewood, N.J.: Ezrat Nashim, 1978). Quoting an unpublished paper by Rabbi Marc Angel of the Spanish and Portuguese Synagogue in New York, p. 27.

7. Adapted from the Talmud, Berachot 17a, translation by Rabbi Lawrence Kushner.

8. Exodus 30:14; Leviticus 27:3–5; Numbers 1:3, 20.

9. *Pirke Avot* 5:21.

10. *Encyclopedia Judaica*, Vol. 4 (Jerusalem: Keter Publishing House, 1972), p. 243.

11. Sukkah 42a, Megilla 23a, as cited in Strassfeld and Strassfeld, eds. *The Second Jewish Catalog* (Jewish Publication Society, 1976), p. 62.

12. Zohar 1:89a.

13. Rabbi Maurice Lamm, *The Jewish Way in Love and Marriage* (San Francisco: Harper & Row, 1980), p. 198.

14. Adapted from a translation by Debra Cash.

15. Philip and Hanna Goodman, *The Jewish Marriage Anthology* (Philadelphia: Jewish Publication Society, 1977), p. 28.

16. From a *get* written by Rabbi Lawrence Kushner and Rabbi Henry Zoob.

17. Tanchuma Buber, Lech Lecha 6, 32a. Although there are some negative comments about converts in the Talmud, they are far outnumbered by the positive.

18. Rabbi Aryeh Kaplan, *Waters of Eden: The Mystery of the Mikvah* (New York: National Conference of Synagogue Youth/Union of Orthodox Jewish Congregations, 1976), p. 35.

19. Sanhedrin, 19b.

20. Lawrence Jeffrey Epstein, *The Theory and Practice of*

Welcoming Converts to Judaism (Lewiston, N.Y.: Edwin Mellen Press, 1992), p. 66.

21. This tends to be an automatic "choice," as a person who knows but makes no reference to her origin has accepted the decision, and the conversion is final. Today, the ceremony of *bar* or *bat mitzvah* is seen as a formal affirmation of Jewish identity.

22. According to tradition, Jews are buried only in Jewish cemeteries or in portions of cemeteries designated for Jews only. Thus, whenever Jews settle in a new place, one of their first communal acts is the purchase of land for a cemetery.

23. Rabbi Rami M. Shapiro, *Open Hands: a Jewish Guide on Dying, Death and Bereavement* (Miami: Temple Beth Or), p. 15.

24. Translation from *Vetaher Libeynu*, p. 119.

25. *Pirke Avot* 4:23a.

26. Ezekiel 24:17.

27. Talmud: Shekalim 2:5.

INDEX